THE HISTORY OF CIVILIZATION

CHIVALRY

THE HISTORY OF CIVILIZATION

General Editor C. K. Ogden

The *History of Civilization* is a landmark in early twentieth Century publishing. The aim of the general editor, C. K. Ogden, was to "summarise in one comprehensive synthesis the most recent findings and theories of historians, anthropologists, archaeologists, sociologists and all conscientious students of civilization." The *History*, which includes titles in the French series *L'Evolution de l'Humanité*, was published at a formative time in the development of the social sciences, and during a period of significant historical discoveries.

A list of the titles in the series can be found at the end of this book.

THE BLACK PRINCE

From a MS. presented to H.R.H. the Prince of Wales, by Members of the
University of London. (See p. ix.)

CHIVALRY

Its Historical Significance and Civilizing Influence

Edgar Prestage

First published in 1928 by Routledge, Trench, Trubner
Reprinted in 1996 by Routledge
Reprinted 2000

2 Park Square, Milton Park,
Abingdon, Oxon, OX14 4RN
&
270 Madison Ave,
New York NY 10016

Transferred to Digital Printing 2009

Routledge is an imprint of the Taylor & Francis Group

© 1996 Routledge

All rights reserved. No part of this book may be reprinted or utilized in any form or by any means electronic, mechanical, or other means, now known or hereafter invented, including photocopying and recording, in any information storage or retrieval system, without permission in writing from the publishers.

British Cataloguing in Publication Data

ISBN10: 0-415-15606-8 (hbk)
ISBN10: 0-415-56905-2 (pbk)

ISBN13: 978-0-415-15606-6 (hbk)
ISBN13: 978-0-415-56905-7 (pbk)

ISBN European Civilization: (11 volume set): 0-415-15616-5
ISBN History of Civilization: (50 volume set): 0-415-14380-2

Publisher's Note
The publisher has gone to great lengths to ensure the quality of this reprint but points out that some imperfections in the original may be apparent.

TO

H.R.H.

THE PRINCE OF WALES

EXEMPLAR IN OUR OWN DAY

OF

THE IDEALS OF CHIVALRY

THIS VOLUME

IS

WITH GRACIOUS PERMISSION

RESPECTFULLY DEDICATED

EDITOR'S PREFACE

THE following chapters formed a course of Public Lectures in the Department of History, delivered at King's College, London, in the Michaelmas Term of 1925. It is hoped that they will prove welcome in book form. The bibliography of chivalry in English is relatively slight and does not correspond to the importance of the subject; moreover, the works that deal with it are all, or nearly all, long out of print. We have no adequate account in our language of chivalry in Germany and Spain, and none at all of chivalry in Portugal; in these respects the present volume fills a gap. The various contributions do not of course pretend to be exhaustive, the limits of space would forbid it, but an attempt has been made to supply the salient facts and ideas under each head, while the list of authorities given by each contributor will enable readers who so desire to pursue their studies further. The illustrations dealing with historical personages and events are as nearly contemporary as could be found, and some of them are reproduced for the first time.

I would express my gratitude to the colleagues and other collaborators who have made my editorial task an easy one.

EDGAR PRESTAGE.

NOTE ON THE FRONTISPIECE

By Sir Israel Gollancz

THE frontispiece, from a manuscript of the end of the fourteenth century or early fifteenth, in gold and colours in the original, depicts the Black Prince kneeling on a cushion, dressed in armour with a sword and coat on which are emblazoned, differenced with a label, the Royal Arms—the Lions of England with the Fleur-de-Lys of France. The Prince is in prayer, uttering the words, " Et hec tres unum sunt ". In the upper compartment of the illustration the Trinity is depicted. It is recorded that the Prince piously kept the Festival of the Trinity " from the first days of his youth, and upheld it all his life zealously, without evil thought ".

On each side of the kneeling figure is a large ostrich feather, in silver, and on each feather is the famous motto, still borne by the Prince of Wales, but in the form " ich dene ", not " ich diene ".

The manuscript from which the frontispiece is taken is a metrical chronicle in French verse by the Herald of Sir John Chandos, dealing with the Life and Feats of Arms of Edward Prince of Wales, the Black Prince. Only one other manuscript is known; but this illustration is unique.

On 5th May, 1921, it was my high privilege at the Guildhall to offer this volume to H.R.H. the Prince of Wales for his gracious acceptance as a gift from members of the University of London, on the occasion of his honouring the University by becoming Honorary Doctor. Subsequently His Royal Highness was pleased to loan the manuscript to the

University, where it is now prized among its choicest literary treasures.[1]

It was my good fortune to recognize the peculiar value of the manuscript, and more particularly of the frontispiece, as corroborating a theory I had advanced that the time-honoured motto borne by successive Princes of Wales was originally "Ich dene", so spelt (though misread as "Ich diene") by the Black Prince himself, as his signature is the only extant specimen we possess of his handwriting. This was his motto of peace, as "Homout" (i.e. "High Spirit") was his motto of war; both were subscribed to the document in question, dated the 25th April, 1370. The present manuscript afforded the only evidence, long sought by me, that his contemporaries recognized "Ich dene" as the correct form of the Prince's motto. I had worked out that from the philological point of view the form "Ich dene" was neither German nor Dutch, but could only belong to a district which included Old Gelderland and Cleves. It is noteworthy that Reinald II— "the Black," as he was called, Duke of Gelderland, one of the foremost princes of the Netherlands of his day, married in 1331, as his second wife, Eleanor, sister of Edward III, and aunt of the Black Prince. Edward the Third's alliances with the peoples and rulers of the Low Countries were, indeed, the prelude to the Anglo-Belgian relations so triumphantly attested during the past years. Both "ich dene" and "homout" belong to the dialect of this district. "Ich dene" (i.e. "I serve"), as the Black Prince himself made clear, was the motto of his "badge of peace"—the ostrich feather, or feathers. Often it was one single feather, as in the present illustration, but as is evident from a passage in a contemporary heraldic Middle-English alliterative poem,[2]

---

[1] Cf. "Ich dene: Some Observations on a manuscript of the Life and Feats of Arms of Edward Prince of Wales, the Black Prince....presented by members of the University of London to H.R.H. Edward Prince of Wales, by Sir Israel Gollancz, Chairman of Presentation Committee": printed by Geo. W. Jones, Gough Square, Fleet Street.

[2] p. 178.

Winner and Waster, which I date 1352, the three feathers were recognized as his more usual badge. Perhaps the number had special suggestion, in view of the Prince's striking devotion to the Trinity.

The popular idea that the Black Prince took the motto, together with the ostrich feathers, at Crêcy, from the vanquished King of Bohemia, does not stand the test of inquiry, nor is there any tradition to that effect. The ostrich feathers seem, however, to be associated with the Prince's victory over John of Bohemia at Crêcy. To the feathers the Prince added the motto of his own choice—" Ich dene "—and took the device as his " badge of peace ". " I serve, Lord ", said that liege, " while my life shall endure," to paraphrase an amended line in the English alliterative poem to which I have referred.

To his contemporaries the Black Prince was the very mirror of chivalry. In peace and war his ideals were well expressed in his two mottoes—" Homout " (i.e. High Spirit, or Courage), the motto of his badge of war—the Royal Arms, differenced with a label—and "Ich dene", the motto of his badge of peace, the ostrich feathers.

It is significant that as his sign-manual he combined these two mottoes, expressive of his ideals of manhood in peace and in war :—

> " In peace there's nothing so becomes a man
> As modest stillness and humility :
> But when the blast of war blows in our ears....
> Stiffen the sinews, summon up the blood."

These ideals of chivalry are still potent and active, and still win whole-hearted admiration and unstinted devotion.

I may perhaps be permitted to record the closing words of my address to His Royal Highness on the occasion of the presentation of the manuscript : " In our choice of a gift worthy of your acceptance we have been inspired by a joyous recognition that the ideals of courage, reverence, and service, acclaimed in the life of Edward Prince of Wales, the Black

Prince, are so nobly exemplified in Your Royal Highness yourself; and we fervently pray that for long years to come it may be vouchsafed to you, by the side of His Majesty the King, to bear the Badge of Peace, and to continue your high offices and graceful service for England, for the Empire, and for humanity."

I. G.

CONTENTS

CHAP.		PAGE
	EDITOR'S PREFACE	v
	NOTE ON THE FRONTISPIECE By Sir Israel Gollancz	vii
I.	CHIVALRY AND ITS PLACE IN HISTORY By F. J. C. Hearnshaw, M.A., L.D., Professor of Medieval History in the University of London.	1
II.	THE BEGINNINGS OF MEDIEVAL CHIVALRY By E. F. Jacob, M.A., D.Phil., Student of Christ Church, Oxford.	37
III.	THE CHIVALRY OF FRANCE By F. S. Shears, B.A., L. ès L. D. de l'Univ., Professor of French in the University of Aberdeen.	57
IV.	THE CHIVALRY OF GERMANY By H. G. Atkins, M.A., D.Litt., Professor of German in the University of London.	81
V.	THE CHIVALRY AND MILITARY ORDERS OF SPAIN By A. R. Pastor, B.Litt., D.Phil., Cervantes Reader in the University of London.	109
VI.	THE CHIVALRY OF PORTUGAL By Edgar Prestage, M.A., D.Litt., Camões Professor in the University of London	141
VII.	CHIVALRY IN MEDIEVAL ENGLISH POETRY By Sir Israel Gollancz, Litt.D., F.B.A., Professor of English Language and Literature in the University of London.	167
VIII.	MEDIEVAL COURTESY BOOKS AND THE PROSE ROMANCES OF CHIVALRY By A. T. Byles, M.A., Lecturer in English at the Exeter Diocesan Training College.	183
IX.	CHIVALRY AND THE IDEA OF A GENTLEMAN By A. W. Reed, M.A., D.Litt., Professor of English Language and Literature in the University of London	207
	INDEX	229

LIST OF ILLUSTRATIONS

Edward the Black Prince	*Frontispiece*
	to face page
Knightly virtues. Rescue of the distressed, exemplified by Perseus	40
Knightly virtues. Loyalty to Comrades exemplified by Hercules	46
Knightly perils. Drunkenness represented by Bacchus	52
St Louis feeding the poor	64
A Tournament	76
The Joust	78
Walther von der Vogelweide	90
Meister Johannes Hadloub	96
Ulrich von Lichtenstein	100
St James on horseback	114
Alfonso II, 'the Chaste'	120
The Castle of Segovia	134
Attack on and occupation of Gor by King Ferdinand of Aragon in 1489	138
Knights of the time of King Alfonso Henriques	148
Vision of King Alfonso Henriques	148
King Alfonso V in the attack on Arzila	158
King Sebastian	164
The Hermit and the Squire	188
An Ordination Ceremony	192
The Cook and the Knight	196
Publius Cornelius and Gayus Flaminius ask of Fulgens the hand of his daughter	210
Lucres declares her decision to wed that suitor who is the more noble	214
Publius Cornelius addresses the Senate	218
Gayus Flaminius replies	224

CHAPTER I

CHIVALRY AND ITS PLACE IN HISTORY

By F. J. C. HEARNSHAW, M.A., LL.D.,
Professor of Medieval History in the University of London.

I

THE subject of this course of lectures is Chivalry. The term is one which requires some definition; for it is a term used in different senses. The *New English Dictionary* distinguishes seven various meanings, while *Lloyd's Encyclopædic Dictionary* furnishes no fewer than ten. For historical purposes, however, both the seven and the ten can be reduced to four, as follows. First, "Chivalry" is used as connoting simply a body of knights or horsemen equipped for battle; as when Sir Bevis of Hamton in the course of his dangerous career remarks, on perceiving a host of mounted Saracens in pursuit of himself and the inevitable princess, "They would after us with wonder-great chevalrie."[1] Here "Chivalry" means no more than "body of cavalry". Secondly, "Chivalry" is employed in the sense of knighthood in the abstract; knighthood as a rank or order; the position and quality of a knight; as, for example, when Chaucer in his *Legend of Lucretia* asks the guilty Tarquin, "Why hastow doon dispyt to chivalrye?"[2] Thirdly, "Chivalry" is found in a technical or feudal sense to signify "tenure by knight service". Cowell, in his *Interpreter*, defines it as "the *servitium militare* of the French *chevalier*", and remarks, "Chivalry is a tenure of service

---

[1] Compare also Wycliffe's version of Genesis, xxi, 32. Where the A. V. reads "chief captain of his host", Wycliffe gives the rendering "prince of his chyvalrye". Note again Campbell's *Hohenlinden*: "Charge with all thy chivalry."

[2] Compare also Shakespeare, *Pericles*, Act ii, Scene ii, 29. "And his device a wreath of chivalry"; so Bacon in his *Essays*, "There be now for martial encouragement some degrees and orders of chivalry"; so Dryden, *Palamon and Arcite*, i, 100. "The faith which knights to knighthood bore, and whate'er else to chivalry belongs."

whereby the tenant is bound to perform some noble or military office unto the lord." Fourthly, and finally, "Chivalry" is used in a broader sense to include the whole knightly system of the later middle ages, with its peculiar religious, moral, and social codes and customs. It was in this last large connotation that Burke employed the term when, in denouncing the French Revolution, he said "The age of chivalry is gone".[1] Perhaps, too, Chaucer had this wide meaning in mind when he said of his "perfight gentil knight" that he "lovede chyvalrye" with its concomitant "trouthe and honour, fredom and curteisie". In this sense Chivalry is well defined by Professor H. W. C. Davis as "that peculiar and often fantastic code of etiquette and morals which was grafted upon feudalism in the eleventh and succeeding centuries".[2] It was, says Mr. F. W. Cornish, "a body of sentiment and practice, of law and custom, which prevailed among the dominant classes in a great part of Europe between the eleventh and sixteenth centuries."[3] It was "more a spirit than an institution" says one enthusiastic eulogist[4]; "less an institution than an ideal," says another and more critical student.[5] It "represented the Christian form of the profession of arms," contends the pious Paul Lacroix.[6] Two other French historians, less devout but more trustworthy than M. Lacroix, substantially concur: "Chivalry," they say, "was a system which modified and completed feudalism. It was not an institution, but an ethical and religious association, shedding a ray of ideal beauty through a society corrupted by anarchy.[7] France was, indeed, its home, and the region wherein it attained to its fullest perfection. It was in writing of France that the scholarly and judicious Dean Kitchin remarked that "at its highest, and in theory, chivalry sets before us the perfect gentleman—gently born, gentle-mannered, truthful, faithful, courteous to women, pure, brave, and fearless, unsparing of self, filled with deep religious feeling, bowing before God

---

[1] Compare Disraeli, *The Young Duke*, bk. ii, chap. 5, "The age of chivalry is past. Bores have succeeded to dragons."
[2] Davis, *Medieval Europe*, p. 106.
[3] Cornish, *Chivalry*, p. 11.
[4] G. P. R. James, *History of Chivalry*, p. 3.
[5] W. H. Schofield, *Chivalry in English Literature*, p. 3.]
[6] Lacroix, *Military and Religious Life in the Middle Ages*, p. viii.
[7] Bémont and Monod, *Medieval Europe*, p. 257.

CHIVALRY: ITS PLACE IN HISTORY

and womenkind, but haughty in the presence of all others."[1] Another learned Dean, analysing Chivalry in this large and ideal sense, finds it compounded of the following elements— a high sense of honour, disdain of danger and death, love of adventure, compassion for the weak and oppressed, generosity, self-sacrifice, and altruism.[2]

We have now got a very long way from our original " body of horsemen equipped for battle ", and it is necessary to return to it in order that we may trace the process by which a military force characterized by the complete barbarism and sanguinary brutality of the decadent ninth century became (at any rate in theory) transmuted and converted before the thirteenth century into a class of " perfect gentlemen " fully qualified in spirit if not in technical skill, to be medical missionaries. We must fix our eye on the word " knight ", which, it will have been noted, occurs in all definitions of chivalry that we have examined. The English word " knight " is, indeed, the equivalent of the French word " chevalier " ; and the English term " knighthood " stands as a synonym for the French " chevalerie ", as for the Spanish " caballeria ", and the Italian " cavalleria ". Now, before the Norman Conquest there was no such equivalence. For the Continental cavalier was, as his name implies, a horseman,[3] and the Anglo-Saxon " knight " was not. The Anglo-Saxon " knight " or " cniht ", was, at first, merely any young man ; later the name was applied more particularly to a young man who acted as *servant* or attendant to a lord ; next it was still further specialized to denote one who rendered *military* service, and it was translated into Latin by the word *miles* which had similarly become specialized in the meaning of *soldier* ; finally, at the time of the Norman Conquest, it had come to signalize peculiarly those subordinate fighting men *of the minor landholding class* who had commended themselves to some lord and so fought under his banner. In short, the term had become feudalized : it connoted the military tenants of earls and thegns, bishops and abbots, and other eminent local potentates. But still the " cnihtas " fought on foot. It was the Normans who brought

---

[1] G. W. Kitchin, *History of France*, vol. i, p. 243.
[2] H. H. Milman, *Latin Christianity*, vol. iv, p. 204.
[3] Latin *caballus* = French *cheval* = Italian *cavallo* = a nag.

the war-horse with them; all their minor landholders were cavaliers, the English equivalent of which was not "knights" but "riders". Thus the Anglo-Saxon Chronicle, A.D. 1085, tells us that in that year "King William dubbed his son Henry a rider". That expression, however, was not used again. For that same Henry married an English wife, and under his influence the two peoples, Norman and Saxon, were intermingled and fused. The Saxon "cnihtas" learned to ride, and the Norman "chevaliers" became knights.

II

The knight of the early Norman period—whether in England or on the Continent—was a purely feudal personage. He held a parcel of land on condition of military service; he was bound by the terms of his tenure to follow his lord into the field forty days each year, fully equipped, and adequately accompanied, at his own expense; further, he had to attend his lord's court, pay certain reliefs and aids, submit to various rights as to worship, marriage, escheat, forfeiture, and so on. He was not an attractive individual. No one loved him. It is difficult, indeed, to say by whom he was most detested—by the King and the officials of the nascent National State; by the Pope and the clergy of the dominant Catholic Church; or by the commonalty of the subject Third Estate of citizens, burgesses, peasants. The King found him an intolerable nuisance: he was useless and inefficient in war, turbulent and rebellious in peace, an insuperable obstacle to tranquillity and good government. The Church suffered incalculably at his hands: he was greedy and aggressive, constantly on the alert to rob bishoprics and monasteries, defiant of ecclesiastical discipline and much inclined to secure control of the spiritual power by putting his creatures into holy orders. To the commonalty he was an unmitigated terror, a mere bandit, unrestrained by any consideration of mercy or of honour.

We have lurid records of his doings in the chronicles of the period; we have traditions of his behaviour in the *Chansons de Geste*; the Germans still perpetuate his memory

CHIVALRY : ITS PLACE IN HISTORY

in a proverb in which "knight" is synonymous with "tyrannical bully"—*Er will Ritter an mir werden,* "He wants to play the knight over me."

Perhaps no more appalling description of feudal knighthood before its conversion and consecration into chivalry can be found than in the closing entries of the Anglo-Saxon Chronicle, which died out amid the anarchy of the so-called reign of Stephen. The writer probably had in mind as he penned his dreadful words the depredations of Geoffrey de Mandeville, the last of the bandits, of whose atrocities Mr. J. H. Round has given us so vivid a picture. "Every peaceful man," says the Chronicle, "made his castles and held them against the King. They filled them with devils and scoundrels, and they seized those persons that they thought had property and put them in prison and tortured them with unutterable torments; for never were martyrs tortured as they were. They hanged them up by the feet and smoked them with foul smoke; they suspended them by the thumbs or by the head and hung armour on their feet; they put knotted strings about their heads and twisted them so that they went into the brain. They put them into dungeons in which were adders and snakes and toads and so killed them," and so on, and so on, concluding with "However a man tilled, the earth bare no corn; for the land was all fordone by such deeds. And men said openly that Christ and his saints slept."

The records of the authentic Geoffrey de Mandeville and his knightly compeers of King Stephen's time can be paralleled in the regions of romance by the achievements of many a feudal hero, for example Raoul de Cambrai, or Ogier the Dane. They had in full measure the virtue of martial courage; they feared no foe in shining armour, nor any number of them; they were utterly contemptuous of danger and death; but at the same time they were treacherous and disobedient to their kings, impious and profane in matters of religion, brutal and cruel in their dealings with common folk, and free from all respect for women. Of these two typical feudal knights of romance, M. Flach says that their qualities were those of the lion and the tiger. "In their savage outbursts of anger, or their cold ferocity, nothing restrained them; neither regard for weakness nor religious fear had any influence over them; they killed unarmed men without mercy; they burned nuns in their convents."[1] Bevis of Hamton was rather better; but even he, though more restrained and discriminating, was almost purely sanguinary. His only considerable activity was homicide. After reading his story I calculated that, apart from the prodigious but untabulated slaughter which he effected in conjunction with others in four great battles, he himself, with his own hand—before he settled down, sated with adventure, in tranquil domesticity—had slain more than 650 human beings. He lived as dangerously as even a Nietzsche or a Mussolini could desire; but of any good that he did, or ideal that inspired him, or end that he achieved, there is not a suggestion. Psychologically he is no more interesting than a modern machine-gun, or any other engine of indiscriminate slaughter.

In the eleventh century, indeed, feudalism had done its work, and the feudal knight had become an anachronism whose abolition or transformation was the most urgent need of the new age. Feudalism as a military system had come into existence in the Carolingian period, as the only possible means of defence of Western Europe against the invading hosts of Saracens, Slavs, Magyars, and Danes, which threatened Christendom with extinction. Based upon the armour-clad knight and the fortified castle, it had sprung up almost spontaneously as a system of local protection at a time when the central government—whether in Frankland or in England, or elsewhere—was too weak to organize an effective resistance to the aggressors. The knights required to beat back such assailants as Saracens, Slavs, Magyars, and Danes during the dark and dreadful ninth and tenth centuries were not " perfect gentlemen " full of piety and poetry, pitiful and proper. What were wanted, and what by the circumstances were evolved, were tremendous bullies, terrific in wrath, overflowing with animal courage and martial fury; men good at the battle-cry and with the battle-axe; such as were Achilles and Ajax in the old days when Greeks fought against Trojans on the wind-swept plains of Ilium.

By the time the millennial year (A.D. 1000) dawned, feudalism

[1] J. Flach, *Les Origines de l'ancienne France*, vol. ii, pp. 567-8.

CHIVALRY : ITS PLACE IN HISTORY

had achieved its purpose. The Saracens had been driven beyond the Pyrenees; the Slavs had been forced back to the Oder; the Magyars had been expelled from Germany and Italy, and had been persuaded to limit themselves to Hungary and to become Christian subjects of the Papacy; the Danes, too, had been compelled to cease from raiding and to settle down as good Catholics in Eastern England or Northern France.

But still the feudal knighthood and nobility remained; the dominant military force in Europe, impregnable in its ubiquitous castles, invincible with its terrible cavalry, and yet at ceaseless war within itself; an insuperable obstacle to tranquillity, peaceful industry, and centralized government. The prime problem of the age—a problem equally pressing upon monarchs, priests, and proletarians—was how to escape from it; how to reduce it to civility; how to convert it to new uses; how to find it something to do; how to save Christendom from devastation and disintegration from within, by discovering a fresh inspiration and another sphere of activity for those dangerously unemployed anachronisms, the feudal knights errant. The solution of the problem was the Crusades.

III

The attitude of the Church towards war had changed much since the days of the Early Fathers. The first disciples had been wholly opposed to fighting. The religion which they professed was the cult of the Prince of Peace; and its symbol, the Cross, was eloquent of sacrifice and submission, in sharp contrast to the violence and self-assertion of militarism. Moreover, service in the Roman armies involved participation in pagan rites which to the Christian believer seemed to savour of idolatry and devil-worship. One of the main causes, indeed, why the Roman Empire departed from its usual policy of religious tolerance, and persecuted the Early Church, was that the members of that Church refused military service and preached pacificism.

The conversion of Constantine, at the beginning of the fourth century, made a marked difference in the situation. Pagan rites ceased to be obligatory; the arms of the Empire became available for the defence and extension of the Gospel; bishops became politicians, and politicians bishops; the two powers, secular and sacerdotal, long sundered, were re-united, and theologians rejoiced at their new ability to supplement the force of argument by the argument of force. Hence St. Augustine did not hesitate to defend the use of weapons in the cause of the *Civitas Dei*, nor did he shrink from calling upon the Emperor to suppress by violence the Donatist schism. People like Tertullian, who continued to preach the primitive pacificism, came to be regarded as tainted with the Manichæan heresy. But, nevertheless, war was still looked upon as an evil, justifiable only in cases of extreme necessity.

A third phase was inaugurated in the seventh century by the rise of Islam. The religion of Mahomet, was from the first, avowedly a religion of the sword. War was its chosen means of evangel, and the warriors who spread its gospel over conquered peoples were assured by the Prophet of an immediate paradise, if they should meet with death in the course of their missionary mélées. Christendom was compelled to defend itself by means of the same weapons as those by which it was attacked; and it was not to be thought of that Christian knights who fought in defence of the Church against the infidel should hold a lower place of honour on earth, or should enjoy a less speedy prospect of celestial felicity, than those accorded to the Moslems. Christianity became militarized. Not only did theologians begin to exalt war—together with persecution, which was its obvious and inevitable corollary—as a normal and proper mode of Christian activity; but priests, abbots, bishops, and even popes began to don armour and themselves engage in military operations.

The climax of this fusion of war and religion was seen at the Council of Clermont in A.D. 1095. There, on the one hand, was proclaimed the first Crusade; and there, on the other hand, was issued the general injunction that every person of noble birth, on attaining the age of twelve, should take a solemn oath before a bishop that " he would defend to the uttermost the oppressed, the widow and the orphan; and that women of noble birth should enjoy his special care". Christian chivalry, as distinct from mere feudal knighthood, had been brought into existence. The Church had found an occupation for the unemployed brigandage of Europe; and more, it had begun to hold out before it noble ideals of sacrifice and service; it had effectively commenced its gigantic task of converting the cruel and debauched savages of the feudal castle into the "perfect gentleman", chaste and pious, of the *Idylls of the King*, who made it their business and their joy to "ride abroad redressing human wrongs".

Into the causes which led to the Crusades it is unnecessary for me to enter here. Suffice it to say that in A.D. 1071 the Seljuk Turks defeated the Byzantine Emperor at Manzikert in Armenia, and followed up their overwhelming victory by occupying Asia Minor and by threatening Constantinople itself. The ancient bulwark of Christendom in the East was broken down, and the Western world was menaced by an infidel invasion. Even before Jerusalem fell into Seljuk hands, Byzantine had sent its piteous appeal to Rome (A.D. 1073), and the great, Hildebrand, Pope Gregory VII, had recognized the necessity of sending aid to the harassed Greeks. The capture of Jerusalem (A.D. 1076), however, was needed before the conscience of Catholicism was touched, or the imagination of Feudalism aroused. Even then, it required the loud and long-drawn plaints of pilgrims, the passionate preaching of Peter the Hermit, fresh appeals from Constantinople, and finally the commanding call of Pope Urban II, before the knighthood of Europe was constrained to take the cross, and to precipitate itself upon Asia with the unprecedented cry "It is the will of God".

IV

The first crusaders—the pioneers of the Christian chivalry of Europe—were by no means suddenly transformed from feudal barbarians into cultivated gentlemen. In spite of the sacredness of their cause, their progress through Constantinople to the Holy Land was marked by orgies and excesses, murders and debaucheries, which were a disgrace not merely to their religion but to humanity itself. The fact that they were assured of a plenary indulgence on the completion of their enterprise no doubt incited them to enlarge indefinitely the list of the transgressions which, according to contract, were to be washed away. "The taverns along the road," we are told, "were dens of vice; the frivolous way in which oaths and compacts were made and broken is held up to execration, not only by the Arabs, but by the better-minded crusaders themselves. And as to cruelties exercised on helpless prisoners, we hear of nothing more absolutely wanton than the crucifixion of the captives in Edessa, or the sending to the Greek Emperor by Bohemund of Antioch of a whole cargo of sliced-off noses and thumbs."[1] Yet even among this horde of sanctified savages—whose abominations scandalized even the Byzantines, and whose ferocities horrified the very Turks themselves—there were knights in whom piety and courage were mingled in the true chivalric blend. Tancred of Sicily was a not ignoble barbarian; but still nearer the ideal was Godfrey of Bouillon, who combined high military skill and superb bravery with enthusiastic devotion to religion and a life of stainless chastity.[2] Perhaps Godfrey may be regarded as the first true hero of Christian chivalry.

From the Council of Clermont, then, and the opening of the Crusades, the Church may be said to have undertaken, not unsuccessfully, the conversion of the feudal knighthood, and its capture for the service of religion. The creation of a Christian chivalry was, indeed, part of the Church's victory over her inveterate enemy, Feudalism, which through the snares of simony, marriage, and war, had at one time all but dragged her into the pit of perdition. She claimed and secured control of the ceremony of knightly investiture and elevated it into a species of divine ordination. She began to impose upon her sword-girt servants an ever-extending series

---

[1] E. F. Henderson, *History of Germany*, i, 104.
[2] Kenelm Digby, who dedicates the first of the four books of his *Broad Stone of Honour* to Godfrey, speaks of him as "that illustrious hero whose kingly rule seems to have corresponded with the very ideal of perfection in the social order, and whose personal qualities were so heroic that, according to an ancient chronicle, an infidel King was heard to say: "Quand tout l'honneur du monde seroit faillie et absorbe, que le duc Godefroy est suffisant pour le recouvrer et mettre dessus" (*Broad Stone of Honour*, i, 9).

of oaths and obligations which, if fulfilled, raised them to a height of sanctity little inferior to that of priests. To say that there was, and that there always remained, a great gulf between the ecclesiastical ideal of Christian knighthood and the militant reality, is merely to say that chivalry was a medieval institution. For nothing more striking distinguishes the Middle Age both from the Classical Antiquity which preceded it, and the Modern Commercialism which supplanted it, than the enormous discrepancies that displayed themselves between its theories and its practices.

Perhaps the most remarkable effort made during the period under review to harmonize the theory and the practice of Christian chivalry was the institution of the great Crusading Orders—the Hospitallers, the Templars, the Teutonic Knights. In them the principles of monasticism were adapted to the pursuit of arms. The Hospitallers began as a charitable order and later added militancy to their programme; the Templars were warrior-monks simply and all the time; the Teutonic Knights combined fighting and philanthropy— the inflicting and the healing of wounds—from their initiation.

1. *The Hospitallers.*—Even before Jerusalem fell into the hands of the Seljuk Turks, in the middle of the eleventh century, when pilgrimages to the Holy City enjoyed an immense vogue throughout Western Christendom, some pious merchants of Amalfi had secured permission from the Sultan of Egypt, who then ruled over Palestine, to build two great Hospitals or Hostels, together with a Church, for the shelter and comfort of pilgrims from Catholic Europe. One of the Hospitals, that for men, was dedicated to St. John the Almoner; the other, that for women, to St. Mary Magdalene. The Seljuk conquest of Jerusalem in A.D. 1076 checked, though it did not wholly stop, the practice of pilgrimage, and it caused the Hospitallers to pass through a period of adversity which severely tested their faith, and extremely acerbated their tempers. The recovery of Jerusalem by the Crusaders in A.D. 1099 opened up for them a new era of importance and prosperity. They had an overwhelming amount of work to do in tending the sick and wounded, and in providing accommodation for the pious hosts who flocked to the Sacred Sepulchre. Wealth poured in upon

them—Godfrey of Bouillon himself, among countless others, endowing the Hospitals with his estates in Brabant. Branch Hospitals were founded in other parts of Palestine, and even in the seaports of Europe whence pilgrims were accustomed to set forth for the Holy Land. Those who served the Hospitals, both men and women, were organized in a regular order, bound by the usual monastic vows, and distinguished by a special costume—a black robe adorned on the left breast by a white cross of eight points, symbolic of the eight beatitudes. It was about A.D. 1118, under the direction of the Second Master, Raymond Dupuy, that the male section of the order, the Brethren of St. John of Jerusalem, added militancy to their activities. In addition to their original duty of providing shelter and service to pilgrims, they took upon themselves, and were consecrated to, the task of defending the Christian Kingdom of Jerusalem. Their new sphere of operation speedily took precedence of their old. They received a fresh constitution according to which they were divided into three classes, viz. first, *Knights*, who were to be men of noble and gentle birth; secondly, *Serving Brethren*, who were not required to be men of rank, whose function was to act as squires to the knights, and attendants in the Hospitals; thirdly, *Chaplains*, who, in addition to the usual clerical duties, shared in the care of the sick and wounded. Slight differences in costume were made—the Knights, for instance, having a red ground placed behind the white cross of the Order. Here, then, at last was the theoretically perfect combination of Christianity and war; the Cross and the sword; Monasticism and Knighthood; Philanthropy and Militancy; God and the Devil. It is unnecessary for us to follow in detail the long history of the Order of St. John of Jerusalem. The Holy City remained its headquarters until Saladin captured it in 1187; then Acre became its base, until that town, too, was lost in 1291; next Cyprus for a short time was made its home, but in 1310 it moved to a more permanent abode in the island of Rhodes, where it made a magnificent defence of Christendom in the Mediterranean, until, in 1522, the power of the Ottoman Turks overwhelmed it. The remnant of the devoted Order received Malta as a place of residence from the Emperor Charles V in 1530, and there it remained, fighting against

CHIVALRY : ITS PLACE IN HISTORY

Turkish admirals and Barbary pirates, until Napoleon occupied the island in 1798. This was virtually the end of the Order ; but it is not even yet wholly extinct. In England, in 1826, there was even an attempt at a revival, and a new benevolent institution was established under the old name, whose main function was " the providing of nourishing food for the outpatients of King's College and Charing Cross Hospitals ". This institution still exists. Militancy forms no part of its programme. It has reverted to the pure beneficence of the original merchants of Amalfi who founded the Hospital in Jerusalem.

2. *The Teutonic Knights.*—Nearest in character to the Hospitallers, and for a long time intimately associated with them, were the Knights of the Teutonic Order. From the first they combined the care of the sick and poor with the profession of arms. Originally instituted, about A.D. 1128, by a wealthy German, who had shared in the hardships and triumphs of the first Crusade, and had taken up his abode in the Holy City, it was not until Jerusalem was lost (1187) and Acre gained (1191) that the Germans wholly separated themselves from the Order of St. John, and became a separate organization, under the title of " The Teutonic Knights of the Hospital of the Blessed Virgin". They assumed as a distinctive costume, a white cloak with a black cross upon the left shoulder. Only Germans were eligible for membership. The fall of Acre and consequent extinction of the Christian Kingdom of Jerusalem rendered the Order homeless (1291). For a time they settled in Venice ; but soon they were invited to move the sphere of their operations from the Mediterranean to the Baltic, and to wage the holy war against the heathen of Prussia, Lithuania, and Esthonia. Accordingly, in A.D. 1309 they made Marienburg their headquarters, and in Prussia they remained with varying fortunes until in A.D. 1525 their Grand Master, Albert of Hohenzollern, apostasized to Lutheranism, and converted his elective Mastership into the hereditary Dukedom of Prussia, held of the King of Poland.

3. *The Knights Templars.*—Very different from both Teutons and Hospitallers, and frequently at variance with them, were " the poor Soldiers of Jesus Christ ", who, from the site of their original house within the precincts of the

Temple in Jerusalem, became commonly known as the Knights Templars. Founded about A.D. 1118, from the first they were a purely military order, pledged to fight in defence of the Holy Places and for the protection of pilgrims proceeding thereto. They were formally recognized by the Council of Troyes ten years later (A.D. 1128), and they received a rule and a series of statutes drawn up by no less a person than the eminent Saint Bernard, who, further, composed a notable treatise in their favour, entitled *In Praise of the New Chivalry*. St. Bernard's patronage of the Templars, and his composition of this treatise, may be said to mark the final act in the consecration of war to the service of religion. The two prime elements in Chivalry—originally and essentially so incongruous—were fused into a single and apparently homogeneous whole. The Templar was a monk of the strictest and most ascetic Cistercian type, pledged to chastity, obedience, and absolute poverty ; but, at the same time, he was a knight bound to wage ceaseless and truceless war upon the infidel, and never to rest until the Church should reign supreme over the world. His habit was a white robe, emblematic of purity, surmounted by a red cross symbolic of the blood which he was prepared to shed in the cause to which he was pledged. The history of the Templars—wholly comprised within two centuries—is one of brilliant achievement and splendid renown, followed by rapid degeneracy, and culminating in a sanguinary suppression by the combined powers of State and Church. Like the Hospitallers and the Teutons, after Saladin's capture of Jerusalem the Templars made Acre their headquarters; but unlike the members of these two Orders, when they were expelled from Acre (A.D. 1291), they found no new centre, and, what was worse, no new work to do. By that time, although the individual knights still remained, in theory, paupers, yet the Order had received so many bequests of lands and revenues that all the members were able to live, and for the most part did live, in regal luxury. They became lazy, self-indulgent, corrupt, proud, quarrelsome, turbulent— a danger and a nuisance to both kings and bishops everywhere. What, in the eyes of fourteenth century prelates and potentates, was still more deadly, was that they had become suspected of heresy. Their long residence in the East, and their contact with the infidel, seem to have tainted some of them with the Manichæan dualism. But whether or not the appalling charges brought against them by venal and interested accusers were true or false, of this there can be little doubt, that they had outlived their usefulness, and that they were a source of cosmopolitan embarrassment to the governments of the nascent national states. The wealth of their possessions, too, made them a desirable prey. Hence it was natural for monarchs like Philip IV and Edward II to attack them. It proved a surprisingly easy task to overthrow and destroy them, even the Pope (Clement V, 1312) lending his aid to their suppression. Nevertheless, however just and necessary it may have been to abolish this once great and brilliant Order, nothing can condone the horrible cruelty with which the work of dissolution was carried out.

It has been said by Heckethorn that " with the Templars perished a world " ; that " Chivalry ended with them ".

V

In the great Crusading Orders, as we have just seen, the two prime elements of Chivalry, viz. War and Religion, were combined. They were similarly combined in the Orders of Monastic Knights which, during the twelfth century, were established in Spain and Portugal for the purpose of fighting the Moors, and recovering the Peninsula from the Crescent for the Cross. Such were the Orders of Avis (1166), St. James of Compostella (1175), Calatrava (1164), and Alcantara (1183).

But these Crusading Orders lacked, at any rate in theory and according to their rules, the third and completing element of chivalry, viz. Gallantry, in the courtly and erotic sense of the term. The military monks were devoted to adoration of the Virgin Mary, and to veneration for the holy women of the calendar, but in respect of the mundane and mortal members of the sex they were restricted by their vows to the rendering of such assistance as might be necessary, owing to female feebleness, in face of the violence and villany of the bandits, giants, ogres, dragons, and other vermin, who, at that period, infested this terrifying and insanitary earth.

It was among the old Feudal knighthood and nobility—which the Crusades had merely diverted, but not converted, to religion—that Gallantry emerged. When, with the dawn of the eleventh century, the stress of the struggle between feudalized Christendom and the hosts of its pagan or infidel invaders—Danes, Magyars, Slavs, Saracens—was over, the knightly and baronial castle became something more than a fortress; it began to be a home and a centre of social intercourse. The knight, no longer so frequently abroad, was thrown more into the company of his wife, and family. The baron in his more palatial hall began to institute a court wherein feminine graces had an opportunity to bloom; to which the sons and daughters of mesne tenants were sent to learn arts and accomplishments proper to demoiseaux and demoiselles; and to which minstrels, pedlars, palmers, and other wayfaring educationists, brought news of the world and the products of their industry. Civilization commenced to flourish again; music, poetry, handicraft, painting, sculpture, architecture began to burgeon forth into new life.

In the midst of this domestic renaissance the position of the women of the knightly and aristocratic order underwent a remarkable change. Within the century A.D. 1050–1150, damehood like knighthood was emancipated from feudalism. The agents of the emancipation, however, were very different. It was, as we have seen, the priests who captured the knighthood for religion; but it was the troubadours who captured womanhood for romance. Feudalism was as deadly an enemy of romance as it was of spiritual religion or efficient central government. The simoniac bishop, or the hereditary count, was no more (and no less) an intolerable abuse, an outrageous anomaly, and an insuperable obstacle to progress, than was the feudal heiress given as a ward to a greedy courtier and sold by him to the highest bidder. Under the feudal regime, as M. Martin well remarks, "On épousait un fief,"[1] to which the women was merely an appendant burden—one of the inevitable incidents or nuisances. In other words, in feudalism, love and marriage were as completely divorced as was piety from ecclesiastical office, or

---

[1] H. Martin, *Histoire de France*, iii, 381.

efficiency from primogenitary membership of the Curia Regis. The wife of the knight or baron of the dark post-Carolingian age was a serf and a chattel. But, like her husband, she was also a ferocious savage, capable of murderous cruelty, satanic blasphemy, and bestial lust. The accounts which the chronicles have left us of such high-placed viragos as Blanche of Navarre, Mabel of Montgomery, Adelaide of Soissons, and the Châtelaine of Cahuzac, show us that little of barbarity remained to be learned or invented by the harpies of the French Revolution or the harridans of modern Bolshevik Russia. When the husband was at home, he kept the wife in order by such severe corporal chastisement as circumstances might require. When he was abroad, the wife disported herself as she thought fit; but she was, as a rule, quite capable of managing affairs in her lord's absence, and even of conducting the defence of the castle, if she were called upon to do so.

It was from this condition of serfdom and savagery that the troubadours, trouvères, minnesingers, minstrels, and romancers generally—as agents of the social renaissance and domestic revolution everywhere in progress—came to rescue the ladies of the châteaux. They effected the rescue, however, not by encouraging the wives to love their husbands, or the husbands to cherish their wives; not even by urging the youths and maidens to make marriages of love regardless of the restrictions of feudal legality. They do not seem to have considered it possible at that time to break the bonds of feudal conventionality, or to convert marriage into anything better than a sanctified contract, beset with civil and ecclesiastic snares. Marriage was, and always remained, to the troubadours, not the sacrament and consummation of love, but its most formidable obstacle and most dangerous enemy. They deepened, indeed, the schism which feudalism had created between the two.

The rescuer provided, and openly recommended in impassioned verse by the troubadours, was the *paramour*. Ladies were encouraged to seek and find the emancipation of illicit intrigue, and were carefully instructed in the ways by which jealous husbands could be outwitted and their conventional fury evaded. Similarly, knights and squires were required, as part of their chivalric duty, to gain the favour of a lady (whether married or not was wholly a matter of indifference), and having won it, to make it the lodestone of their lives. Chivalric gallantry, therefore, as is abundantly evident from the songs which exalt it and the romances which record its doings, was a gigantic system of bigamy, in which every lady was expected to have both a husband and a *paramour*; and every complete cavalier, besides the wife to whom for business reasons he was bound, a goddess, whose commands he unhesitatingly obeyed, and whose cause he upheld against all comers. It is notable that, on the evidence of the romances, in the selection of *paramours* and goddesses, the lady was almost always the one who took the initiative.

It was a strange system, this system of Gallantry; and it led to consequences which made it necessary for political authority to discountenance and suppress it. It is eloquent of a conception of morals so utterly different from that which, thanks to the Puritans, prevails to-day, that it is difficult to understand it, and still more difficult to judge it fairly. From the first the Church did not like Gallantry, and struggled against it. It corrupted and distracted the knighthood, and turned it from its high tasks of fighting the infidel and recovering the Holy Land. But the Church strove ineffectually; for the Church of the Middle Ages was itself deeply tainted and infected with the virus of gross immorality. So Gallantry succeeded in establishing itself securely, but most incongruously, by the side of War and Religion, as the third and completing element in Chivalry. Thus the distinctive qualities of the chivalric knight in the Golden Age of Chivalry were at their best, honour, piety, and love; at their worst, ferocity, superstition, and lust. The virtues of Chivalry were courage, faith, and devotion; its vices, murder, intolerance, adultery.

VI

Which was " the Golden Age of Chivalry ? " It is hard, indeed, to say. Some writers, Mr. John Batty for instance, think that in the fourteenth century " Chivalry attained its

CHIVALRY : ITS PLACE IN HISTORY

perfection as an institution ".[1] This, however, is certainly putting the Golden Age too late; for although Froissart gives, perhaps, the most fascinating of all extant pictures of Chivalry in operation, it is clearly a decadent, self-conscious, and artificial Chivalry which he portrays. A larger body of more authoritative opinion indicates the thirteenth century as the period of Chivalry's prime. We have seen how Mr. Henderson fixes the interregnum (A.D. 1250-1273) as "the end of the Age of Chivalry". Dr. G. G. Coulton would seem to concur.[2] But elsewhere he points out how very far from ideal was the Chivalry as depicted during even this age by the authoritative and sympathetic pen of Joinville.[3] The scenes, indeed, in the Crusaders' camp at Damietta, enacted in 1249, under the very eye of the saintly Louis IX, himself the paragon of chivalric knighthood, would have better become a horde of marauding vikings. Sanguinary dissension, infamous treachery, blasphemous ribaldry, selfish jealousy, shameless profligacy, and scandalous debauchery—the old and deep-grained vices of the unregenerate feudal knighthood—were displayed in a profusion which neither the Court of Honour had elevated, the Court of God eradicated, nor the Court of Love refined. The sheer impossibility of reconciling what we know of the behaviour of the nobles and cavaliers of the thirteenth century with any ideal of decency, causes Mr. Leon Gautier, the greatest of all the historians and apologists of Chivalry, to place the Golden Age of the institution far back in the twelfth century. M. Lacroix, too, is forced to admit that "it reached its apogee soon after its birth", and that it suffered a speedy deterioration. Careful examination, in short, compels every historian of Chivalry to reject his predecessor's "Golden Age" and to seek another concerning which detailed information is more scanty. Unfortunately for MM. Gautier and Lacroix, although we have no records of twelfth century Chivalry to compare with those of Joinville for the thirteenth, or Froissart for the fourteenth, we do know enough to make us very sceptical as to the purity of the institution even in that age of its infancy. For example, Peter of Blois, writing soon after the murder of

---

[1] Batty, *Spirit and Influence of Chivalry*, p. 45.
[2] *Encyclopædia Britannica*, s.v. Knighthood.
[3] Coulton, *Chaucer and his England*, p. 189.

Thomas Becket by four knights, says: "In these days of ours the Order of Chivalry is mere disorder. For he is accounted stoutest and most illustrious among knights whose mouth is defiled with the most filthy language, whose oaths are most abominable, and who most despises God, reviles his ministers, and defies the Church."[1] Another contemporary of Becket, the famous and judicious John of Salisbury, a less violent writer than Peter of Blois, and in a formal treatise not in a private letter, uses words which confirm the gloomy estimate of his fellow cleric. After giving a summary of what he regards as the functions of orderly knighthood, he goes on to say: "Some think that military glory consists in this, that they shine in elegant dress... If they are sitting softly on their ambling horses they think themselves so many Apollos. If you make an army of them, you will have a camp of Thais, not of Hannibal. Each is boldest in the banquetting-hall, but in battle every one desires to do least... They have the first places at supper; they feast every day splendidly if they can afford it; but shun labour and exercise, like a dog or a snake." And so on.[2] These pictures of the Christian Chivalry of the twelfth century do not differ materially from the lurid views of the frankly savage feudal knighthood of the middle of the eleventh century presented by Adam of Bremen and others. There was, in truth, no Golden Age of Chivalry; no period when the lofty ideals which the Church sought to impose on knights were actually realized by the generality of the chivalric order. There was always a great gulf fixed between the standard of the hero of the Cross whose life was dedicated to conflict and suffering on behalf of the holy and the weak, and the horrid actuality of profane, cruel, selfish, and sensual men. Nay, more, there was hardly more accord between the ideal of the courtly *paramours* of the troubadours, and the reality of the beastly adulteries which corrupted the social life of the late Middle Ages.

It must not be suggested, however, that there were *no* knights and noblemen, *no* fine ladies and fair damsels, who rose to the height of the ideal Chivalry. There can be no

---

[1] Peter of Blois, *Epistolae*, No. 94.
[2] John of Salisbury, *Policraticus*, quoted by H. Stebbing, *History of Chivalry*, i, 45.

doubt that the priestly conception of the perfect knight immensely elevated the level of honour, and incalculably extended the idea of dignity in service. Equally little can it be questioned that the poetical conception of the perfect lady vastly enlarged the sphere of courtesy, and wrought an enormous improvement in general manners. Throughout the twelfth, thirteenth, and fourteenth centuries there were always shining individuals who prominently in the eyes of the world exemplified the virtues and graces of Chivalry, and raised the tone of a society painfully emerging from barbarism. Perhaps nowhere outside the realm of fiction could quite so perfect a paragon as Sir Parsifal be found. But it is enough to mention Godfrey of Bouillon, Tancred of Sicily, William Marshall, Saint Louis, the Cid, Sir Walter Manny, Sir John Chandos, Bertrand du Guesclin, the Black Prince, and the Chevalier Bayard, to recall to all who are familiar with the history of the later Middle Ages the careers of a noble company of illustrious men who in bravery, courtesy, integrity, devotion, piety, and chastity, will well stand comparison with the representative men of any age; men whose lives did much to redeem the reputation of the chivalry to which they owed their education and their inspiration.

VII

I have just used the word "education". It is a cardinal word in respect of the institution of Chivalry. For the strength, and the permanent importance of Chivalry lay in the fact that it was a complete way of life, moulding the character and determining the destiny of its subject from the cradle to the grave. As a type of training; as a code of honour; as a standard of good form; as a school of courtesy; as a norm of piety, ceremonious but not enthusiastic; in all these respects, Chivalry made an enduring mark, not only upon the later Middle Ages, but also upon all the subsequent centuries of Western civilization. In England, particularly, it set the tone which has been perpetuated in the great Public School tradition. Freed from ephemeral accidents, and purged from its absurdities and impurities, the system of education established and developed in the baronial castles and knightly hostels of the twelfth century is precisely that system which has been continued and enlarged in the splendid curricula of Winchester, Eton, and the later members of the great group of which they were the pioneers. They did but graft the classical learning of the monastic schools upon the chivalric training in honour, in sport, in military exercise, in social intercourse, in courtesy and generosity, in reverence and devotion, of the schools of Christian knighthood.

The romance of the Petit Jehan de Saintré gives an inimitable picture of the education of the budding knight. Until the age of seven the child was kept under his mother's care. Then he was sent to be a page in the castle of his father's feudal lord. There for seven years he remained in charge of the women, who besides instructing him—rather prematurely the present age would say—in the rudiments of love, taught him to perform all kinds of menial household duties and to render all sorts of personal services. They made him understand, moreover—a notable lesson never learned in pagan antiquity—that in thus humbly serving he was not incurring any loss of dignity. They further instilled into him his duties, in the manner dear to school-mistresses of all ages; for instance, the Dame des Belles Cousines, who took Jehan under her peculiar charge, warned him against pride, envy, anger, idleness, gluttony, and luxury; further, gave him systematic information respecting the seven virtues, the ten commandments, the twelve articles of faith, and the fourteen works of mercy. As he drew near the end of his period as page, he was taught by the men to run, leap, wrestle, and ride; to use toy weapons, to help to arm his lord himself in the implements of his more serious warfare.

At the age of fourteen the page passed out of the tutelage of the women—though not out of the reach of their influence—and became a squire. We are told how, at this stage, Jehan was taken in hand by the maitre d'hôtel of his lord : " Jehan," he said, " you shall be no longer page " ; and, having informed him of his rise in status, and warned him against pride, he

CHIVALRY : ITS PLACE IN HISTORY

solemnly enjoined him " to keep his hands and nails clean, and also the rest of his person, which would be a necessary attention in the duties he had now to perform." These duties were largely of a martial kind—the use of arms, the management of the heavy war-horse, the breaking-in of chargers, the keeping in good order of the knight's equipment. Besides these military duties, however, he had to undergo a strenuous course of exercises calculated to increase his strength and dexterity; he had also to learn skill in various sports, of which hunting and hawking were the chief. Further, in order that he might be able to fulfil the requirements of gallantry in evening hours, the nascent squire had to practise the arts of music and poetry, and to learn to play such games as chess and backgammon. The squire, moreover, still combined such domestic duties as carving the meat, waiting at table, and preparing the hall for dances or charades. In large baronial or princely establishments, where there were many squires, functions were divided among them. There were pantlers, butlers, constables, stewards, chamberlains, and (highest of all) body-squires, or personal attendants of the lord.

When the squire attained the age of twenty-one, he was qualified for knighthood. The ceremony by which this lofty dignity was conferred upon him was in normal circumstances a long and solemn one, elaborated by the Church and assimilated to the ordination of the sacred priesthood. In times of stress, however—as, for example, on the battlefield—knighthood could be conferred by the simple girding on of the sword, followed by the accolade. Chevaliers so instituted were known as " knights of the sword ", and by this title were distinguished from " knights of the bath ", who had gone through the full process of consecration, in which the ceremonial taking of a bath was a prominent feature. In theory, any knight could dub another; for in knighthood all were equal. But in practice, kings found it necessary more and more strictly to limit the granting of knighthood to themselves or their own accredited agents.

To describe the full process of the ceremonial institution of a knight would absorb more space than is at our disposal. It is unnecessary, moreover, since admirable accounts are available in many easily accessible books.[1] The core of the ceremony was no doubt the primitive and barbaric investiture with arms which marked the formal admission of the young Teutonic freeman to the rank of the warriors of his tribe.[2] When the Church had captured and spiritualized the ceremony—the first indication of which process comes to us from a Service Book of about A.D. 1000—the following were the main features of the rite : (1) The bath, emblematic of purification ; (2) the clothing with white tunic, red robe, and black doublet, symbolical respectively of innocence, self-sacrifice, and death ; (3) the fast for twenty-four hours ; including (4) the all-night vigil in the chapel ; (5) confession, mass, and sermon ; (6) the blessing of the sword ; (7) the taking of the vows ; (8) the investiture with armour, spurs, and sword ; (9) the accolade ; and, finally, (10) the fixing of the helmet, the mounting of the horse, and the performance of spectacular exercises. The duties imposed by the chivalric vows were numerous. The following were the most conspicuous :—to fear God and maintain the Christian religion ; to serve the King faithfully and valorously ; to protect the weak and defenceless ; to refrain from the wanton giving of offence ; to live for honour and glory, despising pecuniary reward ; to fight for the general welfare of all ; to obey those placed in authority ; to guard the honour of the knightly order ; to shun unfairness, meanness, and deceit ; to keep faith and speak the truth ; to persevere to the end in all enterprises begun ; to respect the honour of women ; to refuse no challenge from an equal and never to turn the back upon a foe. These vows embody a noble ideal, and if they were even partly fulfilled, they must have done much to raise the tone of military society. But they ignore the existence of "gallantry", and they ask more than the human nature of the late Middle Ages was normally prepared to concede.

---

[1] Cf. Leon Gautier, *La Chevalerie* ; F. W. Cornish, *Chivalry* ; John Batty, *The Spirit and Influence of Chivalry* ; Paul Lacroix, *Military and Religious Life* ; H. H. Milman, *Latin Christianity* ; F. P. G. Guizot, *Civilization in France*, Lecture 36 ; H. Stebbing, *History of Chivalry* ; Kenelm Digby, *Broad Stone of Honour* ; M. de la Curne de Sainte Palaye, *Memoires sur l'ancienne Chevalerie*.
[2] Cf. Tacitus, *Germania*, xiii.

VIII

After the extinction of the Kingdom of Jerusalem (A.D. 1291) and the suppression of the Order of the Templars (A.D. 1312), Chivalry was obviously on the decline. The period of its pre-eminence was, in fact precisely that of the Crusades—roughly the two centuries A.D. 1100–1300. The causes of its decay are not far to seek. In a sense it had always been in decay, since it had never even approximately realized its ideal. It suffered from what Hobbes would have called "imperfect institution". To make a moral trinity in unity out of a fusion of war with religion, and religion with gallantry, as the three were understood and practised in the late Middle Ages, was so flagrant an impossibility that the decadence of chivalry can be discovered in its very idea. No conceivable elaboration of medieval ecclesiastical ceremonial could consecrate medieval warfare or sanctify medieval love. Medieval religion was too irrational, medieval warfare was too cruel; medieval love too gross for any permanent harmonization. It was necessary for religion to be rationalized, warfare to be humanized, and love purified, before it was possible (to use Hallam's words) for "the character of the knight gradually to subside into that of the gentleman".

Apart, however, from the inherent impracticability of the original chivalric scheme, decline was accelerated, and made evident to all the world, by various extraneous causes. First, kings, in their struggle with feudalism, began, even in the thirteenth century, to lavish knighthoods on children (to free them from wardship); on petty landowners irrespective of training (in order to secure a permanent force of royal cavalry), and on wealthy burgesses (who were prepared to pay heavily for the titular honour). Secondly, changes in the composition and constitution of medieval armies rendered the array of chivalry obsolete. A body of knights was, in fact, not an army at all, but a fortuitous concourse of individual adventurers, without coherence, discipline, or common aim. Nothing could have been more hopeless in its inefficiency for any rational purpose. The pages of Joinville and of Froissart are alike eloquent of absurdities of military behaviour little less ludicrous than those of Don Quixote himself, and far more disastrous. The battle of Bannockburn was lost by the English, and the battles of Crecy and Poitiers were lost by the French, because of the chaotic incompetence of the masses of chivalric lunatics who were all seeking personal glory rather than common victory. The national kings, such as Edward III of England or Charles VII of France, found it necessary to set aside the feudal levies almost entirely, and to build up new professional armies of spearmen, archers, and regular cavalry. Thirdly, and above all, gunpowder was fatal to chivalry as a military force. Artillery converted the baronial and knightly castle from an impregnable fortress into an interesting antiquity. The use of Greek fire by the "Saracens" in A.D. 1249 had heavily discounted the value of the armour worn by the chivalry of Louis IX on the ill-starred seventh crusade. When cannon-balls began to hurtle across the battlefield, armour became worse than useless; it became a trap from which its unhappy captive was extremely unlikely to emerge alive.

Another point should also be noted. The chivalrous knight, even when on a Crusade, was out for sport—sport of that particularly dangerous and adventurous kind which alone satisfied the barbaric taste of the age. The purpose of a Crusade did not touch himself or his fortunes so nearly as to spoil the fun of the enterprise. In the fourteenth century, however, when the effective Crusades were over, subjects of dispute came up which to the carnal imagination were too serious for regulation by the canons of the chivalric game. The Hundred Years War, to begin with, involved issues for both France and England that were, and were felt to be, vital. The war commenced, indeed, in the true chivalric way with a challenge from Philip VI to settle the questions in dispute by means of a personal combat between himself and Edward III; but Edward III, while appearing to entertain the suggestion, used the occasion, in a most unchivalric manner, to move his mercenary army to a more favourable position for battle—merely playing with the proposal until the proper moment for general action arrived. Throughout the war—although, as Froissart abundantly shows, Chivalry strove hard to maintain itself—more and more the issue came to be determined by proletarian forces fighting with the organized strength and efficiency of a regular soldiery. The formation of the French *gens d'ordonnance* in 1438 heralded the victorious termination of the war for France in 1453. Then, in England, there followed the dreadful Wars of the Roses, in which all rules of honour and mercy were swept away in a diabolical orgie of dynastic hatred. These, in the sixteenth century, were succeeded throughout Europe by so-called religious wars, in which the very furies of hell were let loose in a pandemonium of assassinations, treacheries, conspiracies, and rebellions, amid which every idea of Chivalry was negated. The problems generated by the dissolution of Medieval Christendom; by the formation of the modern National State-system; by the establishment of strong monarchies; by the rise of a mercantile middle class; by the discovery of the New World—these problems were too vast and far-reaching, they touched too many people too intimately, to be settled by single combats in well-ordered lists between armour-clad knights, attended by squires, and watched by admiring ladies.

IX

But, although Chivalry vanished from the practical art of war in the fourteenth and fifteenth centuries, it lingered in education (where it was firmly entrenched), in manners, in morals, in society, in court, in all the relations of the governing class. So strong a hold, indeed, had Chivalry, as a way of life, secured over the minds and consciences of the baronial and knightly orders, that they were not content merely to retain its general principles of honour, piety, and courtesy, and apply them in new modes to novel conditions; they strove to keep, revivify, and even extend the obsolete institutions of the Chivalry that was gone. They made the training of page and squire more formal than it had ever been before; they elaborated the rules of courtesy between members of the chivalric orders; they developed a worship of woman-in-the-abstract more extravagant than any hitherto known; they celebrated with unprecedented magnificence the entry of their young men upon the knightly career; they organized tournaments upon a scale of splendour unparalleled; they devoted enormous attention to the development of the science of heraldry, which, as armour was discarded, became a useless and meaningless affectation. Literature took up the task of rehabilitation, and aided them in the effort to infuse life into a dying institution. Hector and Achilles, Alexander and Cæsar, the British King Arthur and the Frankish Emperor Charlemagne, all were made knights of romance, clad in fourteenth century armour, furnished with destriers, provided with squires, and launched on edifying careers on behalf of religion and distressed maidens; and against infidels, giants, dragons, and the rest of the infernal host.

But, above all, new orders of ornamental Chivalry were actually instituted, and it was pretended that they were manifestations, not of an ephemeral mode of warfare which had passed with the Crusades, but of an eternal principle inherent in the nature of things. When Francis I invested Henry VIII with the insignia of a French Order inaugurated in 1469, he claimed the Archangel Michael as the first knight. Caxton in his *Book of the Ordre of Chyvalry* maintains that knighthood was the earliest device of the Divine Being for the recovery of mankind from the ruin of the Fall. Serious writers argued that the Emperor Constantine founded an Order of the Golden Angel in A.D. 213; that Prester John instituted an Order in honour of S. Anthony in A.D. 370; that Clovis commemorated his conversion in A.D. 496 by establishing an Order of the Sacred Vial; that King Arthur actually had a Round Table, and that Charlemagne was really encircled by Paladins. Hence, that the immemorial tradition might be sustained, such Orders (now illustrious) as that of the Garter in England (1349); the Annunciation in Savoy (1392); the Golden Fleece in Burgundy (1429); St. Michael (1469), and the Holy Ghost (1578) in France, were instituted with solemn and impressive ceremonies. The number of Modern Orders, indeed, is legion. The diligent M. Perrot, writing in 1820, enumerated 234 in his *Collection historique des Ordres de Chevalerie*, and since then the new creations have been continuous. Nowhere, in fact, so vigorously as in England, has decorative knighthood maintained and extended itself.

X

I should have liked to say something of the revival of the interest in medieval Chivalry which marked the Romantic Reaction against Rationalism and Utilitarianism at the close of the eighteenth century and during the early decades of the nineteenth century. But space fails me to write more than a few words. The movement began perhaps with the publication of Hurd's *Letters on Chivalry and Romance* in 1762; it was accelerated by the appearance of Percy's *Reliques* in 1765, and by the issue of Warton's *History of English Poetry* during the years 1774-81; but it reached its culmination under the impulse imparted by the poems and novels of Sir Walter Scott, and by the same writer's famous *Essay on Chivalry*. The number of books on Chivalry that were published between 1815 and 1880 is astounding: the titles of the more important of them will be found in the bibliography at the end of this essay. The most remarkable among them, undoubtedly, was the devout Kenelm Digby's *Broadstone of Honour* (1822). One feels the influence of its enthusiasm in all the romantic enterprises of the following quarter of a century, until it culminates in the Young England Movement and Disraeli's *Coningsby* (1845).

It would be improper to close this study without some attempt, however brief, to estimate the value of Chivalry as a factor in the evolution of Western civilization, and to balance its merits and defects. Various, indeed, are the views which have been expressed respecting it. The Romantic writers of the early nineteenth century—looking mainly to its theory, and ignoring even there the shadier sides of gallantry—are lyrical in its praise. Mr. Batty, for instance, says that "Chivalry was the development of all that was lovely, graceful, and worthy in human nature".[1] Sir Walter Scott holds that "excepting only the change which flowed from the introduction of the Christian religion, we know no cause which has produced such general and permanent difference betwixt the ancients and the moderns as that which

---

[1] Batty, *Spirit and Influence of Chivalry*, p. 55.
[2] Scott, *Essay on Chivalry*.

CHIVALRY

has arisen out of the institution of Chivalry ".[2] Mr. G. P. R. James, with even less restraint, contends that Chivalry was "the most glorious institution that man himself ever devised", and maintains that it left behind it "a treasure of noble feelings and generous principles ".[1]

In sharpest contrast to these judgments stand the opinions of such Radicals as Dr. Thomas Arnold, Professor E. A. Freeman, Mr. John Richard Green, and Mr. T. H. Buckle. "If I were called upon," writes the great head master of Rugby, "to name what spirit of evil predominantly deserved the name of Antichrist, I should name the spirit of Chivalry— the more detestable for the very guise of the 'Archangel ruined' which has made it so seductive to generous minds." [2] Buckle speaks of it as "a mischievous institution" whose medieval representatives "enlivened the superstitions of monks with the debauchery of soldiers"; and he thinks that it "inflicted the greatest evils on Society ".[3] Freeman condemns it, together with Feudalism, as an institution which "substitutes purely personal obligations devised in the interests of an exclusive class for the more homely duties of an honest man and a good citizen ".[4] John Richard Green, obediently following his master, dismisses Chivalry contemptuously as "that picturesque mimicry of high sentiment, heroism, love, and courtesy, before which all depth and reality of nobleness disappeared, to make room for the coarsest profligacy, the narrowest caste-spirit, and a brutal indifference to human suffering ".[5] Even Bishop Stubbs, the other member of the Oxford triumvirate, in spite of his more conservative sympathies, asks: "What is the meaning of Chivalry? Is it not the gloss put by fine manners on vice and selfishness and contempt for the rights of man?" [6]

An institution which has incurred such strong denunciation from so many judicious historians must have had some apparent defects. What were they? They are not far to seek. Most of them have been indicated in the preceding pages.

---

[1] James, *History of Chivalry*, pp. 14–15.
[2] T. Arnold, *Life and Correspondence*, i, 255.
[3] T. H. Buckle, *History of Civilization*, Robertson's edition, pp. 561-3.
[4] E. A. Freeman, *Norman Conquest*, v, 482.
[5] Green, *Short History of the English People*, p. 182.
[6] W. Stubbs, *Lectures on European History*, edited by Hassell, p. 137.

In its medieval form—that is to say, during the period of its prevalence in the twelfth and thirteenth centuries, and still more during the age of its decadence in the fourteenth and fifteenth centuries—Chivalry was marked by the following vices. First, it glorified war for its own sake; exalted fighting as the only occupation worthy of a gentleman; instituted a love of bloodshed, and a contempt for human suffering; and yet, at the same time, because of its excessive individualism, remained as a military instrument amazingly inefficient, retarding rather than advancing the science of warfare. Secondly, it was an exclusive class-institution; it placed a gulf between the knightly order and the commonalty, and restricted its code of honour and courtesy peculiarly to members of its own caste; it generated a contempt for social inferiors and a disregard for their feelings which explain, if they do not justify, the retaliatory outrages of the Peasants' Revolt and the Jacquerie. Thirdly, its religion was at once formal and obscurantist. On the one hand it was engrossed in ceremonies and external observances; on the other hand, it was merciless in waging war on so-called infidels, in carrying through crusades against heretics, in persecuting and suppressing freedom of thought. The Inquisition found in the knighthood a ready instrument of its worst atrocities. Finally, under cover of its improved and refined manners, it concealed and disseminated a code of debased and deadly immorality; at its worst, in Provence, it elevated fornication and adultery to the rank of social obligations.

These are grave indictments, and they are sufficient to prevent us from regarding Chivalry, in its medieval manifestation, as an ideal way of life. In mitigation, however, of an undue severity of judgment, it should be borne in mind that our standard of comparison ought not to be the more enlightened religion and morality of the present day, but rather the less elevated condition of superstition and barbarism which preceded the emergence of Chivalry. In war, in faith, in manners, and even in morals, Chivalry marked an advance on the savagery of the dark ages which came before it. It was distinctly an upward move; a move towards the light and the air of the more perfect day. It manifested, if sometimes only in a crude and rudimentary form, the elements of virtues and graces which display themselves as the fine flowers of the cultured and Christian society of this later age. Purged of its grossest imperfections, and refined by the educated conscience of Christendom, it has, through the agency of our public schools and universities, our military and naval services, our churches and ethical associations, transmitted to us an incalculably valuable treasure of lofty principle and noble precedent.

What are the typical virtues of Chivalry in its purified and ideal form ? We have seen that Chivalry was a compound of three elements, viz. war, religion, and gallantry. Each of the three respectively emphasized and exalted three qualities as essential to the true knight. The three primary virtues of Chivalry, based on its *military* character, were courage, loyalty and generosity. The three secondary virtues, derived from *religion*, were fidelity to the Church, obedience, and chastity. The three tertiary virtues, *social* in their nature, were courtesy, humility, and beneficence. On the side of theory and principle, at any rate, Chivalry stressed the duties and obligations of knighthood, rather than its rights and privileges. It held up a high standard of honour, and required it to be maintained without any diminution. It insisted on a truthfulness, a trustworthiness, an adhesion to plighted word, a fidelity to engagements, from which no allurement of advantage and no plea of necessity could cause any deviation. It required a liberality which lavished largesses, even though they reduced the donor to poverty. It demanded a regular observance of the offices of religion ; a full acceptance of the Catholic faith ; a complete submission in things spiritual to the authority of the clergy, and, as a council of perfection for the elect, a respect for marriage vows. It instilled a courtesy (*courtoisie*), a code of fine manners based on heartfelt consideration and genuine regard which immensely added to the delight of the intercourse of social life. Courtesy, especially in the relations of men towards women, although it had been anticipated in the Christian Church, was a new thing in the hard and general world. It differed in its grace and charm and geniality from the mere politeness, civility, or urbanity, which (as the words themselves imply) were the forms of good manners evolved amid the crowded and commercial population of the towns. Above all, it inculcated an ideal of social service ; service without remuneration ; service, however humble its nature, free from degradation or disparagement ; service of the weak by the strong ; service of the poor by the wealthy ; service of the lowly by the high.

Thus, even though in the day of its dominance Chivalry had defects grave and deplorable, nevertheless, it remains a glorious and honourable name, and its principles, freed from their medieval accidents, are among the noblest and most splendid that have assisted the progress of the human race.

SOME BOOKS ON CHIVALRY

ASHTON, J.: *Romances of Chivalry.* 1887.
BASNAGE, J.: *Dissertation Historique sur les Ordres de Chevalerie.* Edited by P. Roques. 1740.
BATTY, J.: *The Spirit and Influence of Chivalry.* 1890.
BÜSCHING, J. G. G.: *Ritterzeit und Ritterwesen.* 1823.
CARDUCCI, G.: *Cavalleria e Umanesimo.* (In Opera, vol. xx. 1909.)
CAXTON, W.: *The Ordre of Knighthode and Chyvalry.* 1478.
CORNISH, F. W.: *Chivalry* [the best brief sketch]. 1911.
COULTON, G. G.: *Social Life in Britain.* (Section V = Kings, Knights, War.) 1918.
COULTON, G. G.: *Chaucer and his England.* 1908.
CUTTS, E. L.: *Scenes and Characters of the Middle Ages.* (Fourth Edition.) 1922.
DIGBY, KENELM H.: *The Broad Stone of Honour.* 1822.
DILLON, E.: " The Ordinances of Chivalry " (in *Archæologia*, vol. lvii). 1900.
DORAN, D.: *Knights and their Days.* 1856.
Encyclopædia Britannica, 11th edition, article on " Knighthood and Chivalry ", by G. G. Coulton. 1910.
FERRARIO, G.: *Storia ed Analisi degli Romanzi di Cavalleria.* 1828-9.
FLACH, J.: *Origines de l'Ancienne France* (vol. ii). 1893.
FROISSART, JEAN: *Chroniques*: translated into English by Lord Berners. New edition with introduction by W. P. Ker. 1901-3.
GAUTIER, JEAN: *La Chevalerie.* 1883. (English translation, 1891.)
GUIZOT, F. P. G.: *Civilisation en France* (Leçon xxxvi). 1839.
HAGEN, F. H. VON DER: *Ritterleben und Ritterdichtung.* 1855.
HENNE-AM-RHYN, O.: *Geschichte des Rittertums.* 1893.
HONORÉ DE SAINTE-MARIE: *Dissertations sur la Chevalerie.* 1718.
HURD, RICHARD: *Letters on Chivalry and Romance.* 1762. (New edition by Edith Morley, 1911.)
JAMES, G. P. R.: *History of Chivalry.* 1830.
JOINVILLE: (1) *Histoire de S. Louis.* (2) *Chronique de Du Guesclin.* (3) *Histoire de Bayart.* (New edition, 1867.)
LACROIX, P.: *Military and Religious Life in the Middle Ages.* 1874.
LA TOUR-LANDRY, G. DE: *The Book of the Knight.* (Fifteenth century English translation, published by Early English Text Society. 1868.)
LINTON, E. L.: " The Women of Chivalry," in *Fortnightly Review*. 1887.
LUCE, S.: *Histoire de Du Guesclin et de son Epoque.* 1876.
MALORY, SIR T.: *La Morte d'Arthur.* (Printed by Caxton. 1485.)
MARTIN, H.: *Histoire de France.* (Vol. iii, pp. 334-405.) 1862.
MELLOR, W. C.: *A Knight's Life in the Days of Chivalry.* 1824.
MENESTRIER, C. F.: *Ordres de Chevalerie.* 1683.
MILLS, C.: *History of Chivalry.* 1826.
MONCREIFF, A. R. H.: *Romance and Legend of Chivalry.* N.D.
NEWBOLT, H.: *The Happy Warrior.* 1917.
NICOLINI, G.: *La Cavalleria.* 1861.
PALGRAVE, SIR F.: *The Lord and the Vassal.* 1844.

PERROT, A. M. : *Collection Historique des Ordres de Chevalerie.* 1820.
RENE D'ANJOU : *Le Pas d'Armes.* Edited by Quatrebarbes, 1835.
SAINTE-PALAYE, J. B. DE LA CURNE DE : *Memoires sur l'Ancienne Chevalerie.* 1759.
SCHOFIELD, W. H. : *Chivalry in English Literature.* 1912.
SCHULZ, A. : *Höfisches Leben zur Zeit der Minnesänger.* 1879.
SCOTT, SIR W. : "Essay on Chivalry" (in *Miscellaneous Works*, vol. vi. 1834–40).
STEBBING, H. : *History of Chivalry and the Crusades.* 1829.
STEENACKERS, F. F. : *Histoire des Ordres de Chevalerie en France.* 1867.
TAYLOR, H. O. : *The Medieval Mind.* (Book IV, "Ideal and Actual Society.") 1911.
THOMAS, H. : *Spanish and Portuguese Romances of Chivalry.* 1920.
WEDEL, H. F. P. VON : *Deutschlands Ritterschaft.* 1904.
WOODHOUSE, F. C. : *Military Religious Orders.* 1879.

CHAPTER II

THE BEGINNINGS OF MEDIEVAL CHIVALRY

By E. F. JACOB, M.A., D.Phil.,
Student of Christ Church, Oxford.

IN one obvious sense Chivalry is not confined to the Middle Ages, for many human beings are happily so inclined. If we study it in this period, the reason lies in the fact that people had begun to systematise their ideas about their fellow-men, to gain some notion of the value of individual personality and to react strongly against the wastage and brutality which disturbed life in the period of the great invasions. These appreciations and feelings did not remain isolated in individual thinkers, as had been the tendency in classical times, but were organised and generalised in the eleventh and twelfth centuries of our era. Medieval Chivalry became an institution as well as an ideal. An institution, it was the unwritten convention of a noble or military class, whose members could only reach and maintain their status in it through proper observance of its ceremonies and duties. An ideal, it supplied the rudiments of morality, and served as a means whereby the Church sought to educate the high-spirited and predatory, and to sublimate the acquisitive instincts. It was not law, though it had no small effect upon customary codes. It was not feudalism, had no essential connexion with tenure and vassalage, although it gave the tenurial system some of its coherence and strengthened many of its sanctions. In its earliest stages it is best described as the Christian form of the military life; for then, while it was pervaded by strong religious influences, it represents the compromise of the Church with pagan violence. In its later developments it lost its moral aspect and passed into aestheticism, became unmuscular and largely decorative, much as robust Victorianism gave place to the 'nineties. Yet its best examples in any period are an inspiration of right conduct in their embodiment of valour and gentleness;

and it is one of the gifts of the Middle Ages that such a union is still prized, even where its occurrence confronts us with the dilemma of having to choose between an Oliver and a Roland.

It began as a system of education, the moral and physical training of the future warrior. Its early history is closely connected with that of the bodyguard or school of personal retainers. The word "scholar" in the Roman Empire at the time of Constantine meant a member of the imperial bodyguard, a man disciplined in the service of the Palace. By analogy, each general might have his *schola* or family of retainers, consisting generally of barbarian mercenaries, not aristocrats or Greeks of free social standing. Between late Roman and early barbarian practice there is, however, this distinction to be drawn, that under the Visigoths and, later, the Merovingian Franks the "school" is recruited from free men taken at an earlier age. In Visigothic times a Roman term was borrowed for them; they were *liberi homines in patrocinio*, free men that had placed themselves for training and protection under some powerful individual as patron. Under the early Franks, as we find in Gregory of Tours, the band is designated as "pueri".[1] They were either sons of well-born Palace officials, or the young relatives of local Counts or military Dukes of the Empire. One calls to mind the picture of the *Comitatus* in the Germania and a similar instance in Beowulf: the *adolescentuli*, marked out for the prince's approval by their high birth or by the great merits of their fathers, introduced among the older and more practised warriors, among whom they bore themselves freely[2] and exercised themselves in arms. I am far from suggesting that continuity can be traced between primitive German and early Frankish practice; there are differences in the ceremonies adopted, e.g. instead of the formal "arming" of the young man when he reaches warrior's age, we find among the Visigoths, Lombards, and Merovings, the ritual of the first cutting of the beard, the *capillatoria* or *barbatoria*, and so forth[3]; but by the end of the seventh century, as

---

[1] They should, incidentally, be distinguished from the less refined category of *antrustions*, a class of inferior retainers recruited from strangers and outlaws, whom Gregory of Tours calls by the unsavoury names of "gladiatores", "muriones", "sicarii".

[2] "Nec rubor inter comites aspici."

[3] P. Guilhiermoz, *Essai sur l'origine de la noblesse en France*, p. 411 ff.

the lives of the Merovingian saints show beyond all doubt, the boy of gentle birth at the age of 14 or 15 was regularly sent to receive his education, either at court from the Mayor of the Palace, or at the house of some powerful external prince or duke, and when of sufficient age was formally girt with weapons by his patron and placed among the palatine officials, where he might remain for several years before going home to be married or to succeed to his inheritance. After he had taken his departure, he was liable to be called back to the court of his sovereign, to receive his orders or to accompany him to war. He is not acting here as a *fidelis*, as a vassal bound to his lord by the tie of fealty, but as an old scholar of the college, who returns for periodical or emergency reunions. The same type of training was the rule at the Carolingian court. St. Benedict of Aniane, son of the Count of Maguelone, was brought up *inter scolares* at the court of Pepin the Short. Later on in the feudal epoch, the class of " scholar " was extended to embrace the young man destined for the Church ; for as the domestic chanceries or writing departments of great nobles grew in imitation of the royal administration, the need became the greater for a staff of literate clerks who could send out the baron's writs and make enrolments of deeds and fiscal documents. We need not pursue this class further, except to note that its members shared the common atmosphere of the *familia* and early got to know the men who later were to be their patrons, or even their royal masters.

The *familia* of a great magnate in the twelfth and thirteenth centuries included men described as *valetti, bachilarii, servientes, armigeri*.[1] The usual translation of the first, adopted in some of the Calendars of Public Records, is " yeoman ". But one of the questions asked in the General Eyre gives its meaning more accurately. The answer to the chapter *De valettis* required the jurors to state who in their neighbourhood had twenty or (in 1256) fifteen librates of land and were not yet knights. The *valettus* here is the landholder who, given the extent of his annual income from tenure, ought to be a knight and is not. This meaning fits in well

---

[1] See the analysis of the Earl of Gloucester's *familia* (1267) in my *Studies in the Period of Baronial Reform and Rebellion* (Oxford Studies in Social and Legal History, viii), p. 129 ff.

with the normal use of the word in the Close Rolls to denote the (as yet) unknighted aspirant to full military status ; a status which he does not acquire till at the command of the king or at the request (*ad instanciam*) of the magnate, his patron, he is formally decorated with the cinglet of knighthood, and " takes up " military arms. So, too, with the third of these terms, the bachelor. In some contexts, mostly of the early thirteenth century, he is the young " undergraduate " knight who has not yet come into his inheritance and has not been armed ; in others, mostly of the later thirteenth and fourteenth, he may be a senior person, a man of standing and experience who does not fly his own pennon in the field, but serves under the standard of some great feudal leader.[1] The one point common to these two widely different meanings, the prime constituent of valetry and bachelordom, is the bond of the *familia*. And so, also, to an even greater degree, with the *armiger*, the young squire, whose training in the mesnée is the subject of numerous reflections in the Chansons de Geste and the Romances. He grew up in the martial traditions of an athletic community, that valued prowess above all things. He was taught the management of horses, the care and use of arms, fencing (which developed the lungs and made one " fitter and more erect and much straighter for it "), hawking—a training in natural history—and hunting, in the evenings chess and backgammon, and on wet days a little writing, though writing as an art must be left to the scribe. It would be a particularly accomplished man who, like Aiol, in the romance of that name :—

> Bien savoit . . . lire et enbriever,
> Et latin et romans savoit parler.

It was this profession in embryo to which in the eleventh century the Church had already begun to impart a religious aspect. Warfare she had always abhorred : " he that draweth the sword shall perish by the sword " had been her principle. In her local Councils she had done her best to limit, or, at any rate, to introduce pauses into, the annual campaigning season ; but she had been forced to accept the inevitable, and to support the concession made by St. Augustine : " At

---

[1] Professor Powicke has kindly pointed out to me that Walter de Colevill, described in 1267 as a " bachelor of the Earl of Gloucester ", was important enough to be summoned to Simon de Montfort's Parliament of 1265.

prez te vient en presens . texte . v.
De qui le hault nom est seuu
par my le monde en toutes pars
en sus li cheuaulx appers
Renanche par lair en uolant
et andromada en alant
δ deliura de la bestie
i fu a si fiere uestue
omme bon cheualier euureu
se renoue a ses parens

THE KNIGHTLY VIRTUES

Rescue of the distressed, exemplified by Perseus. Christine de Pisan, Letter of Othea to Hector. British Museum. Harleian MS. 4431, fol 98*v* (fifteenth cent.).

God's word, or at the command of some other lawful authority, certain wars may be undertaken by the just." Churchmen in the eleventh and early twelfth centuries were far removed from the anti-militarism of the age of Origen and Tertullian. We need go no further than Suger's *Life of Louis le Gros* to see with what approving eye the great Abbot of St. Denis viewed the French king's attempt to war down tiresome feudatories of the Île-de-France, such as the seigneurs of Montlhéry and the Counts of Corbeil. Not once nor twice, at the request of the convent itself, were those expeditions undertaken, or Louis blessed for his strong right arm. Yet Churchmen, to their credit, never failed to think of the wars of military conquerors as *latrocinium* or brigandage. The letters of Gregory VII bear testimony to the Christian horror of an imperial victor taking revenge upon his rebellious subjects, of the *superbia* engendered by the lust for revenge. The one hope of restraining the coarsened instincts, the bestial love of mere violence that made the baron of the Puiset type *homo non rationalis, sed pecoralis*, as Suger called him, was to penetrate the knightly order with the Church's teaching, to turn armed force to the service of unarmed verity. The supreme examples of such a conversion are the First Crusade itself and the eleventh century French Crusade in Spain,[1] that diverted love of mere action towards a celestial objective, while it disciplined and made articulate emotional forces that might have wrecked Europe, had they remained in a state of partial suppression. In the *Chanson d'Antioche* the knights are called " li Jhesus Chevalier ", and the old troubadour completes his definition by saying that they are

cil qui Damedieu servent de loïal cuer entier.

There is no better testimony to the religious conquest of knighthood than the various medieval statements of a knight's duty, or than the order for the ceremony of arming the knight found in the *Ordene de Chevalerie*. When in 1247 William Count of Holland, after being elected King of the Romans, asked to receive knighthood before being crowned at Aachen, the following rules were proposed for him: he must every day hear the Office of the Passion of Jesus Christ; he must expose his life courageously for the faith; he must protect

[1] Even here we must not exaggerate. Every crusade had about it something of a joint-stock enterprise.

the Church and defend widows, orphans and the poor. In 1330 William, Count of Ostrevant, received on a similar occasion still more explicit instructions from the Bishop of Cambrai. Every day he must hear Mass fasting; he must die for the faith, if need be, must protect widows and orphans, not make war without good reason, not espouse unjust causes, but protect the oppressed innocent; he must bear himself humbly in all things, and it is his duty to preserve the goods of his subjects and to do nothing contrary to the interests of his suzerain.[1] Religious orthodoxy and religious diligence stand first among all requirements: prayers to the Virgin, periodical confession, attendance at Mass, death, if need be, in the faith on behalf of the faith, defence of the Church. In the Roman *Pontificale* the suppliant receives the sword of Knighthood, which had been lying on the altar, with the words " accipe gladium istum in nomine Patris et Filii et Spiritus Sancti et utaris eo ad defensionem tuam et sanctae Dei Ecclesiae et ad confusionem inimicorum Crucis Christi ac fidei Christianae"; or, as the French more tersely puts it, " Sainte Eglise salver et garantir." The protection of widows and orphans, the *miserabiles personae* of the Canon Law, finds an echo in the *Chanson d'Antioche* where the poet praises the accomplished knight because:—

> Il ne donna conseil petit ne grant
> Par coi preudome deserité fussant,
> Les veves fames ne li petit enfant.

Fidelity to one's suzerain was emphasized as a guarantee of social stability in an age when the peace of society depended on the keeping of feudal engagements. We may recollect, among scores of instances, the advice to vassals given by that good old schoolmaster Fulbert of Chartres in his famous " six points "—*incolume, tutum, honestum, utile, facile, possibile*[2]; the many contemporary commendations of William the Marshal for his feudal loyalty to his Angevin masters, especially to John Lackland, most difficult of all men to serve faithfully and continuously[3]; or the pitiful

---

[1] Léon Gautier, *La Chevalerie*, p. 33.
[2] Cf. the remarks of Miss Hilda Johnstone, " Fulbert of Chartres," *Church Quarterly Review*, April, 1926, pp. 57–8.
[3] On the Marshal see the *Histoire de Guillaume le Maréchal*, ed. P. Meyer, esp. ll. 9845–58, 19125–52, and the analysis of his character in Miss Norgate's *The Minority of Henry III*, pp. 67–70.

patience of Bernier, the outraged vassal of Raoul of Cambrai, the lord whom finally, as the Chanson de Geste relates, he is forced to disavow.

For the ceremonial making of a knight,[1] the formal arming, the *adoubement* (the *adoubs* is the group of arms constituting a warrior's equipment), was all that was originally required. Strictly speaking, this had no essential connexion with the *accolade*, which was given directly afterwards, though by the thirteenth century the Romances can speak of " La collée qui signifie L'Ordre de Chevalerie ", and make this the crucial point in the ceremony. By the beginning of the twelfth the original rite had greatly changed under the influence of the Church. The candidate had a ritual bath, prayed in solitude throughout the night in Church, confessed and made his Communion. Then came the special moment. After the Alleluias of the Gradual, the bishop laid the naked sword upon the altar and prayed for a blessing upon it. This done, he gave it into the knight's right hand and girded it on him as he kneels before him. The knight brandished it thrice and set it back in the scabbard : virtue had passed into it, virtue all the stronger if the hilt contained holy relics, such as were in Durendal, Roland's brand that had " tooth of St. Peter, blood of St. Basil, hairs of my lord St. Denis, cloth worn by the Holy Mary " ; or as were found in Joiuse, Charlemagne's sword, so called because it was honoured by having in its hilt the iron of the lance that pierced the Saviour's side. These ceremonies are related with greater elaboration in the thirteenth century *Ordene*,[2] which purports to be a dialogue between a Christian Knight and his Saracen captor, who is anxious to know the meaning of each stage in the proceedings. The outspoken refusal of the Knight, at first, to tell what he knows, sums up the attitude of the chivalric class to pagans beyond the pale :—

> Sainte Ordre de chevalerie
> Seroit en vous mal emploiie,
> Car vous estes de mal loi,
> Si n'avez baptesme de foi.

Reminded that he is still a captive, he becomes more

[1] See the account in Miss Joan Evans, *Life in Medieval France*, pp. 39–41.
[2] Ed. Barbazan, *Fabliaux*, i, 59–82. It is obviously an explanatory account of the allegorical nature of the ceremony by a rhyming clerk. There is an English translation by W. Morris.

communicative and explanatory. The bath, he recounts, signifies the mystical washing away of sin. After the bath, he continues, the knight is laid upon a fair bed. What does this signify? asks the Saracen :—

> Sire cis lis vous senefie
> C'on doit par sa chevalerie
> Conquerre lit en paradis
> Ke Diex otroie à ses amis.

After lying on the bed he is dressed in white linen and over it a scarlet mantle is cast, to symbolize the need for him to shed his blood for Holy Church. After putting on the black stockings that symbolize death, the white cingulum is fastened round his loins :—

> Sire par cheste chainturete
> Est entendu que vo car nete,
> Vos rains, vos cors entirement
> Devez tenir tout fermement.
> Ausi com en virginité
> Vos cors tenir en netée,
> Luxure despire et blamer.

Then the spurs, the two-edged sword—one side for rich oppressors of the poor, the other for the strong who persecute the weak—the white coif, after which the *colée* itself is given. Then he receives four instructions. He must never have any commerce with traitors; must never give evil counsel to a lady, married or unmarried, but must treat her with great respect and defend her against all; he must observe fasts and abstinences; and every day he must hear mass and make a reasonable offering at the minster. The latter is the point of the contemporary and highly moral tale ("conte dévot" someone has written in my copy) of the knight overdue at a tournament, who insisted, despite his impatient squire, on hearing mass first, and was therefore miraculously aided by Our Lady when it came to the fight. The squire *loquitur* :—

> Volez vous devenir hermite,
> Ou papelart, ou ypocrite?

The knight replies *en bon clerc* :—

> Amis, ce dist, li chevalier,
> Cil tournoie moult noblement,
> Qui les servises Dieu entent,
> Quant les Messes seront tres toutes
> Dittes, s'en irons à nos routes.

BEGINNINGS OF MEDIEVAL CHIVALRY 45

and yet when this scrupulous fellow enters the lists,

> la pucelle
> Qu'en aoroit en la Chapelle,
> Avoit pour lui fet ses cembiaux.

To digress from the main theme for a moment, it is worth noting what were the juridical consequences of receiving knighthood. In some parts of Northern France, during the eleventh and twelfth centuries, it was only in virtue of this *adoubement* that a man of knightly birth attained his legal majority. Orphans did not emerge from wardship and could not enter upon possession of their goods until they had been armed. It was this alone that conferred the right to possess a seal and make valid contracts. But in the thirteenth century the *adoubement* ceased to become obligatory for this purpose, and was replaced, as a sign of majority in the feudal classes, by a fixed age—twenty-one or fifteen, according to the customary area. In England knighting at first often accompanies, but is by no means necessary to the attainment of "full age". In the thirteenth century Bracton makes no mention of proof of age by knighthood. A minor could not claim by writ or right a military fief till he was twenty-one; and if the justices are in doubt whether a man is a minor or not, they must take an inquest of the country.[1]

Such, then, was the Church's idea of knighthood. In its highest forms it was a product of the great period between 1080 and 1180, the period of spiritual and intellectual renaissance, when a great literary language that should embody it was being fashioned by French writers, Thibaut de Vernon in his *Chanson de Saint Alexis*, Aubri de Besançon in the *Roman d'Alexandre*, Richard le Pelerin in the *Chanson d'Antioche*, William IX of Poitiers and his troubadours, the author of the *Mystère d'Adam*, by Wace and Benoit de Sainte-Maure, the period of the foundation of new religious orders, the period of Roscellinus, William of Champeaux, and Abelard, the period when Suger was making St. Denis the centre of European art; in short, the period of the *motio valida*, expressed by M. Joseph Bédier in the unforgettable

[1] De legibus Angliae, ff. 86, 86b. "Full age" for different classes of society was fixed comparatively early in England. The knight came of age at 21; the socman's heir at 15; the burgess's son when he was of age to count pence, measure cloth, and conduct his father's business. Cf. W. S. Holdsworth, *History of English Law*, 3rd ed., iii, 510-11.

fashion which his countrymen alone can contrive : " C'est alors aux alentours de l'an 1100 qu'apparaissent, comme tumultuairement, le premier croisade—et encore le premier arc d'ogive—et encore le premier vitrail—et encore le premier drame liturgique—et encore le premier tournoi—et encore la première charte de liberté d'une commune [1]—et encore le premier chant du premier troubadour : toutes créations inattendues, jaillies à la fois du sol de la France." [2] It is in the *Chansons de geste* that is to be found the fullest exposition of the chivalric ideal in its early stages, and it is most closely connected with the legendary life of the nation that gave it birth. The dominant motive of these early epic songs is that God chose Charlemagne and his Franks to be His champions and to conduct a continual Holy War against the infidel. It is the motive that inspired the anonymous South Norman writer who accompanied Bohemond of Antioch on crusade to entitle his work the *Gesta Francorum* and to include within that category Flemish and Langobard contingents. There is nothing more significant than the opening of the second chapter. "And now the Gauls (*Gallie*, the divisions of the country, not *Galli*, is the reading of the best texts) are far from their homes." One division has even *maxima gens Alamannorum*. They are the friends of Christ, Christendom itself, victorious because of their belief in God, the Three in One. After the Battle of Dorylaeum, the clerk who collaborated with the knightly author of the *Gesta* put into his prose what others recited in their epic verse : " What wise or learned man will ever dare to describe the skill, prowess, and bravery of the Turks ? Who ever thought to terrify the Franks with the threatenings of their arrows as they terrified the Arabs, Saracens, Armenians, Syrians, and Greeks ? But, please God, they will never be as strong as our folk. Yet, indeed, they (the Saracens) say that they originally sprang from the Franks and that no man by nature can be a knight save the Franks and themselves. I will speak the truth which none shall forbid me to utter. Truly, if they had been ever firm in the belief of Christ and in Holy Christianity, and had been willing to confess the One God in Three, and had believed in the Son of God born from the Virgin, suffering

[1] St. Quentin.
[2] *Roland à Roncevaux*, p. 7.

tepte .xxbij.

Se as lojuulo compuignes aurmes
Jusque en enfer ou vont les avmes
Il dois aler secourw les
u la some com fist hercules

Glose .xxvij.

r la fable que pirotheus et theseus
alerent en enfer pour proserpme recouv

THE KNIGHTLY VIRTUES

Loyalty to comrades, exemplified by Hercules. Christine de Pisan, *ibid*.
Harleian MS. 4431, fol. 108*v*.

and rising from the dead the third day, ascending into heaven in the sight of his disciples, sending them in full measure the consolation of the Holy Spirit, and reigning in heaven and on earth, no one would have been able to find stronger, braver, or more skilful warriors in battle than they." [1] It is the climax of simple chivalric belief, that makes the bathos of the disorderly quarrel between Bohemond and the other crusading leaders for the possession of Antioch, or its retention for the Emperor, all the more noticeable. And if we come back to our poetry, we need go no further than the splendid scene where the dying Roland having rescued his sword Durendal from a Saracen, tries to break it and cannot, however sharply he makes the steel cry out. " Ah Durendal how fair thou art, how clear and white ! In the sun how thou turnest and flamest ! Charles was in the valleys of Maurienne when from the sky God told him by his angel to give thee to one of the counts his captains. Then he girded me with it, the gentle king, the Great. With it I conquered for him Anjou and Brittany, with it I won for him Poitou and Maine (think of the effect of such lines on Philip Augustus' men) ; with it I conquered Normandy the free, with it Provence and Aquitaine, Lombardy, and all the Romagna . . . With it I conquered so many, many countries which Charles the white-bearded holds. For this sword I now have grief and pain ; better die than leave it to the pagans. God our father, suffer not that France should have this shame ! " [2] " Entre le preux et le sage faut-il choisir ? " asks M. Bédier, and it is difficult to give any answer to that age-long question.

Yet the fine flower of chivalry might have bitter fruit, and the glory of the monarchy replace the glory of God. St. Bernard, if any other, had known the knightly life in his youth at Fontaines ; by his conversion and the fire of his example he had drawn away from it, one by one, his brothers, and his suspicion of the military profession remained. " What, then, ye knights is this gigantic error, this intolerable madness, to fight with such expense and labour for no reward, save the reward of death ? " But the foundation and recruitment of the Order of the Temple for the rescue of pilgrims and the protection of the Holy Places was of a different nature

---

[1] Ch. ix, ed. Bréhier, pp. 50-1.
[2] Chanson de Roland, ed. Bédier, l. 2316 f., p. 177.

of things. Yet nine years were to elapse before it received the highest form of contemporary advertisement—Bernard's published approval.[1] The *De laudibus novae militiae* which he wrote at the request of the Grand Master, Hugh de Payns, is the justification of the new amalgam of monk and knight. There was no law that forbade Christians to use the sword. The Gospel recommended moderation to soldiers, but it did not tell them to cast away their arms. "The soldier of Christ takes life with safety to himself, lays down his own more safely still." He does not bear his sword without reason: he is minister of God for the punishment of malefactors, for the reward of the good; and Bernard draws a very characteristic contrast between the simplicity of the knight of Christ and the elaborate equipment of the secular knight with his trailing sleeves and gilded saddle. The life of the Templar is then depicted; all vigour, obedience, hard work. No idleness, no games like chess or dice, no hunting, hawking, or theatricals: hair short, for the Apostle said it was a shame for a man to tend his hair. In a few terse words he summarizes the scrubby nobility of the Templar: "Never brushed, seldom washed, hair shaggy and neglected, besmirched with dust, dark in breastplate of steel and scorched by the sun."

This was, perhaps, a little extreme. The more normal Church view of knighthood is to be gathered from the writers who regard the *milites* as an integral rank of society, set there for a definite purpose. "The knighthood," says John of Salisbury, in comparing the organization of the kingdom to that of the human body, "is the armed hand of the State." Its members must be carefully selected, hardy, disciplined, virile warriors, bound by oath to serve the king, but never to the exclusion of their duty to protect the Church. This is their first task at all times.[2] The same idea is to be found in Vincent de Beauvais, who takes up John's metaphor of the hand. "A Christian prince should choose his knights rather for their faith and morals than for their strength." "The use of an organized knighthood lies in protecting the Church,

---

[1] A letter (ep. 81) written to the Count of Champagne (who had left his fief to join the order) in 1125, seems to show that he did not understand how a prince who desired the religious life could prefer the Order of the Temple to the Order of Cîteaux. Cf. the Abbé E. Vacandard, *Vie de St. Bernard*, i, 286–7.

[2] *Policraticus*, ed. C. C. J. Webb, vi, 601b.

attacking disloyalty, reverencing the priesthood, avenging the wrongs of the poor, keeping the country in a state of quiet."[1] In both writers knights are treated not as courtiers or as an upper class whose culture is its own justification, but as responsible officials, the executors of the prince's justice, the armed policemen of the state. The contrast between this and the lay view will be shortly apparent.

During the course of the twelfth century we enter upon a period of literary sophistication when the ruder chivalric virtues celebrated in the Old Epic give place to the more polished courtliness of the novels inspired by Chrestien de Troyes and of the Arthurian Romances. The Troubadours set the fashion. Not that the two forms of writing, the Epic and the work of the romantic schools, did not overlap, so that a strict chronological distinction can scarcely be insisted upon ; yet the feeling is different. The atmosphere has become professional, even in its early stages a little Alexandrian. As Professor Ker, with eyes turned towards his beloved northern heroes, once put it : " [Romance] has come through the mills of a thousand active literary men who know their business and have an eye to the profits "[2]; and the professional interest is, *par excellence,* the art of love. The characteristics of *l'amour courtois* in relation to medieval chivalry are considered from another standpoint elsewhere in this volume, and it is possible only in the briefest terms here to convey the meaning of so complex and varied a concept. The real mark of distinction between the old and the new is the absorbing interest in unfulfilled desire. Love has become a rite, almost a religion in itself. To its implicated votaries it may be merely a matter of physical relationships, or may embrace all sorts of ethical aspirations, and, as in Francesco Barberino and in the poetry of the *dolce stil nuovo,* emphasize spiritual elements to such an extent that it is regarded as a habit of the noble heart, a serene, enabling virtue, sometimes a union with the principle of beauty itself. The important point for the historian of chivalry is that in formalising love, in dictating for it a system of rules and in building round it an aesthetic movement, medieval romantics were, like all

[1] *Speculum hystoriale,* ed. 1740, xxxi, ch. cxxxi.
[2] *Epic and Romance,* p. 324.

other romantics, doing something to spiritualise it. The terms of feudalism were borrowed to frame the new convention [1]—and the result had a considerable influence on the medieval view of woman and her place in society.

The code was a highly artificial product, as we read it, for instance, in the work of Andrew the Chaplain, who lays down thirty-one propositions, the first being that marriage is not a good excuse for rejecting love : a dictum on the lines of a decision of the Countess Marie of Champagne, to the effect that there could be no true love between husband and wife. But all was not like this : in the "conventional" treatment of love there are many distinctions, from the fresh morning music of Provence before the Albigensian Crusade to the great group of works influenced by the sensualism of the continuation (by Jean de Meun) of the *Roman de la Rose*, while in between stands all the literature that has felt the influence of Ovid's *Ars amatoria*, or its translations like that of Jacques d'Amiens, and obeys the rules. Through all the variety, fresh or exotic, of this fertile growth, two characteristics alternate : there is either complete indifference to the ideal of womanhood portrayed in the religious teaching of earlier centuries and in the less ascetic and more soberly useful exhortations of contemporary Churchmen like Humbert de Romans; or—and this occurs particularly in the works addressed to women—there is the attempt to distinguish between the true sort of love and its degeneration, to elevate the chivalric ideal above the corruptions of the school of the *Rose*. It is not unlikely that the worship of the Virgin which took far-reaching artistic and literary expression in the twelfth century is a part of the reaction, although one of its best known religious effects, the Feast of the Immaculate Conception, was an old English pre-Conquest festival.[2] Such an attempt can be traced in poems like the *Ensehamen* of Garin lo Brun, or in the charming *Die Winsbekin* of the anonymous High German writer, who

---

[1] Cf. J. Anglade, *Les Troubadours*, pp. 77–8, examples from Bernard de Ventadour and Peire Vidal.

[2] On which see the remarks of the late Edmund Bishop in Gasquet and Bishop, *The Bosworth Psalter*, pp. 44–5, n. 8. It is certainly true that the cult of the Virgin and the cult of chivalry grew up together, and continually reacted upon one another : cf. Dr. Eileen Power, "The Position of Women," in *The Legacy of the Middle Ages*, ed. Crump and Jacob, p. 404.

depicts a mother advising her daughter to distinguish between the " hôhe Minne ", the honest love " that does not lower the heart ", and the " twingende Minne ", or the passion that does.[1] Joyful indifference therefore divides the spoils with moral considerations, and sometimes there is a complex of the two, as in the charming " Non ci togliete a Dio, femmine provocanti " of Jacopone da Todi.[2] The result is that the medieval ideal of womanhood is a divided and inconsistent one, half ascetic in its pursuit of secluded purity and its occasional depreciation of the married estate, half mundane in its frank enjoyment of the intricacies of courtship.[3] Now, although this latter aspect did not meet with the favour of the Church moralists, it should not be assumed that the view of the matter held by the average Troubadour or romantic novelist had a particularly gross or unhealthy effect upon society. It is better than the austerity that surrounds life with the menace of eternal fire, or the headlong plunge into an existence of physical pleasure. We may condemn such style and polish as artificialities, yet no civilization worthy of the name can dispense with them; they are preferable to the superficial coarseness of the Fabliaux, and lend its most attractive characteristics to the *Roman de la Rose*.

This chivalric conception of love was partly the result of, and in turn partly affected, the condition under which the noble classes lived. Though sanctified by the Church, marriage, besides being profitable to the overlord, was regarded as a convenient way of adding to one's estates, and there were probably more *mariages de convenance* in the Middle Ages than in post-feudal Europe. That the married woman rather than the young girl was the object of attention is partly explained by the facts of her position. Whilst her husband was away on duty or on some warlike expedition, she was suzerain in the eyes of the vassals. She might undertake the defence of her lord's castles if he was hard pressed elsewhere, hold his court and generally supervise his affairs. The life of the château was a responsible one, as Dame Nicolaa, holding out heroically in Lincoln, could have told her

---

[1] Alice Hentsch, *De la littérature didactique s'addressant spécialement aux femmes*, pp. 45-50.
[2] Text in A. Barnardini, *Il Dugento*, pp. 129-31.
[3] Such inconsistency, it should be remarked, is not confined to the medieval period.

deliverers in 1217. The much enduring Enide of Chrestien de Troyes' tale is not a wholly legendary figure, nor Liénor defending her innocency before the Emperor's Court in *Guillaume de Dôle*. Villon when he wrote his *Ballade des femmes du temps jadis* struck the right note for the women of the noble class :—

> Où est la tres sage Helloïs
> Pour qui fut chastré et puis moyne
> Pierre Esbaillart à Saint Denis ?
> Pour son amour ot cest essoyne.
> Semblablement, où est la royne
> Qui commanda que Buridan
> Fust gecté en ung sac en Saine ?
> Mais où sont les neiges d'antan !
>
> La royne Blanche comme lis
> Qui chantoit à voix de seraine ;
> Berte au grant pié, Bietris, Allis ;
> Haremburgis qui tint le Maine,
> Et Jehanne, la bonne Lorraine,
> Qu' Englois brulerent à Rouan ;
> Où sont elles, Vierge souvraine ?
> Mais où sont les neiges d'antan !

An heiress might have a very eminent and exposed existence ; later, if left prematurely a widow, she was liable to be followed about the country by a lordly suitor, just as that great lady, Isabella de Fortibus, the widowed Countess of Aumale, was pursued by the younger Simon de Montfort at the time of the Barons Wars. Women in the thirteenth century were great litigants. No one can read English Plea Rolls of the second half of that period without being struck by their legal acumen and independence, qualities evidently necessary if dower rights were to be preserved.

The precious and elaborate character of much medieval chivalry is accounted for by the fact that before the end of the thirteenth century the knightly ranks were closing. Royalty was claiming the sole right to confer knighthood ; the ceremony itself was becoming a matter of great expense [1] ; and more and more the descendants of noble families were drawing together to keep themselves above the large masses of military tenants who had increased with the growing subdivision of fees ; moreover, as corporal service declined,

---

[1] See the statement of disbursements made for the knighting of Robert and Alphonse, brothers of Louis IX, in *Recueil des Historiens de la France*, xxii, 580-3.

ecclesiastici. viij.e capitulo.

texte. xxvj.

Qui dit Bachus point ne tacorde
car ses condicions sont ordes
on coulpable est ses deipres
ce [?]gens fait atensuier en pres

Glose sur ppi.

Bachus fu un home qui premierement
planta vignes en grece et quant ceulx
de sa contree sentirent la force du vin

PERILS WHICH A KNIGHT SHOULD AVOID

Drunkenness, represented by Bacchus. Christine de Pisan, *ibid*.
Harleian MS. 4431, fol. 106r.

[*face p.* 52

BEGINNINGS OF MEDIEVAL CHIVALRY 53

and the fief and its fractions were regarded in a commercial light, the dividing line that separated the military from the other tenures grew smaller, and the older chivalric families felt a greater need for segregation. In England chivalry in the full continental sense was confined to a limited number of groups, the *entourages* of great captains, where it flourished in as courteous a form as abroad, and remained fully conscious of its position as an international code of prowess and good manners. In the literature of warfare there are few things better to read than Froissart's account of the reception of King John by the Black Prince after Poitiers, and the banquet that evening where the Prince waited on the French monarch and extolled his valour. Yet the very late appearance of a chivalric literature in this country is an important fact of social history. Mr. Ker expressed the literary fact when he said :—

> Many things are attainable in a literature like that of England between the Norman Conquest and the Revival of Learning ; but what was not attainable before Chaucer, and was very feebly remembered after him, was precisely that sort of grace which belongs to a Court, to a refined affected mode of sentiment, like that of the *Romaunt of the Rose*. Before Chaucer and Gower acquired it, the English had not the right of entry into that world . . . Nothing in history is more desperate than the attempts of English writers under the Plantagenets to master the secret of French courtliness.[1]

(Malory, we may agree with Mr. Ker, was indeed worth waiting for.) The social fact, on the other hand, is that the average English knight was too busy serving in the County Court on juries and inquests, or doing his work as Sheriff or in Quarter Sessions, to live the life of courtliness. He was, on the whole, very agrarian, and very much burdened with the public weal. He was doing his job, unlike the Shakespearean Falstaff, who performs (in a way wholly English) the courteous duties of a knight of France—though the Court may be the kitchen. When young Henry V repudiates him in the pathetic scene in Henry IV, pt. ii, an earlier conception of knighthood stands for a moment face to face with the later.

Yet even in France, there were protests from outside the ranks of Church moralists against the tendencies of the Rose School. The most interesting reaction came from a woman,

---

[1] *Essays on Medieval Literature*, p. 137.

Christine de Pisan, the remarkable daughter of a Bolognese professor of astrology. Christine had been brought up at the brilliant court of Charles V; family bereavements left her at the early age of twenty-five with three children and a large household to support, and she became an authoress, at first a writer of lyrics, and later, after 1399, a writer of longer and serious poems. She took up the defence of women against the school of the Rose,[1] and became involved in a long controversy with her opponents, in the cause of which she had the help of Jean Gerson. " Petite clochette qui grant voix sonne," she said of herself, and her moralizations about chivalry and politics were serious and ambitious works. With great and sometimes rather obscure erudition, she pointed to an ideal of chivalry widely opposed to all its corruptions, both in literature and in fact, in the France of 1400. The *Epistle of Othea to Hector*, from the copy of which, in Harleian MS. 4431, the illustrations that accompany our text are taken, was translated (she had many English admirers) as the " Boke of Knyghthode "[2] by Stephen Scrope for the warrior Sir John Fastolf, the very opposite of the " moult sage et vaillant chevalier " that Stephen terms him. It purports to be the address of the Goddess of Prudence to her protégé, Hector, when he was fifteen,[3] in order to incite him to attain virtuous knighthood. The epistle is written in verse divided into a hundred *textes*, each a medium for instilling moral precepts and contains an allusion to some story from mythology, generally the history of Troy. It is full of amusing anachronisms: lessons, for example, are drawn for Hector from the circumstances of his own death, and from the vision of Christ shown by the Sibyl to the Roman Emperor Augustus, and there is even a reference to the expedition of Louis, Duke of Bourbon, against Tunis in 1391. Upon Othea's teaching Christine comments in a gloss or " glose " explaining the illusions, and there dilates in an allegory on its more spiritual meaning. However complicated the mythology, Othea's[4] lessons are direct and plain; they

---

[1] For the contemporary view of women, see Dr. Cartellieri's *Am Hofe der Herzöge von Burgund*, pp. 104–21.
[2] It has been edited for the Roxburghe Club by Sir George Warner.
[3] It was probably written for her son, Jean du Castel, who was that age in 1400. The work was dedicated to Louis Duke of Orleans.
[4] " By Othea we schall undirstond the vertu of prudence and of wysedome whether wyth he was arrayed."

recall the elaborate and brilliantly tired chivalry to the virtues of the early days, to the prowess and the single devotion that she celebrates in some of the most charming of her lyrics. But she was writing in a complicated world, the world of what Stubbs (who, like her, loved the simpler virtues) called " bastard chivalry ". It is easy to quarrel with the term, and to point out that the essence of chivalric culture is to be found in the refined brutality of figures like John Graham of Claverhouse in *Old Mortality* and not in the idealism of Parsifal. But the institution, as I have tried to show, contained many varied types, and it would be equally true to acclaim as chivalric the ideal picture of the soldier in Julian Grenfell's " Into Battle ", for whom

> life is Colour and Warmth and Light
> And a striving evermore for these ;
> And he is dead who will not fight,
> And who dies fighting hath increase.

CHAPTER III

THE CHIVALRY OF FRANCE

By F. S. SHEARS, B.A., L. ès L., D. de l'Univ.,
Professor of French in the University of Aberdeen.

THE foregoing chapters have already shown that chivalry was essentially a French institution. Some of its features in fact seem to have been deeply rooted in the character of the inhabitants of Gaul, judging from the description of the Celts given us by the ancient Greek geographer Strabo. They are easily roused, he says, and always ready to fight. If they are angered, they march straight at the enemy and attack him boldly in the open. They can therefore be easily overcome by cunning. They can be made to fight where one likes and when one likes, the motive matters little. They are simple moreover, and spontaneous, and willingly champion the cause of the oppressed.[1] Such a stock was obviously favourable for the growth of the ideals which were to inspire soldiers and poets during the Middle Ages. Nor is it difficult to understand why these ideals reached perfection in France during the eleventh and twelfth centuries, for they thus belong to that same civilization that created the Gothic cathedral and illuminated all western Europe with its literature and learning, and won for France the appellation of God's chosen nation, like the tribe of Juda in ancient times.[2] Just as French architects were employed abroad for the construction of cathedrals, just as scholars from all countries assembled at the feet of the masters of Mount Geneviève in Paris, so the young noble proceeded to France, "the flower of courtesy, honour and valour," to learn the code of chivalry. "The fame of French knights dominates the world," says the Welshman, Giraldus Cambrensis, in the twelfth century.[3]

---

[1] Strabo, *Geography*, iv, 4.
[2] Bull of Gregory IX, quoted by Léon Gautier, *La Chevalerie*, p. 65.
[3] Funck-Brentano, *Le Moyen Âge*, p. 154.

As for English knights, they were no match for their continental brethren. According to Wace, the Anglo-Norman author of a history of Britain, the tournament, one of the most important features of the age of chivalry, was unknown in England till the time of Richard, and more than a century later, Jehan le Bel, who took part in the early wars of Edward III against Scotland, says that the English knight in those days wore old-fashioned armour and was little esteemed.

I

The first full-length portrait of the knight in France is given us by the oldest French epic, the *Song of Roland*, which dates from the end of the eleventh or the beginning of the twelfth century. The poem refers to an incident in the history of Charlemagne which had taken place some three centuries earlier: Charlemagne, after conquering Spain, was crossing the Pyrenees on his return to France, when his rearguard, commanded by Count Roland, was attacked and defeated in the Pass of Roncesvaux. These were the sober facts of history, but they counted for little with the primitive listeners for whom this poem was sung. It was not the Roland of history, but the Roland of the poet's creation that appealed to them, and the eighth century warrior was transformed by the epic into a national hero who reflected all the ideals and aspirations of the age of the early crusader. Artists and sculptors worked in his honour, and poets for centuries held him up to men as the perfect image of a knight. It is in Roland, therefore, whom the barons of Charlemagne were pleased to call their champion, that we have the first representative of the chivalry of France.

Roland is best seen as he advances against the Saracens at the head of the Christians. He is riding his charger Veillantif; he holds his lance erect and the long white pennon beats around his wrist. His open smiling face reveals youthful self-confidence. He glances proudly towards the Saracens, but humbly and courteously towards the French. As he rides forward, he exclaims to his followers: "My lords, ride slowly; these pagans are advancing to their destruction; great booty shall we win to-day; greater than that won by any king in France."

The *Song of Roland* was written in the early days of chivalry when the coat of mail had only just replaced the primitive leather jerkin. We are not surprised therefore, to find that the word " chivalrous ", which the poet uses for the first time in the French language, to express his admiration for a warrior, refers in the first place to the physical qualities of a knight. " Malprimes," says the poet, " is right chivalrous; he is big and strong and is worthy of his ancestors." Roland has a full share of these qualities: his onslaught is compared by the poet to that of a lion or a leopard, and his blow cleaves an enemy in two from helmet to saddle. Fear is unknown to him: although he has but a handful of men with which to oppose the great multitudes of Saracens, he refuses to sound his horn to warn Charlemagne of his danger, lest, by showing fear of the enemy, he should bring shame upon his family and his country. Three times does Olivier try to persuade him; his words of prudence only inflame Roland's desire to fight the enemy unaided. " God forbid," he says, " that my parents be blamed, or that fair France fall in disgrace through any deed of mine. Mighty blows will I smite with Durendal, my good sword, which is girt at my side; you shall see the blade all covered with blood. It is an evil day for the felon pagans who are now assembled; I pledge you, all are doomed to die."

But it was not for his strength and valour only that Roland appealed to his contemporaries. He fights for the cause of Charlemagne and that cause is the cause of the Christian faith. Charlemagne is God's agent here on earth; he is under God's special protection; the angel Gabriel keeps watch by his bed and warns him of approaching danger. God works miracles on his behalf: when Charlemagne marches against the pagans to avenge the death of Roland, the sun stands still in the heaven, as for the prophet Joshua. The sanctity of Charlemagne's mission, moreover, is symbolized by his sword Joyeuse; in its hilt are fragments of the sacred lance—the lance which had pierced Christ's side, and which had caused such a great sensation in Europe when it was discovered by the early Crusaders. Similarly, Roland's sword, Durendal, which the emperor gave his nephew at God's command, contains a fragment of the Holy Virgin's raiment and other sacred relics.

When Roland sees the vast army of pagans advancing, he is anxious above all to prove himself a worthy vassal of the emperor. "The Emperor gave us this army of Frenchmen, twenty thousand picked men, amongst whom he knows there is not one coward," he exclaims to his friend Olivier. "A man must endure great hardships for his lord; for him he must suffer both cold and heat, for him he must sacrifice both flesh and blood. Strike with thy lance and I will smite with Durendal, my good sword which the emperor gave me. If I die, he who shall inherit it will say: it was the sword of a noble vassal."

At the same time the Archbishop Turpin addresses the assembled barons and prepares them for battle. With stirring words, words which were once echoed throughout the whole of Europe, he appeals to their devotion to the emperor and to the cause of the Christian faith. "Barons," he says, "Charles gave us this task; we must die for our king. Christendom is in peril, lend it your aid. You will now have battle, for you see the Saracens before you. Confess your sins and ask God for pardon. I will absolve you to save your souls; if you die, you will be holy martyrs and will win a place in Paradise the Great." Whereupon, in a pious scene which reminds us of similar episodes in the early Crusades, these primitive warriors all fall on their knees and are blessed in God's name by the Archbishop, who bids them smite the enemy for their penance.

Finally the most impressive and the most characteristic scene of all is that in which the poet describes the death of Roland. Roland has lost his charger Veillantif; his companions are killed, including Olivier and the Archbishop. Wounded and bloodless he lies beneath a pine, his face turned towards Spain in order to show Charles that he died a conqueror. Then, knowing that death is upon him, he thinks of the things most dear to him, of Charlemagne who nurtured him, of the men of his lineage; and striking his breast he prays for forgiveness and holds aloft the glove of his right hand to God, as his sovereign lord, whereupon the angels Gabriel and Michael descend from the heavens and take up his soul to Paradise.

Such is the conception of chivalry which we find in the early writers of France,[1] and it is mainly an outcome of that same religious spirit which inspired most other medieval achievements. The knight of these early times, like Charlemagne and Roland, had a religious mission: from the beginning to the end of his career he was the servant of the Church, and the first article in his code was the defence of the Christian faith. Etienne de Fougères, Bishop of Rennes, in his *Livre des Manières*, written in the twelfth century, says that St. Peter brought two swords to Christ: of these one was for the clergy, who were to punish the evil doer by excommunication, the other was for the knight who was to smite the enemies of the Church; the mission of the clerk was to pray, that of the knight was to defend the faith; hence the knight's sword was sacred; it was consecrated at the altar for the defence of Christ's people and on the death of its bearer it was to be restored to the altar.

II

The early chronicles of France show how the ideals of poet and preacher are reflected in the everyday life of a knight. The knights with whom we are most familiar are those who accompanied the French king St. Louis on his expedition overseas. Thanks to the memoirs of Joinville,[2] we have no difficulty in penetrating the weaknesses as well as the heroism of these warriors, and there is no danger of confusing history and legend. It is not likely, moreover, that Joinville's narrative is too highly coloured from a religious standpoint, for the chronicler was no fanatic. When asked by St. Louis which he would prefer, either to be a leper or to have committed a mortal sin, he declared that he would sooner have committed thirty mortal sins than be a leper. It is not probable therefore that such a

---

[1] W. P. Ker, in *Epic and Romance*, p. 4, assigns the epic to the "heroic age" as distinct from the "age of chivalry", with which he associates romance. Léon Gautier, in *La Chevalerie*, p. 90, takes the opposite view; he considers that the romances of the twelfth century mark the decline of chivalry, the true representatives of which are to be found in the epic. It is obviously impossible to restrict the definition of chivalry to any one of its phases.

[2] Joinville, *Histoire de Saint Louis*, ed. de Wailly, trans. Marzials (Everyman).

man overrated the religious enthusiasm of his contemporaries, seeing that he could speak so frankly of the limitations of his own faith.

Nevertheless almost every page of the memoirs is a testimony to the religious spirit which animated the Crusader. Joinville's departure to the Holy Land is doubtlessly typical of that of many another knight. After pawning all his possessions to pay the cost of the expedition, just as Godfrey de Bouillon had done before him, he set out, he tells us, with his scarf and staff of pilgrimage, not daring to look back, lest his heart should melt at the thought of his castle and the children he was leaving behind. He embarked at Marseilles; "When the horses and all were aboard," he says, "the master mariner called to his seamen and said to them: 'Is all ready?' and they replied: 'Aye, sir! let the clerks and priests come forward!' And when they had come he called to them: 'Sing in God's name!' and they all with one voice sang: 'Veni Creator Spiritus.' Then he cried to the seamen: 'Unfurl the sails, for God's sake!' and they did so. And the wind in a short space filled the sails and carried us out of sight of the land, so that we saw nothing but sky and water."

It is unnecessary to give the details of this ill-fated expedition. The odds against St. Louis and his barons were overwhelming. Encamped in the burning plains of Egypt, with no supplies and in an atmosphere poisoned by their dead, they present a hideous picture of famine and disease. But, like the warriors of the *Song of Roland*, they were willing to endure any suffering for the sake of their religion and their honour, and like Roland, too, they desired to win a place with the saints in Paradise. When, some years earlier, one of these knights was fighting against the Germans, he had prayed to God, the chronicler tells us, to have pity upon him and to deliver him from that war against Christians, in order that he might die in His service and so win the kingdom of Paradise. Elsewhere Joinville tells us of a valiant man, Lord James of Castel, Bishop of Soissons; when he saw that the French were retreating towards Damietta, he, who had a great desire to be with God, felt no wish to return to the country where he was born; so he hastened to be with God and set his spurs to his horse and fell single-handed upon the Turks, who killed him with their swords and thus put him in God's companionship and amongst the number of the martyrs.

How often does Joinville remind us of the example of King Louis himself: his loyalty and devotion to the cause of his people and his determination to share all their sufferings and perils! "As God died for the love of his people, so did the king put his body in peril, many times, for the love he had for his people." When the king's return to France was being discussed, it was strongly opposed by Joinville, who had been solemnly impressed by the words of one of his cousins, on leaving France: "You are going overseas," he was told, "now take heed how you come back; for no knight, whether poor or rich, can return without shame if he leaves in the hands of the Saracens the meaner folk of our Lord, in whose company he went forth."

One of the scenes described by Joinville bears a striking resemblance to the episode of the *Chanson de Roland* in which Roland refuses to sound his horn to summon Charles to his assistance, and it shows that the poet's expression of the sentiment of honour in the knight was but a pale reflection of reality. A large body of Turks had surrounded Joinville and his party, and as many of them were sorely wounded, Joinville saw that there was no hope, except in the help of the saints. At this critical moment one of his knights perceived the Count of Anjou, but would not ask for help without first enquiring whether it was consistent with his honour to do so. Joinville recalls how this knight came to him—a ghastly figure, for he had been struck in the face and his nose was hanging over his lip—and said: "Sire, if you think that neither I nor my heirs will incur reproach thereby, I will go and seek help from the Count of Anjou whom I see yonder in the fields." To this Joinville replied: "My lord Everard, meseems you would earn great honour if you went to save our lives; your life too is in great danger." And the chronicler adds that he spoke the truth, for the knight afterwards died of his wound.

Such scenes of heroism as this are all the more striking owing to the details given by Joinville, which show that the Crusaders were rough soldiers after all and not saints. Not many of these knights followed the king's example of piety in everyday life. Joinville himself declared to the king that he refused to wash the feet of the poor, for it would make him sick to wash the feet of such villains. St. Louis, we are told, did his best to suppress blasphemy; he himself was never heard to swear during the twenty-two years that Joinville knew him; but scarcely anyone else in the realm of France, says Joinville, could open his mouth without mentioning the devil. After the capture of Damietta, in the first flush of victory, the Crusaders' conduct was scarcely less loose than that of most other armies in similar circumstances, and one of Joinville's remarks shows that even the leaders were not above suspicion. These human weaknesses serve only to emphasize the force of the ideals which could bring men to achieve such splendid examples of self-sacrifice. They had accepted the promise of the poets :—

> Ki ore irat od Loovis,
> ja mar d'enfern avrat poour
> char s'alme en iert en pareis,
> od les angles Nostre Seignor.[1]

And the price they paid for their unflinching faith is seen in the passage in which Joinville describes how he heard from his bed of sickness the continual knolling of the bell in the neighbouring chapel, where the bodies of twenty or more warriors were brought daily to the strains of the chant: *Libera me Domine*.

Amongst the many incidents related by Joinville which enlighten us as to the customs and institutions of chivalry, there is one which is of special interest, for it shows in what great respect the person of a knight was held in the thirteenth century. Joinville is commenting on the equity of St. Louis' judgments in Syria. One of the king's soldiers had struck one of Joinville's knights, and Joinville complained of this offence to the king. St. Louis was at first unwilling to take action, saying that the sergeant had only pushed the knight. But Joinville insisted and declared that he would leave the king's service, if a sergeant were to be allowed to push a knight. The king then ordered that the offender should make amends. He was brought forward, bare-

[1] He who goes with Louis will have no fear of hell, for his soul will be in Paradise, with the angels of Our Lord. (These lines, written about 1146, refer to Louis VII.)

ST LOUIS FEEDING THE POOR

British Museum Royal 16 G vi. f. 43b. 1325-1350 A.D.

[face p. 64

footed and wearing only shirt and breeches, and was made to kneel before the knight; he then offered the knight a naked sword, saying: "My lord, I make amends for having laid my hand on you, and I have brought this sword so that you may cut off my hand, if such is your pleasure."

III

St. Louis' expedition to Syria marks a turning point in the history of the crusades. Never again do we read of the same enthusiasm. When the king planned his second campaign, the crusade against Tunis, Joinville, who had been such a faithful servant in Palestine, protested vigorously. To those who pressed him to take the Cross, he replied that it would be more pleasing to God if he remained at home to help and defend his people. Similar objections are expressed by the poet Rutebeuf, a contemporary of St. Louis, in his dialogue between the Crusader and the Non-Crusader. The latter refuses at first to take the Cross because, he says, it would mean selling his possessions for nothing and leaving his children to the dogs, and that, he is sure, is not God's will. Moreover, he adds, it is not necessary to go to the Holy Land to win Paradise; little does he trouble about the Sultan's threats: if the Sultan came to France he would know how to punish him, but he has no intention of going yonder to find him.

At the same time, in the place of this religious enthusiasm, which was on the decline, another and a less stern ideal had established itself in the code of the knight, that of human love and service to women. A poem of Conon de Bethune, one of the leaders of the fourth crusade, shows how the sentiments of even a twelfth century warrior could be divided. The poet does not question a knight's duty: he knows that all who go yonder will win life immortal, yet he grieves at his departure: his sorrow is caused by the thoughts of his lady whom he is leaving, for if his body is going to serve the lord, his heart remains in the keeping of his mistress:—

> Ahi! Amours con dure departie
> Me convendra faire de la meillour
> Ki onques fust amee ne servie!
> Deus me ramaint a li par sa douçour

> Si voirement que m'en part a doulour.
> Las ! qu'ai-je dit ? ja ne m'en part je mie :
> se li cors vait servir Nostre Seignour,
> li cuers remaint del tout en sa baillie.[1]

We have here a sentiment which is unknown in the earliest phase of chivalry. In most of the early poems of France, the knight is intent only on the pursuit of war and is usually indifferent to the charms of the fair sex. "These warriors," it has been said, "thought less of a beautiful woman than of a good lance-thrust or a fine charger." Woman, in fact, was so little esteemed in these early days, that poets sometimes tell us how the lord availed himself of his feudal rights to beat his wife. Even in the *Song of Roland*, which has given us the pathetic figure of the beautiful Aude, the heroine plays an unimportant part, and when Roland in his dying moments thinks of the things most dear to him, he has no thought for his betrothed, who will lose consciousness and die on hearing of her lover's death.

The change in the attitude towards women took place about the middle of the twelfth century. It was due partly to the more settled state of the country and the corresponding increase in prosperity and refinement, partly to the influence of the South, which found its way to the North through the marriage of Louis VII and Eleanor of Aquitaine and through the mingling of North and South in the expeditions overseas. Henceforth the influence of women is predominant, and it brings about a lighter rhythm in life and literature. Poets, imitating the troubadours of Provence, now sing of the perfections of their ladies, crave their pity and seek to merit their grace. The knight now fights to win his lady's favour; Mars and Venus are united and the word *amoureux* comes to mean, not only the lover, but also the general virtues of the knight. Finally the idea prevails that a man cannot be a perfect knight if he is not a perfect lover.

Perfection in the lover is mainly courtesy, the meaning of which is shown by a delightful poem, the *Lay of the Shadow*.[2] A knight and a lady are standing by a well. The knight has

---

[1] Ah ! Love, how cruel it is to have to take leave of the best woman who was ever loved or served ! May God bring me back to her in His goodness, as truly as I do depart in grief. Alas ! What words are these ? Indeed, I do not depart ; if my body is going to serve our Lord my heart remains entirely in her keeping.

[2] *Le Lai de l'Ombre*, ed. J. Bédier (Soc. des anciens textes).

contrived to place a ring on the lady's finger as a sign of his love, but she orders him to take it back again. He does so and as he looks at the ring he says : " Gold is not blackened for having been on such a finger." He then leans over the well and sees the image of his lady reflected in the clear water. " Look ! " he says, " I shall not keep this ring, but my fair friend shall have it, she whom I love most after you." " But," asks the lady, " where have you found her ? " " She is your shadow," he replies, and drops the ring in the well.

It is this blending of gallantry with the older elements of chivalry that characterizes the knight of the Hundred Years' War. Whatever may have been his true reason for fighting, his only avowed motive was the love of his lady, which was the formula that usually accompanied the challenge to combat. All the heroes of the age have a mistress in the background, who uplifts them to acts of valour. It was Love, if we are to believe the poets, that first inflamed the courage of Du Guesclin :—

> Premierement pour Amours fut armé,
> Ce disoit-il, et desir d'estre aimé
> Le fist vaillant.[1]

Even Edward himself, the victor of Cressy, was inspired, according to Froissart, by his love for the Countess of Salisbury.

How " arms and love " were associated during the Hundred Years' War we can see from a score of passages in the Chronicles of Froissart alone. During the expedition to Africa, the French observed in the ranks of the Saracens a young Moorish knight who rode a fresh and prancing steed, which was light to the touch, and seemed to fly through the air. All his accoutrements were black, apart from his white turban, and he generally carried three feathered and pointed javelins which he handled with skill. The Christians, we are told, concluded that his deeds of prowess were inspired by his love for a lady of his nation, the daughter of the king of Tunis, a most beautiful lady, according to the report of some Genoese merchants who had seen her in the town of Tunis. The chronicler adds that during the siege, the French knights took great pleasure in beholding the deeds he performed for the love of his lady, and often tried to capture

[1] Christine de Pisan : *Oeuvres poétiques*, II, 96.

him, but the young Moor was too well mounted to allow himself to be taken.

Another story which is typical of the age is that of Olivier Mauni and the partridges. During the siege of Rennes by the Duke of Lancaster, an English knight approached the walls of the town carrying some partridges he had taken in the fields, and asked to speak with Du Guesclin, who commanded the defence. The Englishman was accosted at the gates by Olivier Mauni who asked whether he would give or sell the partridges for the ladies of the town. The Englishman thereupon challenged the Frenchman to fight for them. Olivier needed no second bidding. Fully armed as he was, he forded the moat and the conflict started beneath the walls of the town, in sight of both armies and of the ladies of Rennes, who looked on with delight from the battlements. Olivier finally overcame his adversary; he then led him, whether he liked it or not, across the moat and into the city, and there he presented him to the ladies, together with the partridges.

The sequel of the story is no less entertaining. The victor had been wounded in the duel and required certain herbs to heal his wounds. So he called his prisoner and promised him his liberty, if he would procure for him a safe conduct which would allow him to leave the town for a month. The English knight came to the Duke who taunted him about the partridges and granted the Frenchman's request. Olivier was then richly entertained in the English camp and was visited daily by Lancaster's own surgeons, and when at last he was cured and took leave of his host, the latter presented him with silver plate and gave him messages for the ladies of Rennes, expressing the wish that they might often have partridges.

Amongst the many other passages of the *Chronicles* which illustrate the gallantry of the times, there is one which has seldom been noted by historians of chivalry. It is all the more interesting moreover, because, if the episode is true, it has an important bearing on English history. When Queen Isabella left her husband, Edward II, and fled to France, she hoped in the first place to get help from her brother the King of France. But she failed in that quarter and she next appealed to William of Hainault and his brother

John, who were regarded by their contemporaries as models of chivalry. This time her appeal was not in vain. When she arrived fugitive and penniless at Valenciennes, knights of Hainault rode out to meet her and jousted along the road for her amusement. There were many who thought that the expedition to England would be too dangerous an enterprise. But John of Hainault was not to be discouraged on that account: "Every knight," he declared, "must do his best to help women and maidens in distress." He had only to die once, he said, and he would as soon die in the service of this noble lady, who had been driven from her kingdom, as otherwise. So the expedition was raised which brought about the dethronement of Edward II and the coronation of his son, the young Edward III.

IV

In spite of this glorification of the spirit of gallantry, religion still remained the foremost article in the code of the knight. Froissart, when he defines the duties of a knight in his poem entitled the *Temple d'Honneur*, states as his first injunction that he must obey the commands of the Church, attend mass devoutly, confess and serve God in fear. Prayers are still said before battle and on one occasion, at least, thanks are returned to God for victory; it is when Don Pedro thanks the Black Prince for his aid: "Give thanks and all praise to God," replied the Prince, "for it was He who brought you victory, not I."

Nevertheless, in the history of the Hundred Years War we see no signs of that religious enthusiasm which inspired the knights of the early crusades. We no longer hear of the desire to win Paradise; "these soldiers," says Froissart of his contemporaries, "bother little about pardons, except in their dying hour." When we read the accounts of the crusades of the fourteenth century we find ourselves forced to agree with Count Albert of Bavaria that the knight's only motive for fighting was "to win the vain glory of this world". This is seen especially in the chronicler's description of the crusade against the Moors of Africa. The Genoese desired this war for purely commercial reasons and they sent ambassadors to France to gain assistance, for as there was then a truce between England and France, they knew that many knights "having nothing else to do" would be glad to join them. The French knights, when they received this invitation, much rejoiced at the prospect of "winning honour" and informed the envoys that they could depend upon their assistance "in their praiseworthy desire to extend the Christian faith". When after the arrival of the crusaders in Africa, the Saracens desired to know on what grounds war had been declared against them, the Christians replied that it was because their ancestors had crucified and put to death the Son of God, called Jesus Christ, the true prophet, without any cause or just reason. But the Saracens were better versed in religious history and received the answer with derision, Froissart informs us, and sent word to the French that they made assertions without proof, seeing that it was the Jews and not the Saracens who had crucified Christ.

In the fourteenth century there were naturally writers who declared that the ordering of battles was in God's hands : one in fact goes so far as to say that the French defeat at Cressy was God's punishment for the wearing of extravagant fashions in dress, particularly the short tunic, which revealed the shape of the person.[1] The more general opinion, however, seems to have been that God had no hand in the scenes of bloodshed and cruelty which were so frequent during the Hundred Years' War. "The Grace of God is indeed good," says Froissart, "but we see few lords nowadays increase their possessions otherwise than by force." The fourteenth century had in fact created for itself a deity more in harmony with the spirit of the age than the God of the New Testament. This deity was Fortune. She had been brought forth by Alain de Lille and Jean de Meung from the *De Consolatione Philosophiae* of Boethius, and she was henceforth sung by a hundred poets and portrayed by numerous artists. She even found her way into the cathedral, where the stained glass representation of her wheel stood as a warning to men not to put too great faith in the prosperity of this world. During the Hundred Years' War, when wealth and power were rapidly changing hands, it was to her that the instability of human affairs was generally assigned. "When they are raised up and think themselves secure, Fortune overturns them

[1] *Grandes Chroniques de St Denis*, vol. v, p. 462.

in the mud and leaves them lower than they were at first," says Froissart of men of mean extraction, and the same theme gives the chronicler his formula for war—"Now down, now up, such is the nature of war." This fickle goddess, therefore, is a sign that a devil-may-care attitude to life had taken the place of the Christian principles of service and self-sacrifice.

Nevertheless, in spite of the weakening of the religious element, the code of chivalry was still a magnificent ideal, the effect of which was to introduce into the methods of warfare a spirit of generosity and fair-play, which we in the twentieth century could never emulate. Victor Hugo, in his *Légende des Siècles*, to recall the age of chivalry, narrates the combat between Roland and Olivier, which he borrowed from the epic *Girard de Vienne*. When Roland has disarmed his opponent, he refuses to follow up his advantage, for he considers that such an act would be unworthy of his rank. So he bids Olivier to send for another sword and a sword of a better temper. The scene is typical of many an episode narrated by Froissart. Whilst Edward was besieging Reims in 1360 a party of English knights laid siege to the castle of Cormicy in the neighbourhood. Unable to take it by assault, they brought a number of miners from Liège and ordered them to mine under the fortress. The shaft was constructed under the moat, as far as the main tower of the keep and was supported with stays. When this was done, the besiegers asked to parley with the French captain and called upon him to surrender, as he valued his life. The French knights laughed on hearing the summons and replied that they were all quite well within the fortress and that there was no lack of stores, nor could they believe that the castle, which was built of good stone and wood, was in danger of falling. In the end, however, the defenders consented to come out, whereupon the miners set fire to the stays, and the main tower, splitting in two, crashed into the moat. So the French surrendered according to their undertaking and thanked the English for their courtesy !

According to the code of chivalry it was of little importance whether a knight was victorious or not, provided he acquitted himself honourably in the face of the enemy. One author, in fact, declares that it is no reproach to a king if he loses a battle; it is an honour for him, on the contrary, to have had the courage to fight a superior enemy.[1] When, after the battle of Poitiers, the Black Prince entertained his royal prisoner, King John, to supper, he insisted on serving him himself, in all humility, and on bended knee he complimented the king on his splendid conduct during the day. "I do not say this to flatter you," the Prince added, "for every man on our side is of the same opinion and all are agreed that the prize and chaplet should be awarded to you, if you will deign to wear it."

It is true that the bravery of the knight of the fourteenth century is open to criticism; the warrior of those days would doubtlessly have been a better soldier had he thought less of personal valour and paid more attention to tactics. But we all have a certain admiration for that youthful impetuosity which makes no distinction between bravery and foolhardiness. Of all the stories of folly related by the historians of the Hundred Years' War, there is none more extravagant than that of the Order of the Star. This Order, says the chronicler Jehan le Bel, was founded by King John in the year 1352, after the manner of the Round Table, which existed formerly in the time of King Arthur. It was to consist of three hundred of the most valiant knights of the realm of France, and each year the King was to hold a full court of all its members, when each was to relate the adventures, glorious or otherwise, which he had encountered since he had last attended the court. And the king was to appoint two or three clerks who would record these adventures, when the court would decide upon the most valiant and the most deserving of honour. And none could enter this company who was not valiant and without reproach and all had to swear that they would never flee from battle. . . . But it happened the following year that a great host of men of arms came from England to succour the Countess of Montfort, and to lay waste the country which was in the hands of Charles de Blois, and the knights of the Star were sent by King John to oppose them. But when the English heard of their arrival they devised an ambush; the French advanced recklessly, and all were discomfited and killed, including eighty-nine knights of the Star, because they had sworn they would never retreat.

[1] *Le Débat des Hérauts de France et d'Angleterre*, p. 45.

This, adds the chronicler, was the last heard of the noble order.

But the most pleasing feature of these wars was the treatment of prisoners. When an adversary was conquered he was treated like a brother, to use Froissart's words, and was allowed to return to his home till a given date, when he reappeared to pay his ransom. It was contrary to the laws of courtesy, moreover, to fix the ransom at such a high figure that it meant ruin to the knight, or prevented him from maintaining his estate. Sometimes, indeed, the prisoner was asked the price he could pay, as in the case of Du Guesclin, after his capture by the Black Prince, and when the Prince expressed surprise at the enormous sum of one hundred thousand francs which the French captain said he would pay, the latter, according to his biographer, declared that not a woman in France who could spin would spare her labour to contribute to his ransom. Such was the etiquette of the age and all who failed to comply with it are severely criticized. The chronicler complains bitterly of the Germans for this reason: it were better, he says, for a nobleman to be captured by a Saracen unbeliever than to fall in the hands of the Germans, for they keep their prisoners in chains and torture them to extort large sums from them, and he considers that no man should consent to bear arms with such people.

We need not allow ourselves to be deceived, moreover, as to the general character of the times by passages such as these. Doubtlessly for one act of generosity in the history of the Hundred Years' War, one could name a dozen acts of cruelty and treachery, but it is not without significance for the history of the fourteenth century that it is these deeds of chivalry that are most emphasized by contemporary chroniclers.

There is one passage relating to the chivalry of this period which deserves special mention, for it probably gives the best description of the investiture that has been handed down to us. It is taken from the Chronicles of the Monk of St. Denis, who relates how Charles VI of France knighted the King of Sicily and Charles his brother. The ceremony took place at the abbey of Saint Denis, which was prepared beforehand for the Queen and her ladies, and for the royal family. In the principal court a hall 64 yards long and 12 yards wide was constructed, and was covered with cloth of white and green and decorated with tapestries of gold and silk, representing various themes, which charmed the gaze of the onlooker. Outside the abbey, a space 120 yards long was levelled and cleared for the jousts and tournaments and a pavilion was erected for the accommodation of the ladies, who were to preside over the jousts and allot the prizes. On the 1st of May the two princes rode out from Paris to St. Denis attired in special garments. According to ancient usage, says the chronicler, they were wearing a wide long cloak of dark grey stuff, and they had no gold either in their dress or their trappings. They also carried, rolled up and fastened behind them, a cloth of the same stuff as their dress, for such was the practice of the squires of old when they set out for a long journey. On their arrival at the abbey they proceeded to the priory and purified themselves in a bath, which had been prepared for them. Then, having changed their raiment for the dress of a knight, they went to the church, where they prayed before the sacred relics of the martyrs. After supper they were lead to the altar to pass the night in prayer, according to ancient usage. The next morning mass was celebrated by the bishop. Two squires from the king's guard, each carrying by the point a naked sword on the pommel of which were hanging golden spurs, entered the church by the door of the cloister. Behind them walked the king, accompanied by the King of Sicily and his brother. When they had taken their places before the altar, they awaited the arrival of the Queens of France and Sicily, and mass was then sung by order of the King. At the end of mass the bishop came forward and the two princes knelt and asked to be admitted to the Order of Knighthood. Then, when they had taken the oath, the king belted on their swords and ordered one of his knights to fasten on their spurs. Finally the bishop pronounced the benediction and the two knights were lead to the festive hall, where they supped in company with the king, the nobles, and the ladies, and the rest of the night was spent in dancing and revelling. The four following days were likewise devoted to jousting and feasting, and the monk who describes these scenes is obliged to add that they ill became the sacred atmosphere of a monastery.

It is hardly necessary to state that the ceremony was not

always so complicated as that described in this chronicle. When St. Louis's crusaders disembarked in Egypt, Joinville knighted a squire in a small boat in the face of the Saracens, so that the ceremony must have been of the most summary kind. Knights were often created just before or just after a battle. This practice is illustrated by an amusing incident quoted by Froissart. When the French and English armies were drawn up at Buironfosse on the day appointed for battle, there was a sudden tumult in the French ranks, so that it was thought that the English had started the attack. Thereupon John of Hainault created a batch of forty knights; but no battle followed; the tumult had been caused by a hare which had rushed through the French camp, so that the new knights were afterwards called the Knights of the Hare.

V

There is a final aspect of chivalry which has still to be considered, namely the tournament. The tournament not only provided an outlet for the knight's martial spirit in times of peace, enabling him to win " honour " in the intervals between his campaigns, it was also the great social event of the age, for it brought together knights from all countries. During the Hundred Years' War particularly, whenever there was a lull in hostilities, we read of a constant coming and going of knights across the channel to take part in friendly tournaments in either England or France, with the same men they had recently faced on the battlefield. Incidentally, too, the tournament was a source of revenue for the successful knight, who carried off from the lists great prizes in horses and arms : the *Fabliaux*, for instance, depict for us a knight complaining of the prohibition of the tournament by the church, for he had thus been deprived of his sole means of livelihood.

The tournament included two kinds of encounters, the single combat or joust, on horse or on foot, and the tournament proper, which was a general mêlée or miniature battle. At the tournament of Chauvency held in 1285 these contests were distributed as follows : the first day, Sunday, was a day of assembly and a general fête ; Monday and

Tuesday were devoted to jousting; Wednesday was a day of rest, when sides were picked for the tournament, and this took place on Thursday. Each evening when the contests were over, the whole company joined in singing, dancing, and feasting.

Froissart's account of St. Inglevert illustrates certain points of procedure in the preparations for a tournament. When Charles VI was staying at Montpellier, taking great pleasure in the company of the ladies of the town, three young noblemen, inflamed by this courtly society of ladies and damsels, issued a challenge, which was approved by the king, in the following terms :—

> In our desire to know the noble gentlemen, knights, and squires of the borders of France, and of distant kingdoms, we shall be at St. Inglevert the twentieth day of the month of May, and shall stay there thirty successive days, and on each of these days except Fridays we shall deliver from their vows all manner of knights and squires of no matter what country, with five courses with lance or rocket, whichever they please, or with both if it pleases them. And outside our tents we will place our war shields and our peace shields blazoned with our arms. And whoever would joust, let him come the day before and touch with a staff whichever he would choose. And if he touch the war shield, he shall have on the following day mortal combat with the one whose shield he has touched; if he touch the peace shield, he shall have the friendly tilt.
>
> And all who come or send to touch our shields must give their names to the persons appointed to the care of them. And all foreign knights and squires who would tilt with us shall bring with them a noble friend and we will do the same on our parts, who will order what may be proper to be done on either side.
>
> And we beg all noble knights and squires who would accept our challenge not to think or imagine that we have undertaken this enterprise out of presumption, pride, hatred, or ill-will, for our sole desire is to have their honourable company and friendship. . . .

This proclamation was published in England, Spain,

A TOURNAMENT

British Museum Addit 12,228, f. 150b-151. 1352 A.D.

[*face* p. 76

Germany, and Italy, some three months before the date fixed for the meeting, in order to give knights from distant parts time to assemble. In the meantime, preparations were made for their reception. Tents were pitched, heralds, trumpeters, and minstrels were installed, and large stocks of good wine and foods were provided for the entertainment of all comers.

We will leave the three French knights to uphold the honour of France, which they did for the space of thirty days, it is to be noted, without incurring hurt or wound, and we will glance at other scenes of the tournament which are described by various texts. The accompanying illustration is taken from a fifteenth century work, *Le Petit Jehan de Saintré*. Saintré arrives at the lists in a veritable procession ; he is preceded by drummers on horseback, minstrels, trumpeters, heralds, and kings-at-arms, by armourers with pack animals bearing cases of armour ; then comes his ensign bearing his colours at the head of a lance, then he himself on richly caparisoned steed, with his pages. Before the combat begins, lances are measured, and the two combatants swear by God, their lives, and their honour that they are not carrying on their persons any charms, herbs, magic spells, or other diabolical contrivances, that they bear no malice or hatred in their hearts, and that they are fighting with the sole intent of winning honour and good renown, and the much desired grace of their ladies. The oath taken, they return to their pavilions to adjust their helmets ; when this is done and they come forth again, Saintré makes the sign of the Cross, and the marshall, standing in the centre of the lists, cries : "Laissez aller!" Whereupon the two champions spur full-tilt at each other, "like two lions unchained."

The spectators watched the combat from galleries, keenly interested in every pass and ready to protest against any violation of the rules of the fight. The eager expression on the face of the lady in our illustration shows the pitch of excitement to which spectators were sometimes brought. One work, in fact, describes how the ladies in their enthusiasm stripped off their sleeves and headdress for the adornment of their knights, and thus found themselves to their shame sleeveless, with their hair in golden masses on their shoulders at the end of the fight ; but when they looked round and saw that their neighbours were equally dishevelled, they soon laughed at the adventure.[1]

The heralds on the flanks of the spectators shouted in support of their patrons and commented vociferously on the proceedings. The poem describing the tournament of Chauvency relates how a herald, after an unusually violent encounter which brought both knights to the ground in a heap with their horses, stepped out in front of the ladies and shouted to them: "See to what misfortune these knights are exposed; for you they pledge their lands and their persons; now you see them in peril of death. . . . At least you should comfort with some loyal encouragement those who serve you honourably and without falseness; and they would be the better for it, for never did God make a clerk so wise that he could teach a knight in sixty years as much as he earns from a lady in fifteen days."

VI

It is difficult to fix even an approximate date for the decline of chivalry. As early as the twelfth century there are writers who state that chivalry was not what it was wont to be, but this merely denotes that the knight never quite attained in the eyes of his contemporaries that standard of idealism represented by Roland. Even when chivalry was "at its height", moreover, we find criticisms of society which could well be matched with that in which Madame de Staël deplores the lack of chivalry in modern France. There is no doubt, however, that in the fourteenth and fifteenth centuries the prestige of chivalry was beginning to suffer from the introduction of more practical methods in warfare. Charles V scorned the chivalric tactics of his father, John, who fought axe in hand at Poitiers, like the hero of a Chanson de Geste; Louis XI was the least chivalrous of kings, and his counsellor Commines declares that he put his faith in the archer rather than in the knight. But chivalry still retained a certain moral force, as we see from the sermons of the chancellor Gerson, who condemns extravagance and gluttony as inconsistent with the efficiency of the knight; or from the writings of

[1] See *La Curne de Sainte-Palaye*, vol. I, p. 102.

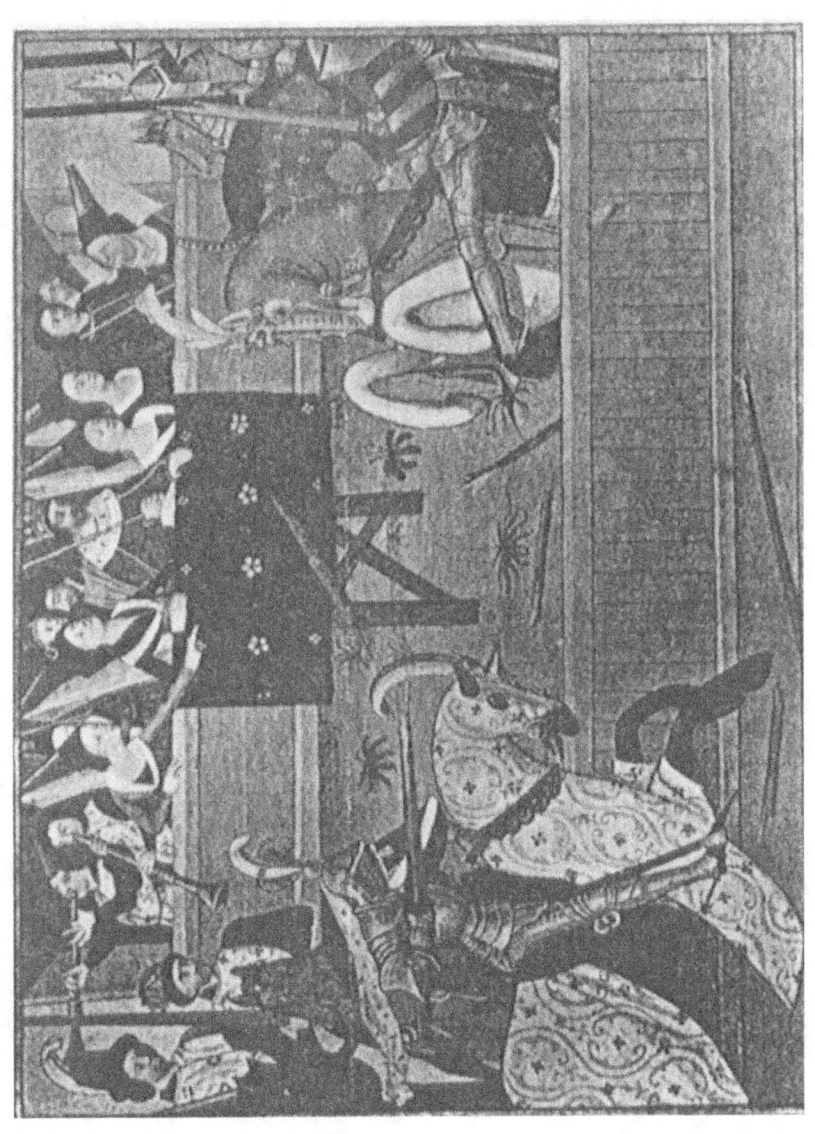

THE JOUST

British Museum Nero D. IX, f. 32b (fifteenth cent.).

[face p. 78

Christine de Pisan, who, in her *Epistle of Othea*, gives a hundred precepts of knightly conduct. It was in 1398, moreover, that the Marshall Boucicault founded the Order of the White Lady for the defence of women and maidens in distress. Even a century or more later there was a chevaleresque flicker amid the "glory and smoke" of the Italian campaigns, as, for example, when Francis I wrote to his mother, after his defeat and capture at Pavia, that all was lost except his honour. But we have only to read Brantôme's description of the entry of Charles VIII in Naples to see to what depths the "Noble Order" had fallen: as the King passed through the streets, Italian ladies, so richly attired that they dazzled the French by their beauty and magnificence, presented their young children and begged him to grant them the Order of Chivalry; "and this the king did not refuse," says Brantôme, "in his desire to please these ladies and to have greater leisure to contemplate their beauty and good graces, and the splendor of their attire."

Nevertheless, it is in the sixteenth century that we meet the illustrious figure of Bayard, the knight without fear and without reproach, who conferred the order of knighthood on his young sovereign Francis I, after the French victory of Marignan. More than four centuries have passed since the ancient poet of France sang the virtues of Roland, and during this time the term chivalrous had come to express many notions; but we have still no difficulty in recognizing in the attributes of Bayard, as recorded by his biographer, the Loyal Servitor, the conception of the ideal knight which we find in the early epic: "All knights ought to have put on mourning," he says, "when the good knight without fear and without reproach departed this life. . . . He loved and feared God above all things, never sware by him nor blasphemed him, and in all his affairs recurred to him alone. . . . His valour was unequalled, in discretion he was a Fabius Maximus, in subtle enterprise a Coriolanus, in strength and courage a very Hector, fierce with his enemies, mild, peaceful and affable with his friends. . . . He was a great giver of alms and he gave in secret, too. . . . In his heart he honoured a worthy gentleman with an income of but an hundred francs as highly as a Prince with an hundred thousand. Of worldly pelf he took no thought at all, as he clearly proved, being at his death little richer than he was at the hour of his birth." [1]

OTHER AUTHORITIES

BRANTÔME : *Œuvres*, ed. Lalanne, 1864–1882.
JAQUES BRETEX : *Le Tournoi de Chauvency*, 1897.
CUVELIER : *La Chanson de Bertrand du Guesclin*, 1839.
CHRISTINE DE PISAN : *Œuvres poétiques* (S.A.T.).
COMMYNES : *Mémoires*, ed. Mandrot, 1901.
CONON DE BÉTHUNE : *Chansons* (Classiques fr. du M.A.).
Le Débat des Hérauts de France et d'Angleterre, ed. L. Pannier (S.A.T.).
ETIENNE DE FOUGÈRES : *Livre des Manières*, ed. Kremer, 1887.
FROISSART : *Œuvres*, ed. Kervyn de Lettenhove, 1867–77.
　　　　Chronicles, Johnes, 1801.
　　　　Poésies, ed. Scheler.
FUNCK-BRENTANO : *Le Moyen-Age*, 1922.
Les Grandes Chroniques de St. Denis, ed. Paris, 1830.
JOINVILLE : *Histoire de Saint Louis*, ed. de Wailly, 1867, trans. Marzials (Everyman).
Le Lai de l'Ombre, ed. J. Bédier (Soc. des anciens textes).
ANTOINE DE LA SALLE : *Le Petit Jehan de Saintré* (Renaissance du Livre).
JEHAN LE BEL : *Les Vrayes Chroniques*, ed. Polain, 1863.
Livre des faits de Jean Boucicaut, ed. Buchon, 1836.
JACQUES DE MAILLES : *L'histoire du gentil Seigneur de Bayart*, 1878, trans. Sarah Coleridge.
RUTEBEUF : *Œuvres*, ed. Kressner, 1885.
Mme. DE STAËL : *De l'Allemagne*.

[1] *Vie de Bayard*, trans. Sarah Coleridge.

CHAPTER IV

THE CHIVALRY OF GERMANY

By H. G. ATKINS, M.A., D.Lit.,
Professor of German in the University of London.

IN treating my subject, the "Chivalry of Germany", I shall confine myself, as far as possible, to aspects of Chivalry and manifestations of its spirit which are peculiar to that country. Previous writers have already dealt with many of the fundamental questions, and so give me the more time for developing my particular theme.

In Germany, as elsewhere, Chivalry had its material basis in Feudalism, and found its ideal field of activity in the Crusades. To the service of the earthly lord was added the service of the Lord of Heaven; the warrior became a Christian knight. When to the service of God and the service of his lord was added the service of his lady, we have the full range of the ideals of medieval Chivalry in life and art—the *Gottesdienst*, *Herrendienst*, and *Frauendienst* of the convenient German phrase.

France is admittedly the country where Chivalry was born. But what of the part played by Germany in its institution, or, rather, in the creation of the conditions which alone made possible its birth? If we go back to the beginnings of the Feudal System, as the necessary condition for the rise of Chivalry, we find ourselves in an age when France and Germany as separate entities did not exist, and when it is therefore impossible to speak of either as having taken the first step along this road.

The Feudal System, initiated under his predecessors, was definitely established by Charlemagne, in place of the older Germanic system, reflected, for instance, in the *Nibelungenlied*, under which the state was regarded as the property of the royal family, and the king was surrounded by a retinue of faithful warriors, bound to him by the common interests of service and reward.

It was Charlemagne, King of the Franks, a Germanic prince, to whom was first granted that overlordship of the Holy City, which the Crusaders attempted to vindicate and turn into a positive reality. As Dr. Barker says [1] : " Charlemagne . . . was closely connected with Jerusalem : the patriarch sent him the keys of the city and a standard in 800 ; and in 807 Harun al-Rashid recognized this symbolical cession, and acknowledged Charlemagne as protector of Jerusalem and owner of the Church of the Sepulchre. Charlemagne founded a hospital and a library in the Holy City ; and later legend, when it made him the first of Crusaders and the conqueror of the Holy Land, was not without some basis of fact."

Under his grandsons the Empire of Charlemagne was, by the Treaty of Verdun in 843, split up into three separate kingdoms, which were to develop into the three modern states of France, Germany, and Italy. It was in the western-most of the three, the *Frankenreich*, Francia, that Chivalry was later born from the contact of a Germanic race with Latin civilization. To the *Nordmannen*, the Normans, who founded their Duchy of Normandy in 911, and from there about the end of the century established themselves in Southern Italy and Sicily, the consecration of feudalism into Chivalry is more immediately to be ascribed. If, then, the Germans in the twelfth century learnt Chivalry from France, they were but learning from their Germanic cousins, and receiving back from them a part of the ancient common heritage, which had undergone the leavening influence of another type of culture.

Feudalism began with the grant of lands to the officials of the Frankish monarchy, which established a privileged class, whose estates and whose rights in time became hereditary. During the wars of Charlemagne and his successors, these landed nobles played a leading part in the state. But with the development of military technique, which gave an ever-increasing importance to the armour-clad knights, it became necessary to expand the numbers of this supreme fighting-class, and from the twelfth century onwards its composition was transformed through the amalgamation

---

[1] Ernest Barker, *The Crusades*, Oxford Univ. Press, p. 6.

with the old free knights of a new class, the *ministeriales*,[1] or *Dienstmannen*, to give them their German name. These were the dependents of nobles or princes, or even of the emperor himself, who in return for military service received fiefs from their lords, and often attained to considerable position and influence. They frequently also acquired the status of free vassals, even though they might still bear the family name of their overlord, as the members of a Scottish clan did that of their chieftain. They might even come to surpass in wealth and dignity the members of the older free nobility, especially if they were in the service of the emperor, and the advantages which they enjoyed induced some members of that order to join their ranks. It was this new class of knights, the *Dienstmannen*, which furnished many of the chief poets of medieval German literature.

Diverse though their origin might be, the knights all belonged to the one privileged class; as knights all, from the emperor downwards, could meet as comrades-in-arms on an equal footing. And not in their own country alone; in all the lands where chivalry was practised they were members of a great confraternity. It was a cosmopolitan caste-system, a manifestation of that striving after universality, after a oneness of the whole known world, which was among the most striking characteristics of the medieval as compared with the modern spirit.

Yet, while within the caste we have a freemasonry that levelled all distinctions of birth or wealth, this privileged class was separated by a wide gulf from the common herd. It was fitted into the rigid framework of medieval society, in which man had his place and his rights, not as an individual, or a human being, but only as a labelled unit of the social organism.

Upon such a society were engrafted the ideals of chivalry learnt by the Germans from their Western neighbours. In France there developed the ritual and ceremonial of a new social ideal; thence came the conception of power that displayed humility, of the " iron hand in the velvet glove ", of voluntary subjection of the stronger to the weaker sex. Much in the code of chivalry is in striking contrast to the characteristic virtues of the German life of earlier periods

[1] Cf. P. Kluckhorn, *Die Ministerialität in Südostdeutschland*, Weimar, 1910.

One can hardly imagine that the chivalric ideal in anything like its actual form would, in any circumstances, have originated spontaneously on German soil. One may venture that hypothesis without any appraisement of the German national character in the scale of moral values. It is a case, not of superiority or of inferiority, but of difference. The essential virtues of chivalry were noble in themselves, and such as to find an echo in the soul of any generous nation, but mingled with the sublime and the profound was much pose and artificiality, features that one would expect less of the Germans than of some other nations, who are better able to carry off the precious with an air. Grace and elegance in social intercourse have never been prominent German national characteristics, as Germans themselves admit. They are, in fact, apt rather to despise than to admire such qualities, and to associate them with insincerity. The motto, *Sein nicht Schein*, " Being, not seeming," voices a very deep-seated German instinct, the contempt for all that savours of artifice.

France, then, was universally acknowledged throughout the Middle Ages as the land which gave birth to the new knightly culture, and in the whole of Western Europe the French were regarded as the masters of courtly etiquette and social polish. The French names for the tourney and joust, for armour, for dress and food, introduced into Germany in the twelfth century, attest this source. It was considered fashionable to use French words in place of their German equivalents, and even good native German words were provided with French endings. And since, at the beginning, the knights of Northern France were the special models, and the Flemish knights, their nearest neighbours, first came under the spell, and as bearers of this new culture shared in their prestige, we find many Flemish words, too, in this courtly jargon.

Still, it must not be assumed that the French customs were always adopted without modification by their German compeers. Even that most important ceremonial of all, the reception into the knightly order, took on a different form in Germany. In place of the French *colée*, the " dubbing ", the tap on the shoulder with the sword, we have in Germany the *swertleite*, the ceremonial girding on of the sword of the young knight. Only later did the *colée*, the *Ritterschlag*, become the symbol of reception into the order.

The Golden Age of Chivalry in Germany was undoubtedly the reign of Emperor Frederick I, the famous *Rotbart*, or Barbarossa, as he was called in Italy. He was the ideal, as he became later the legendary hero of chivalry. The definite establishment of the new order there, and its importance and dignity, were made manifest to all the western world by the magnificent festival instituted by Barbarossa for the *swertleite* of his two sons, Henry and Frederick, at Whitsuntide in the year 1184. It is told that 70,000 knights were assembled, coming not only from all the German lands, but from France and other western countries. For three days all that mighty host were the Emperor's guests; a whole town of tents and booths was built on the plain by the Rhine for their entertainment; chivalry unfolded all its courtly glories of splendid raiment, dignified ceremonial, and knightly skill and valour. And for all his sixty years, Barbarossa himself broke a lance with the best of them. Heinrich von Veldeke, the first poet of the new courtly epic, can find nothing more magnificent with which to compare, in his *Eneit*, the marriage of Aeneas and Lavinia, than this great festival of which he had himself been a spectator :—

>ich envernam van hôtîde
>in alre wîlen mâre,
>die alsô grôt wâre,
>als doe hadde Ênêas,
>wan die te Meginze was
>
>*   *   *   *
>
>dâ der keiser Frederîch
>gaf twein sînen sonen swert.

(I never heard of festival in all the ages so great as this of Aeneas, except it be that festival at Mainz, where Emperor Frederick knighted his two sons.)

Three years later, at Easter, 1187, there was another solemn gathering at Mainz, "Christi Reichstag," a Parliament of Christ, which resolved upon participation in the Third Crusade. There Barbarossa, who forty years before had taken part in the Second Crusade, again fastened on the Cross, and before entering upon the Crusade, like a chivalrous knight he sent his challenge in due form to his enemy

Saladin. From this time the Crusades begin to play a really important part in German thought and in German policy. In the latter field they added another disturbing factor, but on the intellectual life of the country they exercised an enlightening and stimulating influence by bringing German chivalry within the comity of the polite western world.

It is well known to history and legend how the old hero, when within sight of his goal, perished in the waters of the Armenian river Kalykadnus, only to live on as a symbol and embodiment of all those aspirations of the German heart, which found in chivalry a faith, and in the Crusades its not always unworthy expression and realization.

Barbarossa was succeeded by his son, Henry VI. Henry is remarkable in more than one respect. In him we see in an acute form that conflict between the ideal and the real which characterizes many of these heroes of chivalry. As a writer of tender and passionate lyrics, his name is honourably engraved in the roll of the Minnesingers. A poem of his stands at the head of both the great collections of their songs, the Great Heidelberg and the Stuttgart manuscripts, and it is preceded by a picture of the Emperor on his throne with crown and sceptre. In these youthful days he declares that he could better endure the loss of his crown than of his beloved. Yet for all his tender sentiments, he had little of the charm of his father, or of his true knightly qualities. When he succeeded to the throne, conflict and opposition soon revealed the sentimental youth as a harsh and merciless realist. None wielded the might of the empire more vigorously than he—" he was the greatest politician of his day, and in many ways the greatest emperor since Charlemagne." [1] Yet he was capable alike of petty meanness and of revolting cruelties. He is known in England among other reasons as the man who kept Richard Cœur de Lion a prisoner for more than a year in the Castle of Trifels, only to release him on payment of a heavy ransom. When in 1194 he discovered a supposed plot in Palermo, the suspects were put to death with the most cruel tortures, a Count Jordan being placed on a red-hot throne with a red-hot crown nailed to his head, while others were dragged through the streets at horses' tails, hanged, burned, or buried alive. He died in 1197 at

[1] Barker, op. cit., p. 67.

CHIVALRY OF GERMANY

the age of 32, after a reign of only seven years, but his brief career is a good example of the melodramatic contrasts in which the guileless Middle Ages were so rich!

It is not my intention to deal at any length with the Crusades in general or Germany's share in them in particular—the subject has been treated so often and so well, and for a brief account I can refer to Dr. Barker's already mentioned work. There is, however, one matter that perhaps calls for somewhat fuller treatment here. Professor Hearnshaw has already spoken of the great Crusading Orders, the Hospitallers, the Templars, and the Teutonic Knights. Of these the last especially interests us, since not only were all its members natives of Germany, but it played its most important part on the stage of history, far from the Holy Land, on German soil. Founded last of the three, it received a separate organization only in 1198. When rendered homeless by the extinction of the Christian Kingdom of Jerusalem, the *Deutschritter* settled for a brief time in Venice. Thence, commissioned by the Hohenstaufen Emperor, Frederick II, and with the approval of Pope Gregory IX, they set out under their Grand Master, Hermann von Salza, on an important and arduous mission, the conversion and civilization of the heathen Prussians. It was a long and bloody struggle, and only at the end of half a century of warfare did they succeed in consolidating their realm, the German *Ordensland* of Prussia. In 1309 the Great Master established his seat in Marienburg on the Nogat, and from that stately residence Prussia for two hundred years was ruled in model fashion, and became one of the most flourishing of German provinces. Castles were built to ensure the safety of the new territory, and around them developed towns, the most notable of which is Königsberg. The Grand Master in Marienburg was supported by some thirty *Komture* (commanders), who each from his *Ordensburg* administered the district under his sway. The prosperity of the land, and the development of its trade and commerce, reached their highest point in the second half of the fourteenth century. With the fifteenth a gradual degeneration began; the towns aimed at independence, while the nobles outside the Order made common cause with the Poles. In 1410 the Order suffered a heavy defeat at the hands of the Poles in the battle

of Tannenberg, and after a long struggle was compelled by
the Peace of Thorn, in 1466, to cede the half of its territory,
West Prussia, with the residence Marienburg, to the Poles,
while it retained the eastern half, East Prussia, with the
capital Königsberg, as a Polish fief. From now its star sank
ever lower, and East Prussia, too, would have fallen into
the hands of the Poles, whom they had originally set out to
deliver, had not their Grand Master, the Hohenzollern,
Albrecht von Brandenburg, in the year 1525, converted the
Ordensland into an hereditary Duchy held of the Polish king.

An early follower of Luther, Albrecht was the first of the
great spiritual peers to take advantage of the possibility
offered by the reformation of secularizing their domains,
and establishing themselves as temporal princes. The
Archbishops of Mainz and Cologne later attempted without
success the same manœuvre. Albrecht's dynasty was,
however, of short duration. He was followed only by his son,
at whose death Prussia fell to his son-in-law, Johann
Sigismund, Elector of Brandenburg, the grandfather of the
Great Elector. Thus we see the history of one of the great
crusading orders closely bound up with a territorial name and
a dynasty that have been among the most prominent in the
modern European world.

If the knights of Germany, through their contact in the
Crusades with their French compeers, had rapidly acquired
in the twelfth century the new ideals of *courtoisie* in life and
conduct, they were not less quick to follow them in the
literary expression of those ideals. In an astonishingly brief
space of time the new literature, with its artistry and grace,
replaced the simpler, more spontaneous native forms. In
France the "Chansons de Geste" gave way in the twelfth
century to the epics of chivalry of the Arthurian cycle. The
works of Chrétien de Troyes only appeared from about
1160 to 1175, and yet they were introduced into Germany
by Hartmann von Aue as early as 1191 or 1192. The Germans
followed both the Provençal poets and those of the north; the
former in the lyric, and the latter in the epic.

It is, as we have seen, the knightly class that takes the lead
in this new literary movement. In the Great Heidelberg

Manuscript 140 poets are represented; starting with the Emperor Henry, we have kings, princes, counts, and barons, along with simple knights. The poets are no longer monks, or gleemen, but members of the great lay fraternity. And so the literature itself is courtly; *höfisch* is the highest term of praise in this new epoch. These knightly poets are proud, too, of their knighthood in the first place and before all, and regard their poetic achievement as subordinate to the dignity of membership of that great order. Thus two separate works of Hartmann von Aue open with the description of himself as *ein Ritter*, while he takes the precaution of making it clear that his poetic labours only filled the hours not occupied with more serious tasks. Wolfram von Eschenbach roundly declares that the profession of arms is his real calling and makes what are no doubt exaggerated claims to illiteracy.

Under this new influence the poets at first turned their backs on the old national sagas. The rude, grim warriors, the heroines who were swept away over sea and there maltreated, like Gudrun, or who, on the other hand, like Brunhilde, vanquished their suitors in physical contest, were deserted for the figures of this idealized, *politer* world. They returned to them a little later, it is true, furbished them and decked them in the raiment of chivalry, and made them more fit for presentation at court; but for the time Siegfried and Dietrich had to make way for Erec and Iwein, and the other Arthurian knights. The barbaric contests of strength, the stone-throwing, and the javelin play, and the wild chase in the forest, give place to the ceremonial joust and tourney. And there is, too, a great readjustment of social and moral values. The old Germanic virtues of bravery (*mannesmuot*) and fidelity (*triuwe*) remain. But this *triuwe* is no longer the ruthless devastating force, which, as exemplified by Hagen in the *Nibelungenlied*, when loyalty to the liege lord or lady was in question swept aside all other moral claims, and justified lying, treachery, and assassination. It is combined with other gentler and more Christian virtues. *Diu mâze* is now the ideal quality—the observance of due measure, of " good form " on the higher and the lower plane, with its social and moral restraints. In a well-known poem of Walther it is described as the fount of all social virtues. *Hôher muot*, too, is a characteristic of the true knight, stout heart and high emprise. *Staete*, constancy, is also enjoined, while *milte*, generosity, is highly praised in noble lords by the knightly singers refreshed by its golden rain. It was an expansive, free-living world, and the open-handed hospitality of the wealthy patrons of the time is a thing of which we find it hard to conceive the like to-day. It was the golden age for all members of the higher and the lower vagabondage, and the temptations for a man of a roving disposition must have been immense. In one of his poems Walther von der Vogelweide gives us a graphic and amusing picture, coloured probably by disappointment at not sharing himself in the wasted treasure, of the wild doings at the Wartburg, the court of the Landgrave Hermann von Thüringen and the seat of the legendary *Sängerkrieg*.

> If any man sick in the ears you know,
> Bid him from me not near Thuringia's court to go,
> Unless he want his ear-drums split asunder.
> I've joined there in the throng till I can crush no more;
> Before one crowd has left another's at the door;
> That folk can hear at all's the only wonder.
>   The landgrave's built forsooth that way,
> That he must squander all he has on gallants gay,
> A very champion each on his own showing.
> I know his sumptuous mode in fine:
> And if he paid a thousand pound each butt of wine,
> No knight but still would find his cup o'erflowing.[1]

They strove to combine *êre*, honour, with *guot*, worldly possessions, and both with *gotes hulde*, the grace of God, a task the difficulty of which Walther laments in what is probably his best known poem. It was written in the troubled days of internal dissension that followed the death of Henry VI, which explains the gloomy, pessimistic tone of its close. The statuesque pose he describes inspired the famous illustration here reproduced, as well as the variant in the Stuttgart manuscript.

> I once sat brooding all alone,
> Cross-legged, upon a stone.
> One arm upon my knee I dropped,
> And in my hand my chin I propped.
> There I sat, and pondered deep
> Upon the course a man should keep,
> To win and hold upon this earth
> Three things that all men deem of worth:

---

[1] The translations are my own.

WALTHER VON DER VOGELWEIDE

From the fourteenth century "Heidelberger Liederhandschrift," now in the
University Library of Heidelberg.

> Honour and worldly wealth—these two
> Great harm oft to each other do—
> And last God's grace, that yet to-day
> The other two doth far outweigh,
> I'd gladly hold in shrine the three,
> But this, alack, can never be,
> That wealth and honour and God's grace
> In one same heart should find a place.
> Foul treachery in ambush hides,
> Bold Wrong upon the highway rides,
> Justice and Peace they've wounded sore.
> There'll be no safety any more
> For grace of God, Honour and Wealth,
> Until those two are back in health.

The literary works in which these new ideals are reflected, whatever their original source or subject might be, came to Germany from France, the great clearing-house of the Middle Ages. In the centre stands the Arthurian romance, which in France had already been developed into a vehicle for the expression of the ideals of chivalry. The interest no longer lay in the national struggle for faith and country, but was transferred to the individual knights and their fantastic adventures, while as a background we have the Celtic fairy-land, with its dragons, giants, ogres, dwarfs, and wondrous magic castles. It was the Romantic Movement of the Middle Ages. This world has no material or economic basis. The workers are seen only as boors and curmudgeons, the foils of these higher beings, whose code they do not share, and whose etiquette they do not understand.

Yet the Germans are far from being mere translators; they impress in varying degrees their own and the national individuality upon their versions. On the whole the French portray the characters and their actions more realistically, while the Germans idealize more. The French are more objective in their attitude, while the Germans allow their own emotional standpoint to appear. The Germans dwell more on the moral issues involved; where the French are naïve, we find them reflective and metaphysical.[1]

While most of the chief poets of this age were South Germans—Hartmann was a Swabian, Wolfram a Bavarian, Gottfried an Alsatian, and Walther an Austrian—Heinrich von Veldecke, the man who introduced the epic of chivalry

---

[1] Cf. F. Vogt, *Geschichte der mittelhochdeutschen Literatur*, Berlin, 1922.

to Germany, was a native of the Lower Rhine, born near Maestricht. This part of Germany, was, as we have seen, specially affected by French influence, and Flemish knights had taken a prominent part in the first Crusade. It was from the Lower and Middle Rhine that the new fashion spread to the rest of Germany.

Veldecke's *Eneit* appeared between 1180 and 1190. It is not a faithful translation of Virgil, but a free and individual version of the *Roman d'Eneas* of an unknown Norman poet of about 1160. The Frenchman, in the naïve fashion of the time, had already made of the Latin work an epic of chivalry, and Veldecke followed him therein. The importance attached at the time to this first example of the new polished metrical form, is seen from the tributes of his fellow-poets. Wolfram calls him his master, "the wise man von Veldecke," while Gottfried von Straszburg flowerily declares that he grafted the first shoot in German tongue from which there sprang the blossom-bearing branches.

The attraction for contemporaries was not any historical fidelity, which would have left them entirely cold, but the picture drawn of the knightly adventures of Aeneas and his paladins, his romantic and sentimental love-affairs with Dido and Lavinia, the descriptions of armour and tourneys, and all the courtly pomp and ceremony. We saw above that the poet could go no further when describing the splendours of the marriage of Aeneas and Lavinia than to compare it with the great Whitsun Festival of Barbarossa in 1184.

If Veldecke composed the first epic of chivalry, the introduction of the Arthurian epic into Germany was the work of the Swabian, Hartmann von Aue. He is in many respects typical of the poets of the age. As he tells us himself in the opening lines of *Der arme Heinrich*, he was a member of the *Dienstadel*, the vassal of a noble house.

> Ein ritter sô gelêret was
> daz er an den buochen las
> swaz er daran geschriben vant.
> der was Hartman genannt,
> dienstman was er ze Ouwe.

(There was a knight so learned that he could read all he found written in the books. His name was Hartmann, and he was a vassal of Aue.)

He was apparently better educated than most. We know that he took part in a crusade. He wrote two short religious romances, the legendary *Gregorius*, and the idyllic story of *Der arme Heinrich*, which has always been a great favourite, and has incited various poets to retell the tale. It is well known to English readers from Longfellow's "Golden Legend".

We are, however, here concerned chiefly with his versions of two of the Arthurian romances of Chrétien de Troyes, *Erec* in 1191 and *Iwein* some ten years later. *Erec* is of special interest as being, apart from a more primitive *Tristant* of the year 1180, the first Arthurian epic in German literature. In both *Erec and Iwein* we have presented the chief themes of the Arthurian romance, knightly honour and love, and their relation to one another.

Erec, after winning his lady, suffers from excess of love, which becomes a danger to his knightly honour. The story is too familiar to need repetition. Tennyson has told, in his ornamental way, how :—

> He compassed her with sweet observances
> And worship, never leaving her, and grew
> Forgetful of his promise to the King,
> Forgetful of the falcon and the hunt,
> Forgetful of the tilt and tournament
>
> * * * * *
>
> And this forgetfulness was hateful to her.

In short, Erec commits the great crime of the knight of chivalry. To use the German technical term, " er verliget sich." Or to use modern schoolboy slang, which expresses the same contempt for a similar breach of the code, " he becomes a slacker." His knightly compeers " send him to Coventry ", and blame Enîte for his undoing. We know how Enîte won him back to the life of adventure, and the price she paid for it. The chief interest is not to show how heroism wins love, but how true love saves knightly honour after marriage.

This story, then, serves for the thread on which to string a whole series of those strange and excentric adventures which are characteristic of the Arthurian romance, and for an exposition of its ideals of life and conduct. In the end all comes right, and with Hartmann, though not with Chrétien, Erec begs her forgiveness.

In the second part we are shown the reverse picture. Mabonagrin, the Red Knight, *verliget sich*, because his wife in the excess of her love, believing him unconquerable, has gained his promise never to leave their idyllic castle till vanquished in combat. Erec, by conquering him, wins him back for the chivalrous life, and so *two* knights are reclaimed.

In his *Iwein* Hartmann follows Chrétien's *Ivain, ou Le Chevalier au Lyon*. It shares with Erec the moralizing on the dangers of ease, on the conflicts of love and honour. If there we saw a woman who preferred death to her lord's dishonour, here we have one who prefers her own happiness to the honour of her lord. The central theme is fantastic enough even for this fantastic world. Iwein, after having been warned not to *sich verligen* as Erec had done, receives from his wife Laudine permission to ride forth in quest of adventures for a year; but when he outstays his leave she denounces him to Arthur and the Knights of the Round Table! This same Iwein had previously slain her first husband, but she had married him out-of-hand all the same, preferring the victor to the vanquished, and thinking the stronger knight the better guardian of her land. What a contrast to the old Germanic conception of *Treue*, to Kriemhild's life-long, unfaltering consecration to the avenging of her murdered lord. In this world of artifice the moral values are sometimes strangely perverted!

If with Hartmann we find uncertainty in face of the great problem of the age, the reconciliation of the claims of God and the World, of otherworldliness and the joy of life, we have in the greatest work of this courtly epic a picture of the ideal Christian knight, in whom a harmony of the two has been attained. The *Parzival* of Wolfram von Eschenbach is the fullest and the most profound work of the whole period, reflecting all the most important elements of medieval culture. It is based, it is true, on French sources, though it is impossible to tell exactly what Wolfram owes to his predecessors, and what is his own invention. Chrétien's *Perceval* is the only work known to us on which he could have drawn, and that Wolfram knew and was influenced by it is obvious, in spite of considerable and essential divergencies. Yet five of Wolfram's sixteen books, the first four and the last, are not to be found at all in Chrétien's fragmentary work. The

Provençal, Kyot, to whom Wolfram refers as his authority, is very probably a mere poetic fiction. Wolfram's *Parzival* has taken over not a few of the fantastic elements and the arbitrary motives with which the whole genus abounds. Yet it is essentially an independent work, alive with the faith and the philosophy of a great and vital personality.

Wolfram belonged to the lesser nobility. He had a very modest home of his own—he jests himself on his poverty—where he lived with wife and daughters, when not called abroad. In opposition to the prevailing mode, he upheld as ideals of true womanliness married fidelity and wifely duty. He regarded his knightly service as his real profession and dignity : *schildes ambet ist mîn art*, he says in the famous passage at the end of the second book :—

>schildes ambet ist mîn art :
>swâ mîn ellen sî gespart,
>swelhiu mich minnet umbe sanc,
>sô dunket mich ir witze kranc.

>I am a soldier and a knight,
>And were I coward in the fight,
>A fool the woman then would be,
>Who loved me for my minstrelsy.

His statement that he could not read or write is not to be taken too literally. He probably even knew enough French to use the originals to some extent, though not enough to be safe from misunderstandings, especially in the forms of proper names. He was like Walther a guest at the court of Hermann von Thüringen, and we know that the two were there together about the year 1204.

It is impossible here to give even an outline of the story of his vast epic of more than 12,000 couplets, and its main features at any rate are well known. We see Parzival first as a blessed simpleton, in whose childlikeness there slumber qualities that hold the promise of future greatness. It is the first of the great *Bildungsromane*, which form a special characteristic of German literature, romances, that is, which do not deal with an episode in the life of the hero, but trace his development through its various stages from childhood to maturity. It falls into three main parts : Parzival's childhood in the idyllic seclusion of the forest, his period of scepticism and revolt, and his final return to grace, and elevation to the Kingship of the Holy Grail.

All the chief virtues of chivalry are notably exemplified in it: valour, loyalty, fidelity, constancy, generosity, and the rest. It is a great allegory of human life; the story of a man who, in spite of error, through self-conquest finds at last salvation. Religious doubt, wavering, scepticism, is the chief enemy; the whole poem opens indeed with the warning that if doubt creep into the heart it will go ill with the soul. And the great virtue is its opposite, *staete*, steadfastness and constancy in all dealings with one's fellows and in one's relation to God. It is then a kind of medieval Faust, though without a personal Mephistopheles.

Yet, with all his deep religious feeling, Wolfram is no introvert. The whole poem is full of the zest of life; of delight in the pomp and pageantry, the colour and the movement, the extravagant spendthrift ceremonial of this decorative age. He revels in the descriptions of rich armour, or the sumptuous trappings of a horse. His language is fresh, vigorous, direct. Like the sportsman he is, he loves metaphors with a racy flavour; as when he speaks of praise that is not merely lame, but "limps like a spavined horse".

He is no pale ascetic who turns his back on this life in order to win the next. His feet firmly planted on his native soil, conscious of the dignity of his order, he is a true son of the new Church militant, a worthy representative of the sturdy crusading spirit, that never doubted to be pleasing God in spreading by force of arms the one and only true religion.

The fourth of the great epic poets of the period is Gottfried von Straszburg. His *Tristan*, written about 1210, presents a conception of female character in complete contrast to that given by Wolfram. Love with him is supreme. After Tristran and Isolde have shared the love-potion on the voyage to Cornwall, whither Tristan is escorting her as the bride of his uncle, King Marke, all honour and all obligations are forgotten, and they hold the world well lost for love. They respect no law, human or divine, and do not scruple later to deceive by ever fresh devices the man who is husband of the one and uncle of the other. Gottfried displays exquisite art in the portrayal of these emotional, sentimental characters, these *edle herzen*; but the new note which he introduced was

MEISTER JOHANNES HADLOUB

From the "Heidelberger Liederhandschrift."

a disintegrating influence in the conceptions and ideals of chivalry.

The cult of love is, however, most fully represented, not in the epic, but in the lyric. The Minnesong is in England, by name at any rate, best known of all the medieval poetry of Germany. The term is commonly used to embrace all the lyric of the period, but for this it would in its strict sense be too narrow, since love is, though the chief, by no means the only theme. The German formula, *Gottesdienst, Herrendienst, Frauendienst,* gives the main groups—religion, patriotism, and love.

In the older indigenous lyric, as seen for instance with the poet known as the Kürenberger, man was still the lord and master, the proud, untamed falcon, for whom the lady sighed. This is the theme of his best-known stanza :

I reared me a falcon	a year and a day.
But when I had tamed him	and dreamt that he would stay,
And bound his fine feathers	all with golden strands,
He rose aloft towering	and flew away to other lands.

Now the position is reversed. The relationship is conceived in feudal terms, with the *vrouwe* as the feudal lord, and the knight as her humble vassal. It is now he who pines and sighs, and serves humbly for her favour. This is well shown in one of the illustrations of the Heidelberg manuscript, in which we see a lover whose hands are being bound, in token of servitude, by his mistress. When we find Henry VIII in his correspondence with Anne Boleyn normally addressing her as his mistress and calling himself her servant, it shows that these terms belonging to the age of chivalry were then not yet obsolete.

A good example of these sentimental sighing lovers is seen in the accompanying illustration. Hadloub was one of the later Minnesingers, a citizen of Zürich, who died there about 1840. When at last friends persuade his mistress to receive him, he swoons away at the touch of her hand. Dressed as a pilgrim, he approaches her as she is going to mattins and fastens a letter to her gown.

In keeping with this attitude was the tone of lament and melancholy which characterized the German *minne*, at any rate, in its earlier stages. This love-service, and the poetry in which it was expressed, was a conventional thing, its conventions, like its poetical technique, being derived from the troubadours of Provence. Yet, in spite of the employment of a borrowed apparatus, the German Minnesingers expressed thoughts and feelings which were all their own. The mould was foreign, but not its contents. The polished versification, the elaboration of rhyme and strophe are something entirely new, and leave no doubt as to their origin. They represent a greater break with the national tradition than is found in the epic, but on the other hand we find nothing like the same wholesale borrowing of themes as there. The Minnesong is, in the real essentials, far more independent, and one rarely finds direct imitation of a French poem, and very little of that employment of French tags and turns which is there so frequent.

It brought indeed a wonderful blossoming of delight in the sheer artistry of verse. This lyric, like its Romance models, was intended to be sung, as is seen by the manuscripts, where text and melody are handed down together. The poet composed them both, *wort* and *wîse*, and it was his greatest pride and distinction to invent a new *dôn*, or strophic form. The attitude of poet and public to the poem was very different then from now. To-day the interest in the *matter* preponderates, and we are comparatively indifferent to the metrical and strophic form. These poets were content to repeat the same motives, like the old Italian painters. All the subtlety and complexity of the strophe was for them something more than mere virtuosity; in the fine balance of all its parts and in the perfection of its rhythmic movement lay one of the chief charms of the poem.

The conventional gallantry of the age has already been described in previous chapters. It is a commonplace of chivalric romance that the knight was pledged to the service of a lady whose favour he wore, and who might be anyone but his own lawful wedded wife. In fact, it had to be the wife of another, since unmarried girls normally played no part in this service. The Germans took over all this along with other conventions. They, too, wrote *aubades*, which they called *Tagelieder*, in which two lovers are warned by the watchman of the approach of day and the need of parting. Even

Wolfram wrote five of them, though he later took formal farewell of such poems, and was the only one among the Minnesingers to sound the praises of wedded love in contrast to such stolen intercourse. The poets complain of the *huote*, the strict watch under which the lady is kept, and the *merkaere*, or spies, who make difficult their secret meetings. As the lover cannot find his mistress unguarded, he must send a messenger, and poetic missives, *Botenlieder*, often divided dramatically into strophe and antistrophe, developed into a special poetic form.

If we took this love-service literally we might conclude, as some indeed have done, that the period was one of a sanctioned and glorified immorality, such as the world has rarely seen. But, with many of the poets undoubtedly, this licentiousness was largely a pose and a literary fashion, which no more reflected the actualities of real life than a certain type of French or English novel reflects the normal society of its day. To take examples from German literature, one would never guess from their works that Hofmannswaldau in the seventeenth century, and Wieland in the eighteenth, were staid and respectable family men. Rainer Maria Rilke has somewhere a witty phrase about " the troubadours who feared nothing more than the success of their wooing ". And if we are going to accept literature as evidence, we have to take into account no less the courtly epic, in which the usual goal of the knightly adventures is either marriage, or the reunion of those parted by some ill-chance or misunderstanding.

Only great personalities broke the fetters of convention and rose above the artificial standards of their fellows. Like Wolfram, the greatest of the epic poets, Walther von der Vogelweide, the greatest of the Minnesingers, sounds a healthier and more natural note. His ideal, too, is that of the Christian Warrior, who can best find the justification of his order and his calling, the harmony between the claims of this world and the next, of body and soul, in the Holy Wars. We have two crusading-songs of his, full of the most fervent enthusiasm and faith, and though not proof, they at least make it probable that he himself had worn the cross.

Walther's conception of the full round of honour is expressed in the poem we have earlier quoted. He is equally great whether his theme be religion, patriotism, or love. As a political poet he is one of the greatest of all time. He is a patriot in the best sense of the word, not blind to the faults of his country or of his party, but filled with glowing pride for all that is best in his native land, and jealous for its honour. In the stormy days in which he lived he championed boldly the rights of the Empire against the temporal claims of Rome.

As a poet of love and of nature, Walther is one of the sweetest singers of Germany. He prizes true womanliness above the stereotyped qualities of the conventional lady. In a well-known poem he declares that *wip* (woman) is a more dignified title than *vrouwe* (lady), since to be a true woman is more than merely to be of rank. In another he says that he has seen many lands, but the best women he knows are the women of Germany. They are like angels; whoever speaks ill of them is deceived. And in a later poem he complains that slanderers had said he spoke ill of women, whereas he had merely discriminated between the good and the bad, instead of celebrating all alike with unmeaning praise. This again hardly accords with the gloomiest estimate of the life and social manners of the time.

With Walther we see, then, a reaction against the conventionality of this service of dames. He dared to regard woman as a human being, and praise her for her real qualities. He came, too, to treat of themes that fell entirely outside the scope of the older courtly Minnesong—village life and the love of knights and rustic maidens. It is true that it was a country life seen with aristocratic eyes, like that we know so well in the later eighteenth century. Yet in Walther's hands, and in those of his chief successor, Neidhart von Reuental, it represented a great step in the direction of a purely national popular song.

The exaggeration and *reductio ad absurdum* of the fantastic elements of this love-service is seen in a strange Quixotic character, Ulrich von Lichtenstein. In his *Frauendienst*, 1255, the first German autobiography, he gives the marvellous story of his adventures in the service of his mistress. Into it are woven many of his own songs, and they form by far the best part of the work. It is true that fiction is mixed with fact, as in Goethe's famous work, but all the same, his attempt

ULRICH VON LICHTENSTEIN

From the "Heidelberger Liederhandschrift."

to realize the dreams of romance in a practical world remains astounding enough. Ulrich was born in Styria about 1200. Brought up in circles filled with the ideals of chivalry, already as a page he devoted himself in secret to the service of a great lady. Later as a knight he fought for her in joust and tourney, and succeeded in letting her know of his devotion. Hearing that his hare-lip was displeasing to her, he had it removed by what must have been in those days a very unpleasant operation; and when told of her surprise that he still had a finger, which she believed he had lost in a tournament in her honour, he cut off the offending member and had it conveyed to her. Dressed in women's clothes, he travelled in 1227 as Lady Venus from Italy to Bohemia, victoriously upholding his lady's honour in a series of tourneys. On the promise of her favour he waited two days in beggar's clothes among the lepers at her gate, to receive in the end shabby treatment at her hands. After thirteen years of faithful service, he left her in anger at her want of faith and broken promises, and devoted himself to another lady, for whom he undertook in 1240 a quest in the garb of King Arthur. And this phantast was a married man and a father, shrewd and energetic in practical life, a man of action, who played a considerable part in the politics of his native land!

For such a caricature to be possible, it is plain that the true spirit of chivalry must already have been in decline, leaving behind a ritual that was losing its meaning. In fact, before Lichtenstein closed his long life about the year 1275, the decay had already set in. With the rise in importance of the towns there was a gradual shifting of the social balance. The virtual end of the Crusades had deprived chivalry of its great pride and glory, while the end of the Hohenstaufen, and the consequent lack of a strong central power, led to a great increase of the internal feuds which even they had found it difficult to curb. The invention of gunpowder destroyed the fighting value of the armoured knights; the prosperous burghers in the towns had found in it the means of defending themselves against aggression. The castle became of less importance than the neighbouring town. Many knights fell from the high ideals of their order, and developed into quarrelsome bandits. It was the time of the *Faustrecht*—when Might was Right. A graphic picture of conditions about the middle of the century is found in the *Meier Helmbrecht* of Wernher der Gartenaere, which describes how an ambitious farmer's son forces himself, in his snobbish pride, into the ranks of such freebooting gentry, and ends miserably on the gallows.

We are all familiar with the popular picture of the robber knights; how they swooped down from their rocky eyries and plundered the passing convoys, seized the richly laden ships on the rivers, or stormed the towns and carried off the wealthy citizens to hold them to ransom. Sometimes the towns retaliated, attacked the robbers in their strongholds, and hanged them from their own towers. There is, however, another side to the picture. Not all the nobles were such outlaws and parasites on the working world. The tolls which they levied were often in return for services rendered; for keeping up the towing-paths on the rivers, for providing teams to drag the boats up-stream, or for furnishing an armed escort through their territory. Others left their uncomfortable castles on the heights in peaceful times, and had houses in the towns below, hanging their shields with their coats-of-arms above the door, that travellers might know where they could find entertainment and relays of horses. This was the origin of the signs above the doors of inns: The Red Eagle, The Golden Lion, or The Grey Bear. Among the hotels of Innsbruck you will find these very names, interesting reminders of a by-gone age, along with the usual modern meaningless designations. "If you travel in the Tyrol, where old customs linger on, you may find that in a good many places the innkeepers are still noblemen, and that the signs of their inns are still their coats-of-arms. If you go into the churchyards you will see the tombstones of the family of your host, with the arms and with coronets over them, showing him to be a baron, or a count." [1]

So there came about gradually a certain fusion of the old order and the new. The nobles settled in the towns formed an upper stratum of society, and by the accretion of the more wealthy and distinguished citizens there developed the patrician order of the big cities, which was such a pronounced and recognized feature of their life and organization as late, for instance, as the boyhood of Goethe in Frankfurt.

[1] S. Baring-Gould, *Germany*, London, 1887, p. 140.

It will only be possible to touch briefly on the future history of chivalry and the chivalric spirit in Germany. A significant stage is marked by the endeavour of Maximilian I, the Last of the Knights, to revive its ancient glories. He attempted in two works composed under his supervision, and to some extent with his collaboration, to deck out his history and that of his house in the trappings of chivalry. *Der Weiszkönig* (1512) is a prose account of his own public and political life and of that of his father, Emperor Frederick III. Its chief value and interest lies for us to-day in the fine wood-cuts prepared for its illustration by Hans Burgkmair. *Teuerdank* (1517) is a poetical autobiography of Maximilian, written in clumsy rhyming couplets, recounting his adventures in chase and tourney, the whole being involved in a cumbrous allegorical machinery. It was the last product of the courtly epic, and this late after-glow served only to show how dead was its poetical and metrical form, and how far the world had moved from the thoughts and ideals of the Hohenstaufen age.

In the fifteenth and sixteenth centuries, literature, in the hands of the Meistersingers, fully reflected the change of life and thought. It lost its idealistic character, and became practical, didactic and moralizing. It is true the Masters claimed for their art a high and noble descent, and counted among the twelve founders of their order Wolfram and Walther, and other great poets of the Golden Age. But the æsthetic sense, the pure love of beauty, was lost. If these sturdy burghers imprinted upon the last centuries of the Middle Ages a definite and more or less homogeneous stamp, it was that of a sober, utilitarian spirit, in complete contrast to the imagination and grace—the sometimes fantastic imagination and somewhat fanciful grace—of the age of chivalry. We have, it is true, a vast mechanical elaboration of metrical forms. Yet even with the greatest of them, Hans Sachs, the interest in the subject-matter always predominates over the purely artistic interest. For him romantic adventure was so much folly, and Siegfried in his turbulent youth nothing but a prodigal and a ne'er-do-well. For this typical poet of the sixteenth century, as far as his works are concerned, the age of chivalry might almost have never existed at all.

It is not till the middle of the eighteenth century that interest in the age of chivalry begins to awaken afresh. In 1748 Bodmer and Breitinger published in Zurich a selection of songs from the great Heidelberg manuscript, then in Paris; and this was followed later by further specimens of the Minnesong, and a part of the *Nibelungenlied*.

With his *Götz von Berlichingen*, a dramatization of the autobiography of a turbulent knight of the early sixteenth century, Goethe, in 1773, aroused a wild enthusiasm for the "good old days" of chivalrous warfare, when knightly valour spent itself redressing human wrong. For a time the German stage resounded with the clang of armour, and with noble sentiments inspired by the much idealized picture of this full-blooded, loveable, bellicose child. Men saw a welcome contrast to the complexity of their own social and political conditions in this simple-minded crusader, who never doubted the justice of his cause, or his right to draw the sword. According to his own account he had ridden in countless feuds, fifteen on his own score alone. "And having taken part now for well-nigh sixty years, with one hand, in wars and feuds and quarrels," says the Knight of the Iron Hand naively in his autobiography, " I cannot in truth hold or say otherwise than that the Almighty, Eternal, Merciful God has been with me in great and wondrous grace in all my wars, feuds, and perils."

The real revival of interest in the Middle Ages came, however, with the Romantic Movement at the end of the century. The days of chivalry were now seen in a poetic haze, which obscured the harsher outlines of reality. Villains there were of necessity, but with their unfortunate exception the knights were valiant and gentle, the ladies gracious and fair. In such an age Novalis placed the hero of the typical Romantic novel, *Heinrich von Ofterdingen*, whose life was a quest of that " blue flower " which became the accepted symbol of romance. And it was in a world people with pious knights and holy pilgrims that Tieck found the *mondbeglänzte Zaubernacht* and the *wundervolle Märchenwelt* of these Romantic dreams.

The ballad writers, too, played their part; Rückert's *Barbarossa*, for instance, and *Des Sängers Fluch* of Uhland, and countless others, are familiar to all lovers of German poetry. And a good example of the Romantic longing for that world of dreams is Arnim's symbolic novel, published in 1817, *Die Kronenwächter*. These " Guardians " have in their keeping the crown of the Hohenstaufen, and seek out descendants of that imperial house, in order that one day the remembered glories of their empire may be restored.

This Romantic feeling for the Age of Chivalry is still in a large measure alive in the consciousness of the German people to-day. What the direct influence of medieval chivalry has been on German life and character it is hard to estimate. For a long time, notably in the seventeenth century, the direct tradition was pretty completely interrupted. During the Thirty Years War various foreign influences were rampant; French and Spanish modes and customs, above all, were imitated to the detriment of native ideals of culture.

Vogt [1] thinks that chivalry has left traces in the social life of to-day through the courtly and knightly character of its formal training. " Expressions such as *höflich*, *ritterlich*, with their special connotation ; the social privilege of ladies ; *gnädige Frau* as a form of address, along with some formalities of court ceremony, and certain ideas and customs of the officer class, show what deep and wide roots the traditions of that time have struck."

It would be interesting to attempt a comparison between Germany and England, but space is not available for that possibly somewhat invidious task. If it might perhaps be argued that we are nearer to the methods of medieval chivalry in the formal training of our schools, in certain respects the days of chivalry are probably more familiar to German than to English youth. Still in the nineteenth century, says Professor Herford,[2] " German society was that of an old historic land, whose primitive traits had been much overlaid by the slow accumulation of the ages, much defaced by the scars of war, and not a little transformed by its own creative energy. Yet with all this, it retained more traces of primitive structure by far than the society of either England or France. No great metropolis imposed its mundane complexities and corruptions, as a standard to be lived up to, upon the

[1] Op. cit., p. 164.
[2] C. N. Herford, in *Germany in the Nineteenth Century*, Manchester, 1012, pp. 48 f.

nation at large. The small town, the village, remained, even in the first half of the nineteenth century, quaintly old-fashioned; clothed with their heritage of custom and song and legend."

The Rhine is a national possession, the like of which is not to be found here, and its ruined castles and their stories are invested with a glamour whose colouring is largely a romantic tradition. The country in which the great ballad-writer, Uhland, spent his childhood was rich in ruins of historic fame, chief among them the castles of Hohenzollern and Hohenstaufen, from which had sprung two of the greatest dynasties of Europe. Before his native city of Tübingen ran the road along which the German Emperors had led their armies down into Italy. The ducal castle which towered above the town itself was famous for many a siege. Not all German children are so favoured as was that Swabian boy; but all the same the monuments of the Middle Ages are still widely to be found, and what inspired the youthful Uhland is yet present to inspire them, if not always through the intimacy of personal knowledge, at any rate through story, picture, and song.

OTHER AUTHORITIES

Along with the well-known works of Büsching, von der Hagen, Schulz, Henne am Rhyn, and Wedel, already referred to by Professor Hearnshaw, the following may be specially mentioned in connexion with this chapter :—

LÜDERITZ, ANNA : *Die Liebestheorie der Provençalen bei den Minnesingern der Staufferzeit.* Berlin and Leipzig. 1904.

FRANCKE, KUNO : *A History of German Literature as determined by Social Forces.* New York. 1907.

WECHSSLER, E. : *Das Kulturproblem des Minnesangs.* Halle. 1909.

KLUCKHORN, P. : *Die Ministerialität in Südostdeutschland vom zehnten bis zum Ende des dreizehnten Jahrhunderts.* Weimar. 1910.

GOLTHER, W. : *Die deutsche Dichtung im Mittelalter.* Stuttgart. 1912.

HENNE AM RHYN, O. : *Illustrierte Kultur- und Sittengeschichte des deutschen Sprachgebiets.* Stuttgart. 1918.

VOGT, F. : *Geschichte der mittelhochdeutschen Literatur.* Berlin, 3rd ed. 1922.

SCHNEIDER, H. : *Heldendichtung, Geistlichendichtung, Ritterdichtung.* Heidelberg. 1925.

CHAPTER V

THE CHIVALRY AND MILITARY ORDERS OF SPAIN

By A. R. PASTOR, B.Litt., D.Phil.,
Cervantes Reader in the University of London.

TWO accusations, in appearance at least contradictory, have been brought against the Spaniards of different ages. They have been charged with carrying chivalry *ad absurdum*, by preserving the form rather than the substance and by indulging a foolish, almost hysterical sensitiveness where the point of honour is concerned, and also with despising the more practical and humble virtues of social value. Their critics point to the conceptions expressed in the later Spanish drama, more especially in the dramas of jealousy and blood of Calderón, which repel the average modern reader and make it difficult for him to appreciate the artistic effectiveness of these plays.[1] In reply we may say that these conceptions, far from being originally Spanish, represent a revival of the ideas of the scholastic moralists of an earlier age,[2] and that the purpose of this machinery was not a representation of reality, but rather the use (or misuse) of a subject in itself dramatic, for purely æsthetic ends. Calderón himself was conscious of the difficulty when he wrote the lines :—

> . . . ¡ Oh locas leyes del mundo !
> ¡ Que un hombre que por sí hizo
> cuanto pudo para honrado
> no sepa si está ofendido ! . . .

("Oh mad laws of the world ! That a man who did everything he could for his honour, yet should not know if it has suffered ! . . .")

The other accusation is more significant and perhaps more difficult to rebut. It is said that the Spaniards destroyed their

---

[1] We have four of Calderón's more important plays in mind : *El pintor de su deshonra, A secreto agravio secreta venganza, El médico de su honra,* 1635, and *El mayor monstruo los celos.*

[2] See A. Castro, *Algunas observaciones acerca del concepto del honor en los siglos XVI y XVII,* Revista de Filología Española, 1916, vol. iii, p. 1.

chivalry by prosaic commonsense, by ridiculing institutions and ideas of which they seemed only to notice the grotesque manifestations, forgetting the noble origin of these ideas and their value as an inspiration at all times. Everyone knows that this attitude is commonly associated with the greatest of Spanish writers, Miguel de Cervantes Saavedra, in whose mind two eternal types took root, the two extreme forces which act on the Spanish character and which in their incarnations are called Don Quixote and Sancho Panza.

Byron, who was rarely serious and hardly ever profound, thought that Cervantes had " smiled Spain's chivalry away ", repeating the opinion of Defoe's Don Felix Pacheco, who told Captain Carleton that the great novel " was a perfect paradox . . . for, though it must infallibly please every man that has any taste of wit, yet has it such a fatal effect upon the spirits of my countrymen that every man of wit must ever resent . . . And I verily believe that to this, and this only, we owe that dampness and poverty of spirit which has run through all our councils for a century past, so little agreeable to those nobler actions of our famous ancestors ".[1]

We should understand the purpose of Cervantes. To justify fiction, and not to exercise the powers of the imagination, by inventing stories without a pretext, or would-be pretext, has been the purpose of story-tellers from time immemorial. There must needs be a moral, or the story must pretend to be true. Spain produced the apologetic tales, for

---

[1] Defoe's *Novels and Miscellaneous Works*, Oxford, 1840, vol. viii, p. 160. It is curious to notice that Byron's much-quoted lines have never, as far as I know, been related to the general opinion of the eighteenth century. Even W. P. Ker in his admirable lecture on Don Quixote (*Selected Essays*, vol. ii, p. 31), which is one of the most vital, if shortest, English contributions to Cervantic scholarship, speaks of the falsities of Byron and repudiates them without comment in favour of Hegel's famous passage in the *Æsthetics*, vol. ii, p. 214.

It seems that the first to speak in this social-historical sense about Cervantes' work was Sir William Temple in his *Of Ancient and Modern Learning*, where he attributes similar remarks to " an ingenious Spaniard at Brussels " (Sir William Temple's *Works*, London, 1757, vol. iii, p. 464). Steele, in the *Tatler* (No. 219) said that " the history of Don Quixote utterly destroyed the spirit of gallantry in the Spanish nation ". See Alois Brandl's *Palæstra, Untersuchungen und Texte aus der deutschen und englischen Philologie*, vol. xiii. Gustav Becker, *Die Aufnahme des Don Quijote in die englische Literatur*, 1906. This account, however, is not exhaustive, and omits e.g. the important passage in the Preface of the *Serious Reflections during the Life and Surprising Adventures of Robinson Crusoe*, in which *Don Quixote* is described as an " emblematic History of, and a just Satyr upon, the Duke de Medina Sidonia ".

instance the *Apólogos* of the Prince Don Juan Manuel
(1282–1349 ?), a nephew of Alfonso the Learned, the "False
Chronicles", such as the *Trojan Chronicle*, and later the historical
novels which have as their subject the downfall of the Visigothic
monarchy,[1] or the civil wars of the Moorish kingdom of
Granada.[2] The strangeness of the origin of the story, or the
manuscript, was used as a device to awaken curiosity, and
the authors of these romances attribute them to some
fabulous Eleastra, Alanguri, Careste, Rasis, Abenhamin,
or invoke the authority of an ancient manuscript found in
a tomb near Constantinople and brought to Spain by a
Hungarian merchant, as happens in the preface to the
Amadis of Gaul. Cervantes uses these traditional devices
for his complex æsthetic ends, and thus the emphasis placed
on the practical purpose outlined in the preface acquires a
peculiar significance. But it must not be taken as a declaration
of moral faith; it is rather an expression of the pride of an
artist who knows himself to be superior to the ignoble throng
of those who still wrote romances of chivalry, at a time when
this literature had sunk to a low level.

Cervantes was a lover of chivalry, and preserved the
substance of chivalry in spite of his critical Renaissance
attitude. Perhaps an additional proof of this harmony of
contradictions is his life, so tragic and borne with a
fortitude which was not only literary but moral. His
courage during his captivity in Africa, which inspired two
of his plays and several of his tales, his touching pride
at having been present and wounded at the battle of
Lepanto against the Turks, "the most memorable and high

---

[1] *Crónica Sarracina* or *Crónica del Rey don Rodrigo con la destruyción de España* (about 1443), written by Pedro del Corral, who, according to Fernan Perez de Guzmán (1376 ?–1460 ?), the famous author of the *Generaciones y Semblanzas*, was "a frivolous and presumptuous man". His work, which enjoyed great popularity, was an historical novel derived from the *Chronicle of the Moor Rasis*, and was finally ousted from public favour, as late as the year 1592, by *The true History of King Don Roderic*, attributed by its author, Miguel de Luna, a Moor from Granada, to Abulcasim Taric Abentarique. Even an historian like Mariana quotes these novels as if they were history. Both Walter Scott and Robert Southey made ample use of Luna's book, especially the latter in his *Roderick*.

[2] *Guerras Civiles de Granada*, by Ginés Perez de Hita (1544 ?–1619 ?), who attributes his novel to an imaginary Moor Abenhamin. In order to understand that this is a romance and not history, it is sufficient to remember that Perez de Hita makes the Moors worship idols and speaks of a golden statue of the Prophet.

occasion which the centuries of the past have witnessed, and beyond the expectation of those of the future," and finally, his noble conception of the task of a writer in the *Journey to Parnassus*, and in the preface of the *Exemplary Novels*, of the poet as a knight serving a moral and an æsthetic ideal, prove what those who read the *Don Quixote* with an open mind already suspect. It cannot be doubted that he applauds with all the powers of his soul Don Quixote when he rises up " trembling from head to foot " at the banquet of the Duke, and addresses the company in answer to ecclesiastical " infamous revilings ".[1]

However, the two accusations we have spoken of contain a double truth, which must be restated differently. The point of honour, the revival of mediæval conceptions, if not in life at least on the stage, correspond to a devotion to ideas, an insane loyalty to institutions, against all practical considerations, which is characteristic of the later political history of Spain. Yet Byron's hackneyed lines acquire a new significance if they are taken, not in a temporary but in a permanent sense. The attitude of Sancho Panza is the ever-present complement of the idealistic exaltation of which the Spaniard is capable. It is this realism, with its critical and analytical attitude, which gives its peculiar flavour to the most original contribution Spain has made to the literature of the world, the modern novel. And, we may add, that this ever-present anxiety to select the significant fact from experience, and not to invent apart from experience, gives to the earliest works in Spanish literature the value of historical documents.

---

[1] It is the ancient opposition between *arms* and *learning*, the *Clerk* and the *Knight*, which during the Renaissance became an urgent question. A new aristocracy, that of the artists and men of letters was, together with the lawyers, competing to force its way to a privileged social position. In Castiglione's famous *Cortegiano*, the Count expressly condemns the French because they are of opinion that " letters hamper the sword ". Cervantes deals with the subject in many passages, adhering to the view that there are two ways to honour : " one the path of letters ; the other that of arms." Sr. Américo Castro has treated this question in *El Pensamiento de Cervantes*, Madrid, 1925, pp. 218-19. This work develops several fundamental aspects tentatively outlined in W. P. Ker's Essay, already mentioned, of which, however, Sr. Castro seems to have had no knowledge.

CHIVALRY OF SPAIN

The study of the political institutions of the early years of the reconquest of the Peninsula in the ninth and tenth centuries is not far advanced. It presents difficulties not found in the case of France and Germany. And, although there are monographs dealing with special aspects of the problems involved, we still lack a survey which will trace what is peculiarly Spanish and Peninsular as compared with the institutions of other Christian kingdoms.

To understand the beginnings of chivalry in Spain, we must turn to the remains of Castilian epic poetry. Although Castile is not Spain, it is the only kingdom of the Peninsula which expressed itself in epic literature at an early date and imposed its character and institutions on an ever-increasing number of its neighbours. If we make use of these documents, so intensely and so realistically alive with events and personalities of their time, we follow the example of the Castilian chroniclers, who, for instance, in the *First General Chronicle* which Alfonso X, the Learned, caused to be written in the year 1289, inserted, sometimes literally, long extracts from the *Cantares de Gesta*.[1]

This literature has a peculiar character which serves our purpose well. If we compare the French and the Spanish epic, the *Chanson de Roland* and the *Cantar de Mio Cid*, this character becomes clear. The *Cid* was written about forty years after the death of the *Campeador*, in the year 1099, while the *Chanson de Roland* was composed nearly three centuries after the death of the hero. Although the difference in the lapse of time may explain to some extent the fantastic mythology which grew round the French hero, and the Homeric simplicity with which the unknown poet of the town of Medinaceli narrated events which could still be remembered by old people, nevertheless, we notice a difference of principle which corresponds closely to variations in national character.

In the *Roland* the background of chivalry is made up of dreamlike visions. The geography is fantastic. Supernatural forces are closely interwoven in the deeds of men. When Roland dies, prodigies, such as happened during the

[1] In the following we quote from the *Cantar de Mio Cid, Texto, Gramática y Vocabulario* por R. Menéndez Pidal. There is a popular edition of the *Cantar* in the series *Ediciones de "La Lectura"*, Madrid, 1913, with an admirable introduction by the same author.

death of our Lord, take place (*Chanson*, *1423–37*). The deeds of the heroes are beyond all proportion; enormous armies of 360,000 and 450,000 knights go into battle; five Frenchmen kill four thousand infidels; the horn of Roland is heard at a distance of thirty miles; Turpin, wounded by four lances, and Roland with his head split, go on fighting. Probability is sacrificed to romantic magnificence. On the other hand, the Cid is simple, patriarchal, and his prowess does not exceed that of a good Castilian knight. The supernatural element is reduced to the characteristically Peninsular observation of the flight of birds,[1] not so much in order to predict the future, as to produce on the hearer an impression of ominous fatality (*Cantar*, *10–13*, etc.), and to the consoling words of the Archangel Gabriel, addressed to the Cid during the last night the exiled sorrowful hero sleeps on Castilian soil. Moreover, in this case, the poet tells us that it was a dream-vision (*406*) while Roderick was in his "sweet slumber" (*404–10*).

Of course, the Spanish Epic, like all literary works of art, contains *Dichtung und Wahrheit*, but *Dichtung* tends in a direction opposed to that of the *Roland*. Its object is to make us visualize in a simple and intimate way events which are tremendous and heroic. It simplifies and surrounds with a depth of human feeling actual deeds and happenings, which yet are far removed from the everyday life of those who listened to the travelling minstrel who recited the *Cantar*. The ideal of the Cid is the classical ideal of measure in all things.

We look in vain for signs of the inhuman rage which is characteristic of the chivalry of some other countries. It is a significant fact that the Satanism, which is not infrequently associated with French mediaeval chivalry, is not to be found in the Peninsula. The mother of the Infants of Lara, who wishes to drink the blood pouring forth from the wounds of her mortal enemies, is a demented animal, but Raoul de Cambrai is represented as systematic in his ferocity, blasphemy, and sacrilege. He says: "You shall erect my tent in the middle of the Church, you shall make my bed before the altar, you shall place my falcons on the golden

---

[1] It was the duty of an officer called the *Adalid* to observe the flight of birds, especially eagles, and to report to his leader when the favourable moment for the battle had arrived.

DOOR OF THE OLDEST ROMANESQUE PART OF THE CATHEDRAL OF SANTIAGO DE COMPOSTELA

This is probably the earliest Spanish representation in stone of a knight on horseback. The Apostle St James rides *à la brida*, in the northern manner, with outstretched legs. He does not wear the practical, but unsightly, boots *(buesas)* of the Cid, but like his Catalan opponents, only hose *(calzas)*. His tunic *(brial)* is slit and trails almost to the ground. In his hands he holds the sword, his *espada tajador*, which is short and designed to cut coat-of-mail like an axe. His lance is provided with a *pendón*, which was usually white in Castile and not as elaborate as those described in the French poems.

crucifix". He burns the nunnery of Origny and with it the mother of his most faithful vassal. In the *Lorrains* Bégue tears out the heart of his enemy and throws it, still warm, at the head of William ("There you have the heart of your cousin; you can have it salted and roasted"). Elsewhere Gaumadras falls into convulsions when the name of God is mentioned; demons help him in battle; Herchambaut does not deny, but hates God, until diabolism becomes a kind of anti-religion and we find advice such as: "If you find an honest man, dishonour him; burn the towns, the villages, the houses, break up the altars, and knock down the crucifixes."

There is no parallel in the *Cid* to the command for forced conversion given in the Chanson by Charlemagne, or to the manner in which those who resist this order have their throats cut, are hanged or burned alive. On the contrary, the Castilian Poet insists on the kindness and restraint shown by the Champion to the beaten Moors (*Cantar, 541, 802, 851*). When the Cid was told of the outrage committed against his daughters, "He thought and considered for a long while" (*2828*), and the King, after having received the hero's message asking for justice, " was silent and thoughtful for a long time " (*2953*). Roderick is represented as *fermoso sonrrisando*, beautifully smiling, and when the infamous Beni Gomez of Carrión were forced to hand back the two swords *Colada* and *Tizón*, " his body tingled with pleasure, he smiled with all his heart " (*3184*). When he, who has served the King so well, is driven into exile, he does not break out into passionate accusations, but there is a poignant simplicity in what he says to his companions:—

> "Mio Cid sighed for he had great worries,
> Mio Cid spoke well and with much restraint;
> 'Thy will be done, my Lord Father, who art in heaven
> This is what my evil enemies have done to me.'"
>
> (6–9)

Roland is first and foremost a feudal baron of France. The ordinary affections of human life have little place in his world. Roland dies, and the memories that pass before his mind's eye are those associated with his life as a soldier, with his sword, his conquests. Roderick is a patriarchal husband and father. His farewell to Doña Ximena in the early morning of the day when he goes into exile is reminiscent in its

Homeric [1] greatness and simplicity of that of Hector to Andromache; it was "as if a nail was torn from the flesh" (*375*). He is anxious that his daughters should marry well, and hopes to provide amply for them and for his wife.

But it is not only this which makes the chivalry of the Cid so different from the heroism of Roland. There is in the former a certain tenderness and wistfulness which the poet suggests with infinite tact, not explicitly but by delicate allusion, in scenes which show a high degree of artistry. Take, for instance, the meeting with the little girl in Burgos, when the Cid clatters through the silent streets of the old Castilian town at the head of his squadron, and no one will receive him for fear of the wrath of King Alfonso (*23–49*); or the boy, Felez Munoz, who finds the daughters of the Cid, two pathetic fainting girls, after the outrage committed by the cowardly Infants of Carrion—" the tissues of his heart were torn " and he called out: " Cousins, my cousins, Doña Elvira and Doña Sol! Wake up, cousins, for the love of God "; he is greatly embarrassed, and, when one of the girls asks for water he gallantly goes to fetch it in his hat, which the poet adds, " was new and fresh " for he had only just bought it at Valencia (*2785–802*).

It is important that we should note the presence of the most precious of all human possessions, of that peculiar element which has coloured two European literatures— English and Spanish—doubtless in a very different way, a sense of humour. A comic scene from this early life of chivalry has been preserved through the centuries in those short ballads (*Romances*) which are the true successors, in a fragmentary form, of the long epic poems and were enjoyed, as the Marquis of Santillana (1398–1458) said, by " people of low and servile station ", although among them are to be found the most exquisite products of the chivalrous tradition in Europe. One of the frightened Infants of Carrion hides behind a wine press and emerges, all covered with dust, after the Cid has taken an escaped lion back to his cage (*2278–*

---

[1] Ticknor in his *History of Spanish Literature* quotes an article by the poet Robert Southey (*Quarterly Review*, vol. xii, p. 64), who is of the opinion that of all poems written after the Iliad the *Cid* is the most Homeric in spirit— Hallam in his *View of the State of Europe during the Middle Ages*, 1818, (vol. iii, chapter ix, part ii, p. 555) thinks that the *Cid* surpasses everything written in Europe before Dante.

2310), and in the solemn assembly of the Cortes called to do justice to the Cid, one of the noble supporters of the Infants arrives late and noisily, his dress in disorder and his face flushed, " for he had lunched too well." (*3373–6*).

The information supplied by the *Cantar de Mio Cid* concerning the conditions of early chivalry is invaluable, and is, considering the historical character of the poem, information about facts and not about legal theory.

That chivalry in Spain should rest on a broad, democratic basis was a necessity in the secular struggle culminating in the reconquest of the Peninsula. Practical considerations imposed a constant check upon the baronial magnificence so typical of the French knight. Spanish chivalry partakes of the popular and anti-feudal character of all early Castilian institutions. In practice everyone was a *Caballero*, who served in war with a horse, even if he was not a *Hidalgo*. In the *Cantar*, after the distribution of the booty, " those who went as foot-soldiers became knights " (*1213*). Alfonso VII granted a privilege to the citizens of Toledo according to which " he who wished to ride on horseback should do so and adopt the manners of a knight." These were the *Infanzones de Fuero*, who became increasingly numerous in the thirteenth and fourteenth centuries. They formed a municipal aristocracy which was exempted from tributes, and became an oligarchy which monopolized the administrative dignities of the towns (*Portiellos*).

The horse became the emblem of chivalry; it prolonged the legs of the knight and gave him an immeasurable superiority over the lightly armed foot-soldier. Although the early version of the story of the Cid is not very explicit about the famous charger *Babieca*, a later version, called *Las Mocedades del Cid*, describes in a telling anecdote the acquisition of the animal, which was buried outside the church of St. Peter of Cardeña where the Champion was laid to rest. In the time of Sancho the Elder, King of Navarre (970–1035) the knight had his horse in the same room in which he spent the night with his wife.[1] In Castile the horse-loving Countess of Garci Fernandez looks after the horse of the

---

[1] See R. Menéndez Pidal, *L'Épopée Castillane à travers la Littérature Espagnole*, traduction de Henri Mérimée, Paris, Librairie Armand Colin, 1910, p. 128.

heroic and rebellious Count of Castile, who liberated his country from the suzerainty of the aristocratic Crown of Leon.

Yet then, as later, chivalry was in its essence a sacrament, an Order and an international fraternity. The King of Bohemia said to William of Holland when he made him a Knight : *Te in nostro Collegio gratanter accipio,* and the oldest liturgical book, previous to the later form *De benedictione novi militis* of the *Pontificale Romanum,* containing the prayers for the ceremony of conferring Knighthood, belongs to the early eleventh century. The Cid is frequently called " he who girded on his sword in a happy hour ", which means that he had been knighted. As we now know, he had received his arms from St. Ferdinand in Cordoba. But although this sacramental character of chivalry was recognized in the Peninsula, it remained a *desideratum* rather than a universal practice. Spanish sovereigns knighted themselves. St. Ferdinand took his arms in the monastery of las Huelgas in Burgos, Alfonso X knighted himself in Seville, and Alfonso XI in Santiago de Compostela, where machinery was so arranged in a statue of St. James that the King received the accolade from the Apostle. That the *Siete Partidas*, the legal compilation of Alfonso the Learned, should have been insistent on this abuse proves its universal acceptance, especially if we take into account the ultramontane and un-Castilian character of Alfonso's legislation, which delayed for several generations even its partial acceptance by the people of Leon and Castile.

The social position, together with the preferences of the poet, appear clearly in the poem. The sympathies of the author go out to the class of his hero, and this mirror of Castilian chivalry did not belong to the highest aristocracy. He is an *Infanzon* (later called *Fijodalgo* or *Hidalgo*), the *miles* or *nobilis* of the Latin documents, and this is true of the historical Cid, a squire, whose only source of income was from his mills on the river Ubierna. When the Infants of Carrion, who belong to the powerful family of the Beni-Gomez, think of marrying the daughters of the Cid, they consider them inferior to themselves, and say that they would only be good enough to be their concubines (*2759 ; 3276*). The Infants were *Ricos homes* (*richi homines, principes, potestates terrae, proceres, magnates*), who, according to Don Juan Manuel, often " marry their sons and daughters to the sons and daughters of Kings ", and, the Cantar adds, " daughters of Emperors " (*3297*). Amongst these the first rank is occupied by those called in the Diploma of Eslonza (A.D. 929) *omnes proceres palatii* (elsewhere *primates, magnates togae palatii, optimates aulae vel scholae regis*).

The members of these two degrees of aristocracy had the right to be judged by their peers and, in the case of the Cid, the *Cortes*, convoked by the King to judge the case of the Cid against the Infants, are not a political assembly but such a court of justice,[1] in which the King declares that a case for a challenge (*riepto*) has arisen and arranges for the *Gottesgericht*, which brings the poem to a dramatic end. Such judicial duels, called *barralia*, were frequent, and the legal way of dealing with a personal insult. The prudent Cid is careful to tie up his long and beautiful beard, lest one of the partisans of the Beni-Gomez should be tempted to pull it at the *Cortes*, where passion runs high. Such a supreme insult would lead to further bloodshed. This insult was recognized by law and the *Fuero* of Alhóndiga says, *quisquis messaverit alium* shall be punished.

The knight who loses " the love of the King " has to leave the country within a stated time and go into exile, where " he changes his nature " (*desnaturarse*) and can enter the service of some other lord. This custom, and the great difficulties in which it places the victim, gives the stimulus to the Cid for his epoch-making military and political career, when he joins the Moorish king of Zaragoza and has, in accordance with the standards of his time, no scruples in offering his as yet small army to an enemy of the Faith. He does, in fact, exercise a kind of protectorate over the weak Prince of Zaragoza. About the legality of his action there can be little doubt. Even at a later date a law of Alfonso X, the Learned, lays down the procedure to be followed, which differs in the case of the vassal who is a knight from that to be observed by one who is not.

There has been much exaggeration as to the influence of the East on Spanish civilization ; the tendency was rather

[1] The first *Cortes*, in the sense of a political assembly, were held in Nájera in 1137 under Alfonso VII. But in this case no representatives of the towns, far less of the people, took part in what was a gathering of noblemen presided over by the king, which continued the ancestral tradition of the *Concilia* the *Conventus*, and *Congregationes*, but without the presence of ecclesiastical representatives.

to react against the Orient. Yet the Spanish knight was constantly meeting Arabs and Berbers (they must be clearly distinguished), and his attitude towards a race which was that of the enemy, but not infrequently that of a personal friend, was necessarily different from that of a Frenchman, who could see in the Infidel nothing but a monster. The Cid was the greatest foe of the Moslem. The conquest of Valencia was a long step towards the final victory of the Cross over the Crescent, and it stirred the imagination of Europe in an extraordinary way. That Valencia should have been lost after the death of the Cid, proves his unique genius as a soldier and a politician. A fresco from the Palace of Amra in Syria, which was studied and described by the Imperial Academy of Vienna, represents the princes who are considered the chief enemies of the Caliph. Over one of them (the face has been destroyed) we read in Arabic and in Greek *POΔOPIKO*. But, at the same time, the Roderick represented in the poem had trusted friends amongst the Mohammedans, for instance the Moor Abengalvon, whose liberality and loyalty contrast with the sinister machinations of the Lords of Carrion (*2648-2688*). His gentleness and kindness towards the Moors he vanquished are, as we have seen, insisted upon by the poet, a typical case being that of the taking of a small town, Alcocer, where he protects the lives of the inhabitants against the cruel fate of war.

The chivalry of the Cid was felt from the beginning to be national, in a sense that transcends the geographical limits of Castile. The author of the Cid does not continue the secular Castilian hatred of the Kingdom of León. But the regions of the north-east of the Peninsula had been for too long without contact with the remains of Visigothic power in the north-west, and were rapidly developing in accordance with their own national temperament, so different from that of Castile or even Galicia. It is true that we should look in vain for any allusion to " Spain " in the manner in which the poet of the Roland speaks of " France " (one hundred and seventy times), giving this name to the whole Empire of Charlemagne, which, according to the Chanson, consists of Bavaria, Germany, Normandy, Brittany, Poitou, Auvergne, Flanders, Fresia, Lorraine, and Burgundy. Aix la Chapelle is in France, and the traveller crossing the Pyrenees

ALFONSO II, "THE CHASTE," KING OF OVIEDO, LEON AND
GALICIA, DIED A.D. 842

He fought successfully against the Amirs Achacam I and Abderrahmán II and tried to form an alliance with Charlemagne and his son Louis, which was opposed by the turbulent nobles of the Asturias and of Galicia. He restored partially the Visigothic administration and founded towns and churches, amongst them Santiago de Compostela, the shrine of St. James, which soon became the most important centre of pilgrimage in Europe. The illumination reproduced belongs to the *Libro de los Testamentos* of Oviedo, which was probably compiled between 1126 and 1129 and is one of the most significant Spanish illuminated manuscripts of the Middle Ages. The King is represented praying, with his shield-bearer standing behind him.

sees the plains of France spread before him. The French are the chosen people, superior to all other nations and to them God has entrusted his sword. As the *Couronnement de Louis* (Louis VI) has it : " The crown of France must be so highly placed—that all others should belong to it—God ordered the first King of France to be crowned—By his angels singing nobly—Then he commanded him to be his Sergeant on earth."

Menéndez Pidal says " the *Cid* is not national because of the patriotism displayed in it, but rather as a picture of the people amongst whom it was written ". Prescott in his *History of the Reign of Ferdinand and Isabella* observes that in the same way as the Homeric poems were the most important bond between the Greek States, the *Cid*, which gave expression to some of the greatest national memories, affected profoundly the national feeling of solidarity. The Cid feels *quant grant es España*; the Emperor Alfonso rules over Portugal, Galicia, León and Castile, and one of the most constant and most touching characteristics of Roderick is his loyalty and devotion to his Sovereign. After he has been driven into exile, he yet sends presents to Alfonso, sharing with him the spoils of battle. In the scene of the reconciliation, the incomparable hero humiliates himself to the dust before the Emperor. " He bites the grass, tears stream from his eyes. So great was his delight " (*2022–3*). The King-Emperor of Castile is a national symbol.

This wider patriotism grows naturally from a deep attachment to the soil. *Castiella la gentil* is for ever in the thoughts of the exile. If we want to find a parallel to this simple and intimate attachment to the home, the county, the town, the native village or castle, we must think of the Count of Flanders contemplating the desolate landscape round Jerusalem and saying : " I am greatly astonished that God, the son of Holy Mary, should have lived in such a desert. Oh, how I prefer the great castle of my town of Arras!" of Roland, who, when all the Christian barons are dead, says : " Land of France, thou art the sweetest country !" or of William of Orange, who, dying, bared his chest so that the wind coming from France might kiss it.

Chivalry arrived at maturity when the ideal of the soldier and the religious ideal were blended harmoniously. *Non nobis, non nobis, Domine, sed nomini tuo da gloriam*, said the Templars. We have already shown that the Castilian temper does not easily take to mysticism, and perhaps it may be argued that the power and importance of the religious-military Orders in Spain were due, not only to the necessities imposed by the struggle against the Moors, but also to a certain reluctance to accept the extreme metaphysical consequence of chivalry, an attitude which the discipline and organized life of the religious Orders were deliberately designed to overcome. One Order, that of the Ribbon, was created by Alfonso XI, at a late date, in order to strengthen chivalry in the Peninsula and counteract the degeneration of feudal ideas.

Alfonso X, the Learned, in his constant efforts to acclimatise foreign institutions, endeavoured to make the Castilian rural knights courtly and instil into them those feudal ideas [1] which he so greatly admired. When he began

---

[1] Was there or was there not a feudal system in Spain? Recently it has been stated that the not infrequent mention of donations by the King to *Ricos hombres* and *Hidalgos* is a sufficient proof that a feudal system conditioned the social hierarchy in the Peninsula as in France and Germany; but these indications must be properly understood. Dukes and Counts independent in the enjoyment of their *Fief de dignité* were not known in Castile. The fief proper was a grant which established a special bond between the donor and the vassal who received the fief; it was hereditary, although the feudal lord retained some rights over it, and the vassal had the right of jurisdiction over his fief, uniting in his person, property and political power. The feudal lord could in his turn grant fiefs. He was part of a hierarchy which reached from the serf to the Emperor and so to God.

Conditions in León, Castile, and Galicia were quite different. The recipient of a royal donation did not owe his King a special allegiance which differentiated him from other subjects. The King was, and remained, the supreme judge and only law-giver, and, if occasionally powerful Barons in the north-west of the Peninsula became immune from royal interference on this point and acted as judges of their people, it was thanks to special privileges which, even in these cases, forbade the would-be feudal lord to maintain a prison on his territory, and did not prevent his dependents from appealing to the tribunal of the King. Feudalism, therefore, such as it was known in Central Europe and in France, differed radically from the Peninsular *señorío*, even if Kings with foreign connexions tried to impose it against the feeling of their country.

It is curious to observe that, whereas in France and in Germany feudalism arose as a decentralizing force hostile to the Crown, in Spain it was, on the contrary, favoured by the Kings, more especially during the last thirty years of the eleventh century when Alfonso VI became the protector of the Order of Cluny. The ideas of this remarkably active man, whom the poet of the *Cid* did not consider a "good Lord", at least in the first part of the *Cantar*, illustrate this development. Before the conquest of Toledo he called himself already *Rex* (in a document of the 19th February, 1085). Two years later, in a Privilege granted to the Cathedral of Astorga, he styled himself *Imperator Adephonsus*, and six years later he took the title of *Imperator totius Hispaniae*, and considered himself the Doyen of the Peninsular Princes, his relations

to codify Castilian law in his *Siete Partidas*, he laid down that a knight should be poor, and should not crack jokes; that knights must not eat garlic nor onions; that they must consider it their greatest happiness to be in the entourage of the King, and their deepest punishment not to be allowed in his presence. But Alfonso, the dreamer, who hankered after the Imperial Crown, and spent his substance in the attempt to be elected Emperor, died of a broken heart and the rustic knights continued to eat onions and to indulge their natural sense of humour.

In Spain, as elsewhere, the Church had originally condemned all participation in war, but the evolution of a different idea was comparatively rapid, although from time to time the original attitude was restated. The Council of Arles excommunicated deserters and conscientious objectors, but the Council of Kiersy (858) sent forth the injunction that " we must war against our sins and vices and hold peace with our brethren "; and even as late as the year 1514 the Lateran Council pronounced that " nothing is more pernicious, nothing more disastrous to the Christian Republic, than the inhuman rage of war." War is always satanic, but soon it is recognized that it serves purposes of expiation and preparation. The Church regulated war, as in the rules laid down by Nicolas I when, in the year 865, the Bulgars consulted him whether or not it was permissible to continue war during Lent. On one point the Church of the earlier Middle Ages was emphatic, namely, upon the prohibition of the use of bow and arrows during battles between Christians, a verdict clearly stated in the Lateran Council of 1139. The consequences of this affected England, and gave employment to the bands of English and

towards them being similar to those of the Holy Roman Emperor towards the Dukes of the Empire.

But these illusions and ceremonial pretensions were short-lived, and the consequences of feudal anarchy were, for this period at least, avoided, although they became acute towards the end of the fifteenth century, just before the Catholic Queen began to raze the castles of the barons to the ground and to stamp out disorder by her " frightful anatomies ". Only in one kingdom of the Peninsula which was united to the crown of Castile, Galicia, are the evil consequences of such baronial semi-feudalism noticeable. Here the Count of Monterroso, Don Munio Peláez (1121) terrorized the neighbourhood unchecked, the Count Don Garcia Perez (1130) made a large income out of his robberies of the merchants from England and Lorraine, who were on their way to Santiago de Compostela, and the Count Don Fernando Perez had his castle of Raneta besieged and destroyed by the troops of the energetic Archbishop of Santiago.

Scottish archers who were utilized consistently by Castilian and Portuguese Princes, but were held in slight esteem by the chivalry of these countries, although their effectiveness was never under-estimated as in France.

Already St. Augustine had distinguished between just wars and unjust wars and Vincent de Beauvais, in the reign of St. Louis, had stated the three conditions which were necessary to make war permissible; the authority of the Prince, a just cause, and an honourable intention. Finally military prowess became meritorious and the gallant knight might hope for a reward in another world. St. Bernard's famous letter to the Knights of the Temple is the final, and perhaps the noblest, expression of this change. John of Salisbury said that the military profession had been instituted by God; for peace is the gift of God and the soldier brings peace.

Two ideals, the military-chivalrous and the religious-monastic, crystallize in the form of the military Orders which played an important and peculiar rôle in the history of the Peninsula. The same reason which made chivalry spread through different social classes, the urgency of the appeal against the Infidel at the doors, gave strength to these associations when they had long lost their vitality in other countries. It was not necessary to travel across the sea to Palestine in order to take part in the meritorious work of liberation. After the conquest of Sevile by St. Ferdinand in the year 1248, the urgency of this appeal gradually diminished, and the Orders were the instrument for keeping alive a spirit which was degenerating amongst multitudinous interests of more immediate practical consequences.

The power of the military Orders and their social prestige were based not only on their wealth, but on the fact that they have always represented in Spain the aristocratic principle of chivalry, while the chivalry which did not combine the functions of a monastic order with a military organization was, as we have seen from the beginning, profoundly democratic. It is not astonishing that at a later date, during the last quarter of the fourteenth and more than half of the fifteenth century, the military Orders should (nearly always) have been opposed to centralizing influences and the controlling hand of the king or his minister, and been found taking the part of the feudal barons in their innumerable risings against the absorbing policy of the Crown. A member of such an Order was both noble and a knight, and was backed by the immense power of an organized society. This preponderance of the Orders became in the end the very cause of their downfall.

The Order of the Temple, the first to be established in the Peninsula, was already in Calatrava, in the year 1189, and was followed immediately by the Knights of St. John of Jerusalem. Fifty years after the foundation of the Temple, the Knights were present at the conquest of Cuenca by Alfonso VII; at the height of their power in Spain they owned twelve houses in Castile alone. But at the battle of las Navas de Tolosa they suffered terribly; the Grand-Master Gomez Ramirez died after the encounter, and the *Anales Toledanos* remark laconically: " There they died all." The Order recovered, however, for it took a prominent part in the conquest of Sevile by Ferdinand III, the Saint, which broke the power of the Spanish Moslem. After that event the remaining Moorish kingdoms in the south never emerged from a state of intermittent vassalage. The problems to be faced by the Christian princes of the Peninsula became political and social rather than military, until, during the favourable moment of the union between Aragon and Castile, Granada, the last remaining stronghold of Moorish power, the Constantinople of the Occident, was taken by the combined forces of Castile and Aragon.

The activities of the Orders were, from an early date, not only external but internal. Already in the time of Alfonso X, the Learned, we find the Templars supporting the rebellious prince Sancho against the King, who, in order to bring about a reconciliation, handed over to them the town of Fregenal (March, 1283). They had established themselves in Aragon soon after their first appearance in Castile, and contributed to the conquest of the Balearic Islands in the spring of 1229, a conquest which was of the greatest importance for the Catalan trade in the Mediterranean, since the Balearic Islands had been a centre of piracy from time immemorial.

By the year 1290 the Aragonese conquests were completed and the Order was about to disappear. In the following year it was expelled from Jerusalem. The King of France had the French knights tried with the help of Pope Clement V, the first Pope to reside in Avignon, and the Order came to an end in an appalling scene in Paris when the Grand-Master, with fifty-nine of the knights, was burnt alive. In Castile a special tribunal was formed and before it appeared in the town of Medina del Campo in the year 1310 the Grand-Master and the Knights. There was a difference of opinion, which continued at the provincial council of Salamanca. The accusations brought against the Temple were considered by the Spanish judges to be unfounded, but they did not dare to contradict the Pope, and on the 14th of March, 1312, a Papal Bull extinguished the Order. In Spain, as in France, the immense estates of the Order were confiscated, and the blow which destroyed one of the most powerful organizations in Christendom tended to weaken other Orders, as events soon showed. External circumstances, such as the weakness of the Moorish enemy and the appearance of the Turks in other parts of Europe, made their ultimate loss of effective power inevitable.

During the first half of the thirteenth century military Orders in the Peninsula were very numerous. Perhaps one of the oldest is that of the Knights of Trujillo (*Freiles Trujilleses*), which had been founded in Palestine and confirmed by Alexander III, who took a special interest in these Orders. It was organized according to the Rule of St. Basil, and the Knights wore a white dress with a red band and a cross similar to that of the Templars. Alfonso IX invited those who had settled in Valencia to come to Castile and gave them the town of Trujillo in the year 1191. When Trujillo was lost to the common enemy, the Order disappeared, and the King handed its estates over to the Order of Calatrava, which was growing daily more powerful. Alexander III also confirmed the Order of Montjoye, which had been founded in Palestine (1180) by a Spaniard, Count Roderick. This College of Knights was short-lived, for after a quarter of a century the ever-growing order of Calatrava absorbed it. But in a short time it had acquired great wealth, owning, as early as 1180, important estates in the Peninsula. Originally these Knights wore a somewhat spectacular dress, a red mantle and a silver star attached to a chain; later they are represented with a white mantle and an octagonal cross.

These Orders had been international, but, besides them, we find a great number of regional Orders, limited to certain kingdoms. Thus, in Navarre various associations were formed such as the " Knights of the Oak ", the " Knightly Order of the Lilies ", and the " Order of the Terrace "; in Aragon the " Knights of the Stole " and " of our Saviour " are mentioned. Some Orders are associated with certain towns, such as Avila, and in Toledo we find the " Order of Our Lady of the Rosary " (about 1213), specially formed for warfare against heretics. The Knights of this latter order took some part in the Battle of Muret against the Albigensians. From some of the Orders women were not excluded, and in Catalonia, in the town of Tortosa, we find at least one Order, the " Order of the Axe ", which consisted entirely of women. All these Orders have disappeared, usually absorbed by more powerful institutions.

It was a failure of the Templars which gave rise to the Order of Calatrava, for when in the reign of King Sancho the Moors threatened Toledo, the outpost of Calatrava, which was difficult to defend, was abandoned by the Knights of the Temple, and the King offered it to whomsoever would undertake to defend it. Diego Velazquez, said to have been then a monk, but in his youth a soldier who remembered the times of Alfonso VII the " Emperor ", persuaded Raymond, Abbot of the Monastery of Fitero, near Toledo, to lead the undertaking. The Abbot, so the story goes, preached with superhuman fire, raised an army of 20,000, and gained a complete victory over the enemy. The Order was formed immediately and confirmed, by the same Alexander who had granted rules to so many other Orders, in the year 1164. The knights fought desperately at Las Navas (1212).

After the dissolution of the Temple, the estates of the Spanish houses were handed over to the Knights of St. John of Jerusalem; but protests were raised and the King of Aragon, James II, sent a certain Vidal de Vilanova to the Papal Court at Avignon suggesting that a new Order should be created to take up the heritage of the Temple. After some time, for the matter met with much opposition, the Order of Montesa was created, and the new knights, with a black cross on their shields and a green cross on their breasts, were soon to be seen in the Peninsula. They came to a final agreement with the Prior General of St. John of Jerusalem in Valencia concerning the distribution of the rich remains of the Order of the Temple, and the Order was finally approved by the Pope John XXII.

The foundation of the Order of Alcántara is described as follows in an old document. When Estremadura was in the hands of the Moors, a certain Suero, a native of Salamanca, decided to war against them for the service of God, and in the month of September *al reir del alba* (when the dawn was smiling), Suero and his men found a hermit called Amando, who lived in the Church of St. Julian, near the river Coa. In his youth he had served under the " good Count Henry ", Alfonso's Burgundian son-in-law. He now advised them to impose some religious discipline upon themselves, and the Bishop of Salamanca gave them, at their request, the Cistercian Rule. The place of foundation near Castel Rodrigo abounded in pear-trees and there was a specially large one near Amando's church, which was called *San Julián del Pereiro*, " St. Julian of the Pear-tree " ; this, then, was the first name which the Order took, in memory of that smiling dawn when they had met the bellicose hermit.

Meanwhile, the King of Castile, Alfonso IX, conquered Alcántara and gave it in the year 1217 to the Order of Calatrava, who soon found that it was not possible to attend to both the kingdoms of León and of Castile. Alcántara was therefore handed over to the Knights of St. Julian, who took the name of their new stronghold.

Of all the Peninsular Orders, that of St. James rose to heights of power, which at one time made it into a State within the State. It is difficult to date its origin. The story goes (but it is not confirmed by trustworthy documents) that King Ramiro I appointed thirteen Knights to look after the pilgrims who were on their way to Santiago de Compostela. The number was meant to be symbolical of our Lord and His apostles.

There is another story, which is repeated in the preface to the Rules of the Order. According to this version the founders of the Order were twelve adventurers and criminals, but this version is certainly of a very late date, and was probably invented to give a romantic meaning to a conventional sentence in the Bull of Confirmation, which tells us that the companions " were inspired by celestial grace and touched to the quick by the suffering of their hearts on account of the many crimes they had committed ". It is said that in the year 1170 the knights found a retreat in the monastery of St. Eloy (Hoyo or Loyo) and observed the Rule of St. Augustine, but they did not have a fixed centre, as they are to be found in Cáceres, a little later in Alarilla, and in Veles in 1175.

It seems that the true history of the Order differs from this official account. During the turbulent minority of Alfonso VIII it was founded by some pious gentlemen who established themselves in Cáceres, and were called *Freires de Cáceres*. Ferdinand II of León granted them Cáceres in 1172, when the Order was already extending into Castile. In 1173 the Papal Legate Hyacinth journeyed to Spain. He was met at Soria by the knights of the newly founded community, who asked for the protection and recognition of the Church. This they received from the Order-loving Alexander III in the Bull *Benedictus Deus* in the summer of the year 1175, doubtless through the intercession of the Bishop of Salamanca, who, as we have seen, was also a keen advocate of these Orders.

The community spread over the Peninsula and owned Monte Santos and Abrantes in Portugal, but the division into a Castilian and a Portuguese Order of St. James took place in 1290, in accordance with the wishes which King Dinis of Portugal had expressed to Pope Nicolas IV. The whole Order was wiped out at the Battle of Moclin, and reconstituted after the incorporation of the Order of St. Mary, which had been founded by Alfonso the Learned and was unique amongst the Orders of the Peninsula in being essentially a naval order.

In the beginning the Order of St. James maintained its number of thirteen *Freiles*, professed knights who had taken the voluntary vow of chastity, but after the year 1350 a substitute, *Emienda*, could take the place of an absent Knight in the Chapter. The Chapter had the power to depose the Master. Later we find thirteen Commanders and a varying but large number of knights, who are partly in Holy Orders and partly laymen. At first their dress was entirely white, but later the *Santiaguistas* adopted the red cross of the Crusaders. While the Peninsula was not homogeneous and national solidarity was slow in developing, they represented an international-Peninsular attitude and acted as a corrective of conditions under which it was not uncommon for a Christian Prince to see the invasion of a neighbouring kingdom with indifference or even with pleasure.

The tenth chapter of the Rules sums up the religious military ideal of the Order of St. James: "Never cease in the defence of your people and comrades and Mother Church. There is nothing more glorious, more agreeable to God, than to lay down one's life in the defence and preservation of His Law and to perish by the knife, fire, water, captivity or any other danger." The knights were to be lions in battle and lambs in their convents. They had to resign some of their personal rights. The married ones lost their *patria potestas*; they and their families became, nominally at least, the property of the Order. They were not only Crusaders on the field of battle, but they regulated in many ways the relations between the Spanish monarchs and the Moslem world of Spain and North Africa. They were the first to organize on a large scale and in a permanent way the rescue and ransom of captives, a great work which was later continued by the Monks of Mercy. The Knights owned ten clearing houses to deal with prisoners, *Casas de Merced de Redención*, in Toledo, Cuenca, Teruel, Las Tiendas, Zaragoza, Alarcón, Moya, Castrotorafe, Talavera, and in Castiel.

At the same time considerable privileges were attached to the permanent status of Crusader enjoyed by the Knights. Their estates were inviolable while the owners were engaged in military expeditions; no debts could be collected from them and they could sell land which under normal conditions was inalienable. The privileges granted to colonists of the frontiers against the Moors led them to despise the fear of raids and pillage by the enemy. For ten years they were exempted from taxes, if they undertook to remain on the frontier for another ten years after the period of grace. The Order concerned itself with the education of the children of the knights, making provision not only for the military training of the boys, but for the upbringing and marriage of the girls.

The wealth of the Orders was one of the causes which contributed to their incorporation in the Crown. It was inevitable that their estates should become immense, for they had the power to acquire property but not to alienate it. At first these properties paid taxes, but at an early date the collection of taxes by the officers of the King ceased. The Crown was, and had been, fully aware of the serious dangers implied in this system. Ecclesiastical foundations had been forbidden. Alfonso VII in the Cortes of Nájera, in 1138, denied the right of ecclesiastical communities to own land, except in cases where a royal privilege had been granted. This was the national attitude, which was many times re-stated in the early *Fueros* of Castile, the *Ordenamiento* of Alcalá, and the *Fuero Real*, which is a contemporary of the *Siete Partidas* of Alfonso the Learned. But these protests became increasingly ineffectual and the estates of the Orders grew into cancerous latifundia, the possession of which poisoned the political and military life of these institutions. The economic legislation of the Chapters is a constant effort to dispose of these gigantic tracts of land. Thus, for instance, the Chapter of Uclés of 1440 orders that the peasants who redeem waste land are to keep it. Two sales of properties and rights, by no means the most important, which took place in accordance with two Bulls of Paul V, produced 2,400,000 ducats. Even in 1636 when the Grand-Masters were raising a loan and treating with Johann Jacob Holzapfel and Johann Christoff Everlin, agents of the imperial bankers, the house of Fugger in Augsburg (*rico como un Fúcaro*, as Cervantes had said) the annual income of the *Encomiendas* was still 588,000 ducats. The remaining property of the four surviving Orders was sold, or, rather, thrown away in the " Amortization " of 1847.[1]

[1] The literature on the Orders of Chivalry is as extensive as it is unsatisfactory. The following works have been consulted :—
Fr. F. Rades y Andrade : *Crónica de las trés órdenes y cancellerías de Santiago, Calatraua y Alcántara*, Toledo, 1572.
Historia de las Ordenes militares de Santiago, Calatrava y Alcántara. Ordenado por el Licenciado Francisco Caro de Torres, Madrid, 1029.
A. F. Aguado de Cordova : *Bullarium equestris ordinis S. Jacobi de Spatha, etc.*, Madrid, 1749.
I. J. de Ortega : *Bullarium ordinis militiae de Alcántara olim San Julian del Pereiro*, etc., Madrid, 1759. *Bullarium ordinis Militiae de Calatrava*, Madrid, 1761.
W. Lippert : *Des Ritterordens von Santiago Thätigkeit für das Heilige Land*, 1889.

From very early times, parallel to the hard-working, efficient and human chivalry of the Cid, there appears another chivalry, arrogant, theatrical, mystical without religion, and unpractical without idealism, which, since the Gothic revival in the eighteenth century to the days of pre-Raphaelite affectation, has been admired by lovers of the picturesque, who are innocent of historical knowledge.

The personality of the Cid himself suffered through this change. Already in *Las Mocedades del Cid* he is represented as a diabolical youth, ill-treating his father and insulting his King, who, not without cause, remarks that Roderick is a *pecado*—a sin, a demon.

A number of non-Castilian and non-Peninsular influences were at work. The youth of the thirteenth century borrowed ideals of French and of Provençal origin and was inspired by the example of Charlemagne and his peers, whose deeds were celebrated in Spain in the Chronicle of Turpin, written most probably in Santiago de Compostela in the twelfth century. This work became the father of an innumerable progeny, which include the *Noble cuento del emperador Carlo Maynes de Roma e la buena emperatriz Sevilla*, only to be found in a manuscript in the library of the Escorial, the *Historia de Enrique, fi de Oliva* (Seville, 1498), the *Historia de Carlo Magno y de los doce Pares* (1525), and many others.

In the fourteenth century the Celtic romanticism of the *Matière de Bretagne*, already acclimatized in Galicia and Portugal, where the national temperament was favourable to this individualistic, lyrical outlook upon life, reached Castile and filled the imagination of every man and woman, until there was not a camp follower who did not dream of the Knights of the Round Table, of Erec, Gawain, or Lancelot, no lover who did not wish to emulate Tristan, no girl who did not aspire to the passionate love of Iseult or the perfection of Oriana. Many a noble Portuguese called his daughters Iseu, Genevra, or Viviana, and chose for his sons the names of

Escudero de la Peña: *El Archivo de Uclés, Boletín de la Academia de la Historia*, 1889, vol. xv, p. 299.

F. R. Uhagon (Marqués de Laurencin): *Ordenes militares*, Acad. Hist., Madrid, 1898. *Indice de los documentos de la Orden Militar de Calatrava existentes en el Archivo Histórico Nacional*, Madrid, 1899.

B. Martin Minguez: *Regla de la Orden de Santiago*. Academia Heráldica, 1917 (on pp. 4, 9, 25, 30, 57, 61, 73, 70, 104, 110, 127 y 137, the rules are compared with passages taken from the *Cid*).

Tristão, Lançarote, or Percival,[1] although in Castile the references to Celtic stories are few before the fourteenth century. They derive from the popular Latin Chronicle of Geoffrey of Monmouth, which tells of Merlin and of how Arthur battled against the Saxons, the hereditary enemies of the Celts. From Alfonso the Learned onwards, who mentions Tristan in his poems, familiarity with this romantic chivalry increases and grows into a passion for gallant love and the point of honour. So grave a personage and so eminent a writer as the Grand Chancellor of Castile, Peter Lopez de Ayala, confesses that in his youth he was carried away by the fashion when he read and re-read *Lancelot of the Lake*. There are fragments of an early Spanish Tristan, and with the anonymous knight Cifar appears the first Peninsula Romance of Chivalry, written some time between the year 1299 and 1305 and characteristic of this process of adaptation in its mixture of chivalrous, didactic and hagiographical elements.

Towards the middle of the twelfth century the simple hard-fighting cavalry soldier of the Cid was ceasing to be an ideal, for one important section at least of the Peninsula. The Court of Alfonso VII, " the Emperor," had become the most splendid in Europe, and was considered a model for all others; a madrigal attributed to Frederick Barbarossa says :—

> Plaz mi : cavalier franzez
> E la dona cathalana
> E l'ouvrar del ginoez
> E la cour de Kastellana.

Here the noble but rustic friends of the Cid would not have met with a good reception, and the ladies would have turned away from them and smiled upon some adventurous knight who had shown his prowess in foreign parts. In this world women were not like Doña Ximena or the gentle silent daughters of the Cid. They were about to be raised to a false and barren heaven of romantic perfection by knights who rode in search of adventures, invoking their lady at the command of fashion. The Cid had found strength in the thought that his wife and daughters were watching him go

---

[1] See Henry Thomas, *Spanish and Portuguese Romances of Chivalry*. Cambridge University Press, 1920. p. 23.

into battle from the walls of Valencia. Now love had become sensuous, and at the same time was surrounded by a pedantic ceremonial, culminating in the erotic conventional poetry of the fifteenth century, which fills the *Cancionero de Baena* with its uninspired strains.

If love and ladies had in one sense become more subtle, individual and interesting, war had become theatrical and monotonous. The tactics and strategy of the Cid are full of variety, while the later Romances abound in monstrous charges, infinite repetitions of superhuman displays of strength and valour, which tire the modern reader and shock the military historian. The knight was becoming a knight errant and many Spanish *Caballeros* visited foreign countries. Already the Emperor of Constantinople, Alexander Commenus, had employed the services of a Leonese knight called Guzman. The Catalans went on their momentous expedition to the Balkans; adventurers innumerable jousted and fought in France and in Germany, until Hernando del Pulgar could say with truth that more Spaniards went north in search of adventure than foreigners came across the Pyrenees for the same high purpose. This was not the only contact with foreign chivalry. The Black Prince and his English knights, Duguesclin and his Frenchmen, John of Gaunt in Galicia, English Queens and gentlemen contributed to this change, although their influence has, doubtless, been exaggerated. Marriages with foreigners were frequent in the royal family even at a very early time. Alfonso VI had five wives; the first, Ines, was the daughter of Guido, Duke of Aquitaine; the second, Constance, was a daughter of Robert of Burgundy; the third, Bertha, came from Tuscany, and his two last Queens, Isabel and Beatrice, seem to have been French.

There is perhaps no better example of adventurous chivalry, romantic and yet tempered constantly by a Castilian common sense and complacency in popular wisdom, than the life of Don Peter Niño, which was described in a Chronicle by his squire Gutierre Diaz de Gamez (1379 ?–1450), entitled *Victorial*.[1] He tells us of the early education of his Lord, of

[1] *Crónica de don Pedro Niño, Conde de Buelna*, ed. Eugenio de Llaguno Amírola, Madrid, 1782. See also, in the series *Varones Ilustres de la Marina Española*, *Vida de Don Pedro Niño*, by Don Josef de Vargas y Ponce, Madrid, 1807.

THE CASTLE OF SEGOVIA

On a precipitous rock above the rivers *Eresma* and *Clamores*. Originally an Arab stronghold, it was rebuilt by Henry IV during the years 1352 to 1358 and used by the Court. Here Isabella and Ferdinand were proclaimed. The building was partially burnt down in 1862, and restored from 1882 onwards.

[*face p.* 134

his first military exploits, and amongst others of his expedition to England with three galleys in the company of the French sailor, Charles de Savoisy (*Sebasil*). They first attacked Cornwall (*Cornualla*), but the prudence of the Frenchman prevented Don Peter from landing in Falmouth (*Falmua*), where another Breton sailor had lately met with a hot reception. The artillery of *Plamua* (Plymouth) was formidable, but at Portland the raiders were successful, although they met with a spirited defence. The inhabitants, so the chronicler says, were poor people, and most of them had taken refuge with their women and children in the natural caves of that island. The Frenchmen began to set fire to their houses, but " the Castilians did not want to do so "; on the contrary, they prevented more fires from being lit, as the inhabitants of the island were poor. They knew that it was the wish of their captain, " to be gentle with the weak and strong with the strong," [1] A battle was fought in Poole (*Pola*) against the advice of *Mosen Charles*, which after many difficulties proved a victory for the Spaniards, who recovered there the famous cross of Santa Maria de Finisterre which English sailors had removed from the Galician shrine. Don Peter was about to retire to his winter quarters in France, but before doing so he visited *Antona* (Southampton), where he nearly burned a Genoese vessel, thinking it a prize taken by the English. He was only prevented from doing so by the entreaties of the owners, who pointed to the traditional friendship of their Republic with the King of Castile, and added that they were not leaving the ship in English hands as the king had already ordered her to be returned to them. London, " which seemed a large city in a plain," is situated on the river *Artamisa*. As soon as the Spaniards landed, " there came immediately so many archers that they compelled them to make for the sea in haste ".

Don Peter returned to France and spent some time in the Castle of Serifontaine (he calls it *Girafontayna*), which belonged to the French admiral Renaut de Trye (*Arnao de Tria*). Monsieur de Trye was old, and he had as a wife the most beautiful lady in France. Needless to say, Don Peter fell in love with *Madama la Amiralla*, who seemed to the Spanish knight a vision from those romances of chivalry

[1] *Crónica*, p. 108.

which he remembered so well. Here was a fair lady to be conquered by gallant deeds, such as the tournament in Paris in which he vanquished every opponent. The life in the castle is described in detail.[1] The lady and her damsels got up early and went into a neighbouring wood, each one with her book of hours and her rosary, and they sat by themselves and said the canonical hours and they did not speak a word while they were praying; later on, picking little flowers and violets, they repaired to the Palace and went to chapel to hear mass. After breakfast Madame would go for a ride, and with her knights and gentlemen. Again they picked flowers and foliage and listened to *lais*, and *delais*, and *virolais*, and *chazas*, and *reondelas*, and *complaintas*, and *baladas*. A banquet followed, and was attended with much ceremony and followed by a dance, in which the lady of the castle danced with Don Peter. After the siesta everyone went a-hunting, Madame on her beautiful horse, with a noble falcon on her glove. When the hunt was over, an al fresco picnic was arranged in a meadow, attended again by songs and flowers.

But the lady of the old admiral did not keep him for more than a season, although Don Peter did not forget her quickly. He returned to Spain, and made love to Beatrice, a daughter of the Infant Don John of Portugal, married her secretly, and suffered disgrace until the King, John II, recalled him to the Court and conferred on him the earldom of Buelna in 1421.

It is interesting to observe how Diaz de Gamez sums up the national character of the English and of the French.[2] "The English are a people very different in character from other nations with whom they live at variance. The reasons for this are many: firstly because it happens to be the nature of their ancestors; secondly because they live in a country which is rich in produce and in metals; further because they are many living in a comparatively small space, I mean the population is very large, although the island is considerable. They say that in that country mortality is low and that their harvest is rarely bad. Besides they are encircled by the sea, and for this reason they don't fear anyone." "The French are a noble nation; they are wise and learned and expert in all things that appertain to good breeding, courtesy, and elegance. They make a brave show in their clothes . . . They

---

[1] *Crónica*, chap. xxxi.   [2] *Crónica*, chaps. xviii and xxx.

love to please and honour greatly all foreigners; they know how to praise and greatly extol high deeds. They are not malicious; forget worries ... are courteous and gracious in their speech; are very gay, love pleasure, and seek it. Both sexes are much given to love and pride themselves on it ... and these qualities are natural in them, for the climate of their country depends on a star called Venus. ..." Curiously enough, it was England and not France which survived in the imagination of Spaniards as a country of romance and of chivalry. England was the home of King Arthur and his Knights of the Round Table. England supplied an enchanting, if nebulous, background for the adventures of Amadis of Wales, and when Philip, not yet the second of Spain, came to England to marry Mary Tudor, the few chosen gentlemen who accompanied him were in an ecstasy of delight when they visited the parks of English country houses, which reminded them of the novels of chivalry; when they saw the table of the Knights of King Arthur, which was shown to them at Winchester, and which they mistakenly or courteously believed to be genuine; when they witnessed the astonishing spectacle of the daughters of English squires riding on horseback unaccompanied, managing their mounts as though they were men and as if they had escaped from the pages of one of those Romances which abound in wandering damsels and enterprising maidens. But after a short time they found pork and beer poor fare; the ladies they thought on closer examination disappointing, and finally one of them wrote in a letter that " he would rather be amongst the briars and brambles of the kingdom of Toledo than in the bowers of Amadis.' [1]

During the second half of the fifteenth century many

[1] See *Viaje de Felipe II á Inglaterra, por Andrés Muñoz, impreso en Zaragoza en 1554, y Relaciones varias relativas al mismo suceso*, ed. Pascual de Gayangos, Bibliófilos Españoles, Madrid, 1877. In an anonymous letter dated from *Rigamonte* (Richmond) on the 17th August, 1554, it is said that " He who composed the books of *Amadis* and other Romances of Chivalry must doubtless have known the customs and strange manners of this kingdom when he described those flowery fields and pleasaunces. For who has ever seen in any other country women riding alone on their palfreys and even sometimes galloping along with the skill and nerve of an experienced rider ? And thus, your Grace may well believe that there is more to be seen in England than is described in the Romances of Chivalry, for the pleasaunces in the country, the rivers, hills, woods and delightful meadows, strong and beautiful castles, and everywhere so many fresh springs, are well worth seeing and, especially in the summer, most enchanting."

causes contributed first to the weakening, then to the death, and finally to the rebirth in a new form of chivalrous ideals. The death agony was still rich in dreamlike exploits, which were becoming increasingly sterile and amounted to a kind of insanity, for instance, in the case of the knight Suero de Quiñones, who, in order to be freed of a vow to wear an iron ring round his neck as a sign of servitude to his lady, undertook with his companion at arms the defence against all comers of the passage over a bridge.

The last occasion in which chivalry displayed itself with all its romantic trappings, and, let us add, with a strange and almost melancholy self-consciousness, was when the combined forces of Castile and Aragon, united through the marriage of their sovereigns, finally consummated the inevitable expulsion from the Peninsula of the last vestiges of Moorish political power.

In the cathedral of Toledo the carvings on the choir stalls, a series of fifty-four reliefs forming the backs of the stalls, give a vivid account of the great events described by the contemporary chroniclers Diego de Valera, Alfonso de Palencia, Fernando del Pulgar and Andrés Bernaldez.[1] These reliefs were begun by a German artist in the year 1489, under the auspices of the Archbishop, the Grand Cardinal Don Peter Gonzalez de Mendoza, one of the most prominent figures of the Spanish Renaissance. The German adapted himself to the realistic standards customary in Spain, however much the fortified towns he depicts may be un-Moorish and northern. The story they tell is the story of chivalry becoming a ceremonial display, serving as a ritual in the surrender of the keys of vanquished cities, a kind of military etiquette reduced to impotence by the devices of the engineer and the gunner. On most of these reliefs some artillery is in action. We assist at the conquest of Alhama, at the surrender of Alora, the conquest of Ronda and of Moclín, and many others, and in every one of these incidents in the conquest of Andalucia, artillery is the decisive factor, and the artist was well aware of its importance. The historical value of this collection is immense. The King, Don Ferdinand of Aragon, is represented over thirty times in different attire, in armour

[1] See on the subject of these wood carvings, J. de M. Carriazo, *Los Relieves de la Guerra de Granada*, Archivo Español de Arte y Arqueología, No. 7.

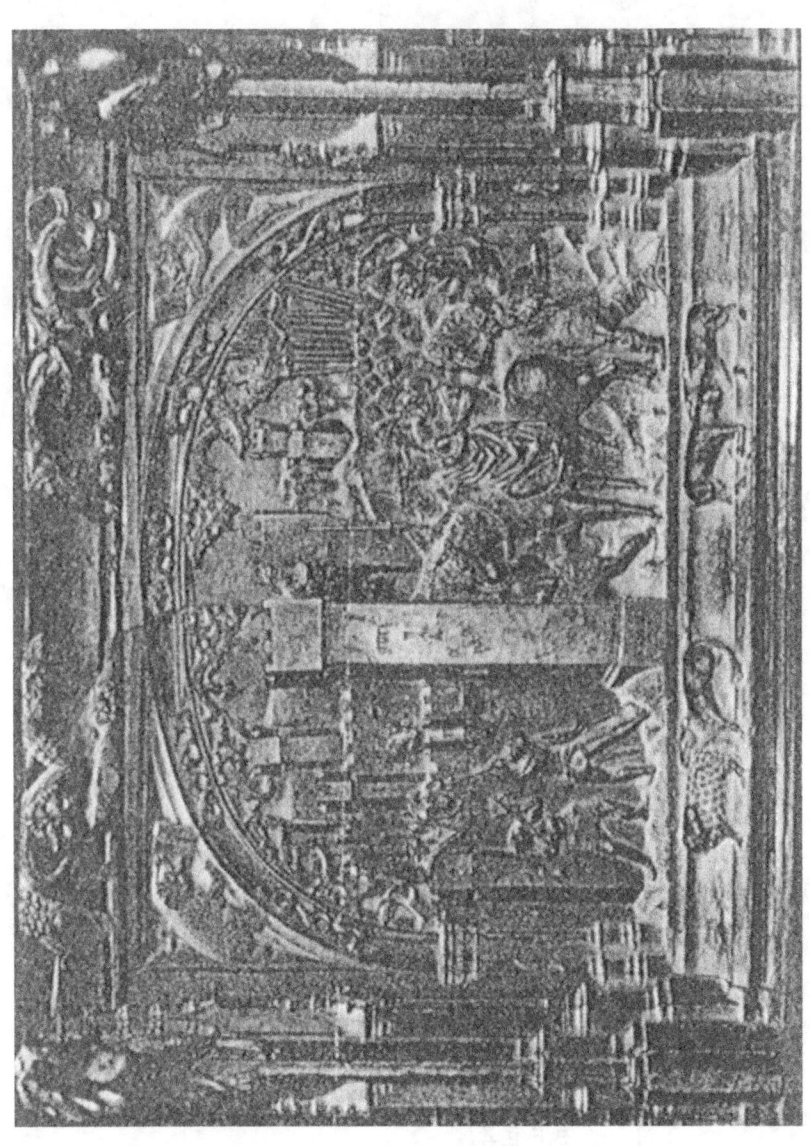

ATTACK ON AND OCCUPATION OF GOR (BETWEEN BAZA AND GUADIX) BY FERDINAND OF ARAGON IN 1489

The town is represented as well fortified. On the left two Christian soldiers attack three Moors. At the same time the Spanish army enters the city gate, while a Moor shows the key above it. The King rides in armour, enveloped in a large mantle and accompanied by knights and soldiers. In the corners a pig and a monkey are chanting the Office and looking into the choir-books. This wood-sculpture is on the back of one of the choir stalls of the Cathedral of Toledo.

[face p. 138

and a royal mantle with a helmet, a hat or a crown, riding in the European fashion (*á la brida*), and in the manner copied from the Moors (*á la jineta*), which the Spaniards had adopted more generally after the battle of Higueruela. Amongst the portraits there are many of the Catholic Queen Isabella, of the Cardinal Mendoza, of Don Alvaro of Portugal; of the Counts of Cabra and Tendilla, of the King of Granada, Boabdil, of his uncle El Zagal, of the defender of Málaga, Hamet el Zegrí, and of the murderer Abraham Alguerbi; of the Marquis of Cadiz, the real leader and Chief of Staff of the expedition, and last, but not least, of the *Conde inglés*, Earl Rivers, who went to Spain and joined the Christian army, partly to save his soul and partly for his own sweet pleasure, and who, according to the chronicler Valera,[1] behaved gallantly during the attack on Loja, where " he had three teeth broken and twenty of his men killed ". When the King sent a messenger to express his regret that he should have been injured, he answered that it was not much to lose three teeth in the service of Him who had given them all.

Granada fell on the 3rd January, 1492. There are many descriptions of this great event, amongst them one by a Frenchman, an eye-witness, which is included in the famous *La Mer de Histoires*. Six hundred hostages having been assembled in the Christian camp, Gutierre de Cardenas took possession of the Alhambra and other fortresses of Granada, and placed the Cross on the highest tower; " this Cross was raised three times and every time the infidel Moors inhabiting the city wept, groaned, cried and broke out into great lamentations. . . . The herald called from the tower Santiago, Santiago, Santiago; Castilla, Castilla, Castilla; Granada, Granada, Granada; for the most high and powerful Lords, Don Fernando and Doña Isabel, King and Queen of Spain, who have won this city of Granada, and all its lands through the might of their arms, with the help of God and the glorious Virgin His Mother and the blessed St. James, and thanks to the help of our most holy father, Innocent VIII, and the aid and loyalty of the Peers, Prelates, Knights, Hildalgos, and Corporations of their Kingdoms."

[1] Mosen Diega de Valera, *Crónica de los Reyes Católicos*, Anejos de la Revista de Filologia Española, viii (p. 201).

"As the herald ceased, it seemed as if the tower shook with the great roar of cannon and mortars, which were all discharged together as a sign of joy and victory. Then we heard the sounds of trumpets and clarions and all kinds of martial music to show our joyful happiness."

The herald had not only announced the final fall of the Crescent in Spain. His words were spoken on the day on which chivalry died, for the metamorphosis which chivalrous ideas underwent during the Renaissance was such that we must rather look for reaction and contrast than for continuity. Castiglione's *Cortegiano* was translated into Spanish by the poet Boscán (1534), and this classic translation, one of the masterpieces of Spanish prose during the Empire, profoundly affected educational and moral ideas.

Yet the ideal of the Renaissance was at one moment an ideal of self-expression, of heightening the potentialities of character, regardless of consequences. A generation later the beginnings of the Counter-Reformation shattered a short-lived optimism. In the seventeenth century, a Jesuit, Baltasar Gracián (1601–1658), a pessimist much admired by Schopenhauer, evolved the outlines of the modern gentleman. He adopted as guiding principles measure, restraint, taste, and the education of the will-power rather than of the intellect. He distinguished Persons from Individuals. Perhaps this idea of the modern gentleman is one of the three great contributions Spain has made to the patrimony of the human race. I leave it to the reader to identify the others.

CHAPTER VI

The Chivalry of Portugal

By Edgar Prestage, M.A., D.Litt.,
Camões Professor in the University of London.

IT is a commonplace that we must penetrate the ideas and environment of those who are remote from us in time, if we desire to comprehend their actions. This is certainly true of the theme, chivalry in Portugal, and of the Middle Ages in which the institution was born and flourished. Let us try, therefore, to forget for the moment that we are living in an age, in which men and women all over Europe have different religious creeds, or none at all, and imagine an epoch when there was a Christendom united in belief under the successors of St. Peter; when life beyond the grave was known to be of supreme importance and the present a passing show, and when hardly anyone questioned the literal truth of the words of our Lord: " What doth it profit a man if he gain the whole world and lose his own soul." For our purpose it does not matter that too often this belief was not translated into practice; it none the less existed and the spirit of dogmatic Christianity permeated and moulded law, customs, and daily life.

Chivalry is best defined as the medieval knightly system, with its religious, moral and social code. The Crusading spirit, translated into action by chivalry and by those associations of warrior monks, the Military Orders, exercised an enormous influence on the foundation of the Kingdom of Portugal, and on the oversea discoveries and conquests to which that country owes its place in world history; hence the religious side of chivalry, as being the most important there and the basis of the others, will be the principal subject of this chapter.

Knighthood was contemporaneous with, but independent of, feudalism, and though it had its rules, did not constitute a class apart from the rest of society; it was a dignity which rewarded some notable achievement, and, later on, was conferred upon conditions set out in the codes, after a novitiate. The spirit of fraternity united these champions of a common ideal, but they were under no authority and had no centre or special sphere of action. Each of the initiated, if he took his obligations seriously, sought always and everywhere, but independently, to fulfil the oath he had sworn when he was created a knight.

The Holy Order, as it has been called, is as old as the Portuguese monarchy, but it was not until the thirteenth century that it obtained a written rule in the Peninsula. This is contained in the *Siete Partidas*, one of the great medieval legislative codes, promulgated by King Alfonso the Wise of Castile, the main provisions of which were incorporated in the *Ordenações Afonsinas*, published in 1446.[1] It enacted that only men of good stock and not very poor were to be received, and a trader was not judged worthy to be girt with a sword, but this rule cannot have been strictly adhered to, for in his *Chronicle of King John I*, Fernam Lopes tells us that in his time sons of men of low estate were kinghted for their good services and toils.[2] Criminals, weaklings, and traitors were expressly excluded and the dignity could not be bought. Candidates had to be Christians, for the chief duty of chivalry was to maintain the Catholic Faith, and they must possess high qualities of mind and body. The usual age for admission was 21, but the first King of Portugal, Alfonso Henriques, assumed the honour at 14, John I was knighted at 7, and John II at 16. The ceremony usually took place in a church, palace, or castle, at one of the great ecclesiastical feasts, but sometimes knights were created before or after a battle; John I exercised this privilege on the eve of Aljubarrota in 1385, while, after the capture of Ceuta in 1415, he knighted his sons and they did the same for their noble retainers who had earned the dignity by prowess. The Spanish sovereigns were accustomed to knight themselves, and Alfonso Henriques, when only Infant, followed this procedure in 1125, by taking his arms from the altar in Zamora Cathedral, " as is the custom of Kings," [3] but it was

---

[1] There is a modern edition in 5 vols. Coimbra, 1780; the chapter on knighthood will be found in vol. i, p. 360.
[2] Pt. i, chap. 163.
[3] *Monarchia Lusitana*, vol. iii, liv. 9, chap. 14.

CHIVALRY OF PORTUGAL 143

an abuse, according to the *Siete Partidas*, for no one could give what he did not possess. We find this doctrine applied in 1382 to King Fernando; he was preparing to attack the Castilians on the River Caia, and began to create knights from among his own followers, and the English auxiliaries. After he had made thirty-four, he was told that though a King he had exceeded his prerogative, not being himself a Knight, whereupon he consented to receive the honour from the Duke of Cambridge, and went through the ceremony again. Subsequently, however, the *Ordenações Afonsinas* recognized that a King became a Knight *virtute officii*.

As the royal power grew, monarchs began to claim the exclusive privilege of conferring knighthood, as being the proper fountains of honour; by an edict of 4th May, 1305, King Denis decreed that no citizen could receive it save from himself, or by his order, and this was confirmed by the *Ordenações Afonsinas*,[1] but a simple knight had permission to create another in time of war, if the sovereign or his heir were absent.

Zurara, in the *Chronicle of Guinea*,[2] quotes a case which would come under this exception. During one of the Henrician exceptions to the West African coast, a *fidalgo*, Suerio da Costa, *alcaide* of Lagos, had performed some gallant deeds, but was not yet a knight, though he had fought all over Europe and been in the battle of Agincourt. Pressed to receive the honour, he consented, so long as he obtained it from the hand of a comrade, Alvaro de Freitas, "since he knew him to be such a knight that his own knighthood would be beyond reproach." The Chronicler continues "and so that noble man was made a knight, and I marvel at his toiling thus long in the profession of arms and being so eminent therein, without ever having been willing to receive the honour of knighthood till then. Surely I believe that though Alvaro de Freitas was such a noble knight and it had befallen him to create others like him, yet never had his sword touched the head of so great a man, nor was he a little favoured by the fact that Suerio da Costa sought to be knighted at his hand, when he could have obtained the same from very honourable Kings and great Princes." Aspirants usually sought the distinction from men of mark, as indicated here; King Manuel I, for instance,

[1] Vol. i, p. 376.   [2] Chap. 55.

bestowed it on three Polish nobles who had come to Portugal for the purpose, attracted by the fame he had gained by his navigations, and wars with the Infidel.[1]

The ritual to be observed in the creation of a knight is set out in the *Ordenações Afonsinas*.[2] At mid-day, on the eve of the solemnity, squires came to conduct the candidate to the symbolic purifying bath. Next they stretched him on the fairest bed that could be provided, where knights of authority dressed him in rich raiment. After his body had been cleansed, it was the turn of his soul. He was taken to church and begged God to pardon his sins and guide him to do his duty in the dignity he was about to receive, that he might defend His law, for, as is here observed, the vigil of a new knight was not established for play, or anything else, but to ask God and those present to direct him, as one who enters upon a career of death. After this, always kneeling, the candidate gave himself up to prayer and meditation, watching alone in the sanctuary until dawn, when he heard Mass. His godfather, or consecrator, then appeared and asked him if he wished to receive knighthood and on his reply in the affirmative, fixed on his spurs and armed him, save as to the head, which remained bare. He next girt him with a sword, drew it, and placed it in the candidate's right hand, making him swear not to fear death for his law, natural superior, and land. After the oath had been taken, the officiating knight gave him a blow on the neck, saying: "God guide you in His holy service and grant you to carry out your promises," and then kissed him in token of the faith and brotherhood which ought to reign among members of the Order, and all present did the same. This liturgical formula of consecration, copied from the *Siete Partidas*, is evidence that the rites of the Order in the fifteenth century were simpler and more severe than in Italy or France.

Sometimes, however, outward pomp accompanied the ceremony, as when King Pedro knighted John Alfonso Tello. Fernam Lopes relates that the King ordered 600 arrobas of wax to be prepared (1 arroba was equal to 32 lb.), and of this 5,000 tapers were made, and when the Count was to watch over his arms in the Monastery of S. Dominic in Lisbon, the same number of men holding these tapers lined the route

---

[1] Goes, *Chronica de D. Manoel*, pt. iv, chap. 4.   [2] Titulo, lxiii.

CHIVALRY OF PORTUGAL

from there to the Palace, which is a good long way, as the Chronicler says. The King with many *fidalgos* and knights went through their ranks, dancing and taking pleasure, and in this wise they spent a large part of the night. Great booths were set up in the Rossio Square, containing piles of baked bread and casks of wine, with cups to drink from, while oxen were roasted whole at the fires and every man who cared to eat could do so, for none were denied; so they remained while the festivity lasted, and during it other knights were created.[1]

The rites referred to above were impregnated with symbolism; the bath signified purification from sin as by baptism, the bed pre-figured the repose conceded by God in Paradise to valiant knights, and so on. An emblematic significance was also attached to the various articles of apparel worn by the neophyte; the white shirt reminded him to keep his body pure, the red tunic that he must be prepared to shed his blood for Christ, and the Church; his boots were dark, to match the earth of which we are formed and to which we have to return. These allegories came down from early times and chivalry copied some of them from the Catholic liturgy. External signs are needed to impress upon the mind the meaning and importance of spiritual acts. The man of the Middle Ages possessed faith; it was their moral wealth, and the deeds of heroism and self-sacrifice they performed were the fruit of an instinct which the Church sedulously fostered. The religious aspect of knighthood attained its full development in the ritual *De benedictione novi militis* contained in the *Pontificale Romanum*, but there seems to be no evidence that this was followed in Portugal; in that country a layman girt the neophyte with his arms and gave him the blow; the priest only blessed them and invoked the Divine assistance.

The dignity could be lost by ill conduct, and, according to the *Ordenações Afonsinas* [2] the knight was to be dismissed from the Order for the following, among other reasons: when he sold or ill-used his arms or horse, lost them at play, gave them to bad women, fled from battle, deserted his lord, or the castle which had been entrusted to him. Once degraded, he could never hold any public office and the privileges he

[1] *Chronica d'El Rei D. Pedro*, chap. xiv.   [2] Vol. i, p. 375.

enjoyed were taken away; these included exemption from torture, save when he was guilty of certain capital crimes, and from imprisonment, unless he had committed an offence entailing the death penalty.

The chief business of chivalry was the Crusades. The first was undertaken in 1095 at the bidding of Pope Urban I, to deliver the Holy Places in Palestine from the Infidel, and, as a derivative for the internal struggles which afflicted Christian states. But while designed for the common good, the individual was not overlooked, and in his discourse at the Council of Clermont, the Pope appealed to his hearers to redeem their souls by sacrificing their bodies. At that time a sincere and even exalted religious feeling dominated all classes, and though the evils were many and great, a superior virtue was able to overcome many of them. The worst sinners feared, not Hell only, but the judgments of God in the present life, and remorse led them to attrition and confession; even powerful monarchs submitted to the severe penances imposed on them to purge their crimes. Fighting was the main business of feudal times, and the Crusades offered men an ideal worthy of their mettle and promised them the reward of fame in this world, and of Paradise in the next. Hence they appealed equally to the good and the bad for spiritual reasons, although among the millions who took the Cross, a large number, to judge by their conduct, must have done so for plunder or mere adventure.

Long before the Crusades a similar struggle had commenced in the Peninsula to deliver it from the Infidel, and one that was destined to have more lasting results; the Kingdom of Portugal came into existence during the strife of seven centuries between Christian and Mohammedan, which, commencing shortly after the battle of the Guadalete in 711, only ended by the conquest of Granada in 1492. The domain of the Cross grew little by little, and before the first half of the eleventh century new Christian kingdoms occupied a considerable area; in 1072 Alfonso VI united under his sceptre León, Castille, Galicia, and Portugal, and in 1085 he took Toledo, after Cordova, the chief city of Mohammedan Spain. Many French and Norman knights, animated by the Crusading spirit, came to join him, among them Henry of Burgundy, to whom he gave the hand of his daughter,

Theresa, and the government of the county of Portugal, in or about 1094. Henry found the Order of Knighthood already in the enjoyment of a respectable tradition, for it is said that the Cid received the dignity in the Mosque at Coimbra after the capture of the city by Ferdinand the Great, and Henry himself took the Cross and went to Palestine in 1108. The Military Orders, which represented the systemization of chivalry, were born before Henry's son Alfonso Henriques, the first King of Portugal, ascended the throne; being organized and disciplined bodies, they were more useful than individual knights in warfare against the Moors, and were not as in other countries overshadowed by feudal barons, because the feudal system never took full root in Portugal. The great landowners had no obligation of military service, but, on the contrary, it was one of their privileges to be exempt from it. Portugal knew only Kings and subjects; the continuous struggle against the Infidel needed one directing head, which was found in the Monarch, and he carried it on by the aid of *milites villani* and the Military Orders.

In 1128 Alfonso Henriques assumed the government, and shortly after began to style himself King; his title and the independence of the country were recognized by Alfonso VII of Castile and Leon in 1143, and in the following year, to secure both, he offered Portugal to the Holy See and declared himself the Pope's vassal. Lucius II assured him of protection, but it was not until 1179 that Alexander III extended full recognition to the new monarchy. During his long reign of fifty-seven years Alfonso Henriques exhibited courage and political skill of a high order, and he found vassals worthy of him. Among these was his tutor, Egas Moniz, paladin of the point of honour, a product of chivalry and inculcated by its code, according to which the word of a knight was sacred and no less binding than an oath.

In 1127 Alfonso Henriques, then only Infant and in revolt against his mother, was besieged in Guimarães by Alfonso VII, and to save him, Egas Moniz promised that he would recognize his cousin's overlordship. On hearing of the engagement made on his behalf, the young prince refused to ratify it, whereupon his tutor did what he could to remove the stain on his own honour. Accompanied by his wife and children, he went and presented himself, clad only in a shirt and barefooted, with a rope round his neck, to the King of Castile, offering to redeem the broken oath by his death; moved by his honourable conduct, the latter released him.[1] This exemplary act, recorded in the Chronicles, eulogized by Camões in *The Lusiads*, and known to every Portuguese schoolboy, proved fruitful, and had it not been so, the struggle for independence against the neighbouring states, and for expansion against the Moors, could hardly have succeeded; collective aspirations only triumph after many individual sacrifices. A similar instance of fidelity is reported of certain subjects of Sancho II. When this monarch was deposed by Innocent IV in 1245, at the Council of Lyons, and the regency conferred on his brother, afterwards Alfonso III, the latter ordered the governors of castles to surrender them to him. Some refused to break the oath they had taken to Sancho, and two held out until his death. One of these, D. Martim de Freitas, hearing that his master had passed away in exile at Toledo, obtained leave to go there and see if the news were true. On his arrival, he had Sancho's coffin opened, placed the keys of Coimbra castle under the dead man's arm, and kneeling told his story. Only then did he hold himself absolved from his oath. Taking back the keys, he returned to Portugal and handed them to the King *de facto*, who was now King by right.[2]

The pages of the early Chronicles are filled by details of the struggle for the separation of Portugal from Leon, but the Crusade was the national vocation. At first warfare against the Moors consisted merely of forays, because Alfonso Henriques, occupied with defending himself against his Christian neighbours, could do little more than hold his southern frontier in the centre of modern Portugal, but in 1139 he took the offensive and fought the battle of Ourique. The legend of the vision of our Lord granted him on this occasion played so important a part in subsequent history that it must be told here. When the King retired to his tent to rest on the eve of the battle, he opened his Bible and came upon the passage in Judges relating the victory of Gideon over four Midianite Kings. Then he fell asleep, and

---

[1] Duarte Galvão, *Chronica d'el Rey D. Afonso Henriques*, chap. x.
[2] *Monarchia Lusitana*, vol. iv, liv. 14, chap. 30.

KNIGHTS OF THE TIME OF
KING ALFONSO HENRIQUES

From the *Comentario a Apocalypse de Lorvão*, Torredo Tombo, Lisbon

VISION OF KING ALFONSO
HENRIQUES

From the *Portuguese Drawings*, British Museum.

an old man appeared, assured him of success on the morrow, and told him he would presently see the Saviour of the world. He was awakened by his chamberlain, who announced the arrival of a messenger with important news, and when the latter entered, the King recognized the subject of his dream. The old man repeated the words he had previously uttered, and asked the King to go out at midnight, when he heard the bell of his hermitage ring. The King obeyed, and saw our Lord on the Cross, who said that he would found a kingdom for Himself in the person of Alfonso Henriques, and that his descendants might know from whom they derived it, the King was to take for arms the price paid for man's redemption.

The first vestige of the legend appears in a contemporary Chronicle, the *Vita Santi Theotonii*, which attributes the victory of Ourique over the five Moorish Kings to Divine aid,[1] but the actual vision is not mentioned earlier than the fifteenth century, and is first described at length by Duarte Galvão in 1505, though he did probably little more than modernize the language of an earlier work. The legend is enshrined in *The Lusiads* and came to be almost an article of faith. Some modern historians have pronounced it an entire fable, but while it is rash to despise tradition altogether, even when it has been written down late, we are not concerned to defend the authenticity of the story; we will merely quote a dialogue in one of Disraeli's novels: "But Don Quixote never existed." "He lives for us." The belief in the miraculous foundation and preservation of the kingdom was a factor in its liberation from Infidel rule, and in the winning of the overseas empire, and the Portuguese were persuaded as late as the seventeenth century that they enjoyed a special protection from on high. In 1655 de Jant, French minister in Lisbon, reported of them: "They confide so much in Providence, as regards the preservation of Portugal, that the Turks believe not more deeply in predestination, nor the Jews in the coming of the Messiah."[2]

The national flag, which has remained in essence unaltered through every change in regime, and still waves over the Republic, testifies to the Christian origin and feeling of the

---

[1] *Portugaliae Monumenta Historica, Scriptores*, p. 80.
[2] Tessier, *Le Chevalier de Jant* (Paris, 1877), p. 137.

country. Alfonso Henriques took as his arms five shields, arranged in the form of a cross, on each of which he put bezants in the self-same form. In modern times there has been much controversy as to the meaning of these arms. There is no doubt that the cross symbolized the Redemption, but while some authors see in the bezants the price for which our Lord was sold by Judas, others, like Dr. Antonio de Vasconcellos,[1] point out that the coins varied in number from twenty-five to sixty, and consider they represent the money spent by the King in good works, such as the foundation of churches and the redemption of captives. In any case, we shall be correct in saying with D. Thomas de Vilhena [2] that the consensus of opinion, both Portuguese and foreign, has seen in the banner another Labarum of Constantine.

The capture of Lisbon in 1147 was effected by the aid of a crusading fleet of 164 vessels, carrying 13,000 men from different countries, which put into the Tagus on its way to Palestine. Some of the victors rejoiced at the triumph of the Cross, others at the gold, silver, and beautiful women which fell into their hands. In the accounts of the four months siege from the pens of eye-witnesses, there is one incident worthy of record here ; a German knight named Henry, fell in the final assault and was buried in St. Vincent's Church, erected in the Christian lines ; on three separate nights he is said to have appeared to the guardian, to ask him to translate to a place near him a devoted servant of his, who had been laid in a distant and humble grave.[3] As D. Thomas de Vilhena remarks, this reflects the chivalrous idea of fraternity in arms ; both men died for the Faith, and having made the same sacrifice, deserved equal honour.

The task of conquering Portugal south of the Tagus was entrusted by Alfonso Henriques to the Military Orders ; they obtained from the King and his successors extensive grants of land, which they reduced to cultivation, and the castles they built for defence became the nuclei of towns.

---

[1] *O escudo nacional portugues* in *Lusitania*, vol. i, pp. 171, and 321.
[2] His *Historia da Ordem da Santa Cavallaria em Portugal* (Coimbra, 1920), vol. I, which embraces the period down to the conquest of the Algarve, has been of much use for the present study ; the subject has been difficult to treat, for the old authors tell us less than we might expect.
[3] *Chronica da fundação do Mosteiro de São Vicente*, in *Portugaliae Monumenta Historica, Scriptores*, p. 410.

The struggle continued under Sancho I, who, by the aid of two crusading fleets, took Alvor and Silves, the capital of the Algarve, but could not hold them, and Portuguese knights fought in the Christian defeat at Alarcos (1195) and in the victory of las Navas de Tolosa (1212). Alcacer do Sal was taken by Alfonso II in 1217, with the aid of another crusading fleet, Sancho II submitted various places in the Alemtejo; the Algarve was definitely won for the Cross under Alfonso III, and about 1249 the country attained her furthest European limits.

The Military Orders had been the chief agents in the national crusade; they included the Templars and Hospitallers and two Spanish Orders, the Knights of Calatrava and Saint James. Though their members were mainly Portuguese, difficulties arose from the fact that they were subject to superiors abroad, and successive Kings endeavoured to obtain their exemption from foreign jurisdiction. In the case of the Order of Saint James King Diniz in 1318 pointed out to Pope John XXII that it possessed castles near the frontiers, by which the Castilians might invade Portugal, unless these were held by his subjects, and he obtained the desired separation. It had already been granted in the case of the Templars in 1288, while the Portuguese Knights of Calatrava were, in fact, independent of their Spanish brethren from the beginning, and the Order acquired the name of Aviz from the place of its seat. On the extinction of the Templars, the same Pope, by agreement with King Diniz, founded in 1319 a new Order, that of Christ, which took over the property of the former. The mission of the Military Orders as a whole came to an end with the conquest of the Algarve; in many cases a life of ease dissolved the bonds of discipline and religious austerity, the vow of poverty became a dead letter, and later on the Knights obtained leave to marry. Men sought admission as a means of livelihood and to escape civil jurisdiction, and at the Cortes of 1472 the Third Estate asserted that even criminals entered the Orders for the latter purpose; similar complaints were made in the Cortes of 1481. As early as 1361 their fortresses were in ruins, and they so continued a century later. The Grand Masters ceased to be elected by their brethren, and were usually members of the royal family; John I obtained the headship of Aviz at the age of seven, and in 1551 the Masterships were united to the Crown.

The Orders would have been saved from this *débâcle* if it had been possible to use them as organized bodies in the overseas conquests; ideas, however, had changed. In 1456 Pope Calixtus III directed them to furnish members to reside in and defend Ceuta against the Infidel, and Pius II repeated this command in 1462, but the Infant D. Fernando, Grand Master of Christ and Saint James, opposed the execution of the Bulls.[1] Knights of rank considered it unfitting their dignity to pass their days in Africa, nor could such self-exile be expected from married men; they declared that they would dissuade aspirants from entering the Orders, if the obligation were imposed and it was accordingly revoked. King Manuel I, however, in 1503, ordered thirty *habits* with *commendas* to be reserved for those who lived in Africa, "that the Moors, enemies of our Holy Faith, might see in those parts the sign of our Order (Christ), and know that it was founded to make war on them," and a final attempt to restore the Orders to their original purpose was made by King Sebastian, who decreed that all *habits* and *commendas* should be filled by men who had served in the wars of Africa and India and in fleets against Infidels and Heretics. That some such measure was necessary is shown by a declaration in two documents of 1551 that Knights refused to render military service. This arose in part from the lack of scruple in the bestowal of *commendas*, which were given as royal favours to persons devoid of merit, and even to minors. King John III more than once had to obtain absolution from the penalties he had incurred for this reason.

After the decline of the Military Orders, the traditions of chivalry were carried on by individual knights, whether belonging to them or not. A Portuguese contingent contributed to the victory of the Salado (1340), and the combatants are said by a contemporary writer to have encouraged one another by crying: "This is the day when we must imitate our ancestors who conquered Spain; this is the day of our

---

[1] The Infant obliged them to serve at their own expense in the expedition of 1462 against Tangier, but this led to a protest on their part that they would never do so again and the Infant bowed to it. Zurara, *Chronica de D. Duarte de Menzes*, chap. 152.

CHIVALRY OF PORTUGAL 153

soul's salvation. Remember, Sirs, how Jesus Christ died to save us, and we must do the same for Him and seize the chance to preserve His Faith. Those of us to die to-day will be with Him in His Heavenly Kingdom, where there are mansions so noble that tongues cannot describe them." [1] These are echoes of the doctrine preached by Urban II two and a half centuries earlier, and here, as in other battles, a relatively small force, by virtue of faith and patriotism, overcame largely superior numbers.

In such an atmosphere it was natural that the wars of King Fernando against Castile at the end of the fourteenth century should produce deeds like that of the squire Nuno Gonçalves, *alcaide* of the castle of Faria; they would now be called patriotic, though essentially chivalrous, for the greater includes the less. This man went out with his men to meet the enemy and was captured. Fearing that his son, whom he had left in charge, would surrender the place to liberate him, he asked to be taken in front of the walls, pretending that he would order a capitulation; instead he charged the youth to yield to no one save the King. His loyalty cost him instant death, but his son held out, and when peace came, refused a reward for his successful resistance, and gave the rest of his life to religion in the priestly state.[2] To the same period belongs D. Nuno Alvares Pereira, greatest of Portuguese knights, the very mirror of chivalry, generous to his foes, a hater of cruelty, champion of women, protector of the weak, in fine, a man of God and recently beatified. He began his career as a soldier in 1371 at the age of thirteen, was the right hand man of John I in the struggle for independence, led the van as Constable at the battle of Aljubarrota, and won those of Atoleiros and Valverde (1384-5). When he was sixteen, his father desired to marry him to a lady of rank, but found the youth strangely unwilling, for, as his Chronicler says : " He had great relish for and was often wont to hear and read story books, especially that of Galahad, and because he found that by virtue of virginity this man had accomplished great deeds which others could not achieve, he wished to imitate him and remain a

---

[1] *Livro de Linhagem* No. 8, in *Portugaliae Monumenta Historica, Scriptores,* p. 186.
[2] Fernam Lopes, *Chronica de D. Fernando,* chap. 79.

virgin, if it pleased God." [1] He had, however, to yield, and became the founder of the House of Braganza, but when his wife died at an early age, no one could persuade him to a second marriage. His anonymous biographer records some of the actions which won the admiration of contemporaries; among them, how he saved a blind man at the siege of Torres Vedras by taking him up behind him on his mule; how he restored a cauldron, which his men had carried off from a church, when he heard of the theft many years later; how he punished a knight who had pulled out a villager's beard, and taken wine without payment, and how he gave all the bread he had to eat to some hungry English knights. In the administration of justice he paid no regard to rank, relatives, servants or friends, which earned him the dislike of the grandees. Chaste in desire and deed, he heard two masses daily and three on Saturdays and Sundays, rose at midnight to recite the Canonical Hours, fasted three days a week, and gave a tenth of his income to the poor. Before entering the Carmelite Monastery in Lisbon which he had built, he distributed all his property, and left himself with nothing but the clothes he wore. He organized the first standing army in Portugal, and revolutionized the art of war in the Peninsula by recognizing the superiority of foot soldiers to horsemen; dismounting the latter, and forming them in square, he won his first battle at Atoleiros over the chivalry of Castile. After this he went barefoot on pilgrimage to a neighbouring shrine, and finding the church choked with dirt from the animals the Castilians had stabled there, he did not content himself with ordering it to be cleansed, but was the first to carry out the dung. This act of humility is the more remarkable as practised by a man of high lineage.

The influence of the Arthurian legends, evident in the *Livros da Linhagem*, and in the life of Nuno Alvares, is also seen in an incident at the siege of Coria. John I, dissatisfied with the conduct of some of his followers, said half in jest: "We had great need to-day of the good knights of the Round Table, for surely, if they had been here, we should have taken

---

[1] *Cronica do Condestabre de Portugal*, cap. iv. Professor W. J. Entwistle says of this biography that it may be considered as in a sense the finest effort of Arthurian prose. *The Arthurian Legend in the Literatures of the Spanish Peninsula*, p. 239.

the place." On hearing these words Mem Rodrigues de Vasconcellos could not restrain himself and naming some of his friends who were as brave as Galahad, Tristam, and Lancelot, he declared that what they needed was King Arthur, who knew good servants and bestowed many favours on them, so that they might seek to serve him well.[1]

One of the motives which impelled the Portuguese to the oversea conquests, beginning with that of Ceuta in 1415, was the spread of Christianity. Desiring to confer the Order of Knighthood on his sons, John I planned a festival year of jousts and tourneys, to which knights from every country were to be invited, but the young men urged that it would not be to their honour to receive the dignity in such a way, and, aided by Queen Philippa, they prevailed on him to attack one of the Mohammedan emporia of North-West Africa. Henry, the greatest of the Infants, obtained from his father two privileges, that he should be one of the first to disembark at Ceuta and when the scaling ladders were raised against the walls, he should be the first to mount. The national enthusiasm for the Crusade was such that a noble knight aged ninety came with his men to take part in it. The Queen, who died of plague on the eve of the expedition, had swords prepared for the ceremony of knighting her sons, and when they took leave of her, gave to each of them a piece of the True Cross, commending the people to Duarte, the service of ladies and maidens to Pedro, and the care of knights and squires to Henry.[2] On the way to Africa the fleet put in at Lagos, where Frei João Xira preached, and in the course of his sermon declared that he who thought himself a Catholic and true Christian and did not defend the Holy Faith with all his strength, was not a true knight, but worse than an Infidel.[3] The prowess of Henry at the assault led the Chronicler Zurara to call him the " flower of chivalry ". The organizer of modern discovery by sea, to which he devoted his life, his desire to spread Christianity and combat Islam were no less strong than his craving for a knowledge of the unknown world, and he died a virgin. He devoted the revenues of the Order of Christ, of which he was Governor,

---

[1] Fernam Lopes, *Chronica de D. João I*, pt. ii, chap. 80.
[2] Zurara, *Cronica da tomada de Ceuta*, chap. 41.
[3] Ibid., chap. 52.

to the work of discovery,[1] and the caravels which sailed down the African coast bore on their sails the red cross, the symbol that Portuguese knights showed on their armour.

The sentiments of the sons of John I are well illustrated by the letter D. Pedro sent his brother, D. Duarte, when the latter ascended the throne in 1433, and by the reception it met with. He counselled him to thank God, abase himself for fear of his judgments, and labour to be an obedient and faithful servant of the Lord, from whose hands he had received the dignity. He set down the virtues a King ought to possess, the first being that he should be Catholic and very firm in the Faith. Duarte esteemed these counsels so much that he had them entered in a book he always carried with him.[2] Among the opponents of the disastrous expedition to Tangier in 1437 was the Infant D. John, who observed that good judgment and chivalry were different things, because judgment forbids a man to leave the certain for the uncertain and peace for war, while the rule of chivalry is one of adventure.[3] In the retreat to the ships, two of the leaders, though hard pressed by the Moors, contended with one another, each wishing to be last, an example of the perfection of honour in these knights to which Ruy de Pina calls the attention of his readers.[4] Some of the survivors went to visit King Duarte in sad coloured garments, and pretended to be more injured than they were, in order to obtain favours, but D. Alvaro caz de Almada, Knight of the Garter, who had fought at Agincourt, did quite otherwise, though he had lost much and reaped no small glory. Dressing himself in his gayest attire and newly shaved, with a joyful face he went before the sovereign and told him he should not grieve at the captivity of his brother, the Infant D. Fernando, who was one man only and mortal, but rather rejoice at the fame he had earned

---

[1] Without these resources the work could not have been carried on ; hence the Order deserves part of the credit for the success of this new crusade.

[2] Rui de Pina, *Chronica d'el Rei D. Duarte*, cap. 4. When Duarte's page was buckling on his master's armour at Ceuta, he exhorted the Infant to do some great deed for love of his lady. The reply was that he would, if reminded, when the opportunity came. Zurara remarks that this showed Duarte was not much of a ladies' man, for had he been so in truth, he would have needed no other reminder than the mortal torment which true lovers ever carry with them, *Cronica da tomada de Ceuta*, chap. 69.

[3] Pina, *Chronica d'el Rei D. Duarte*, chap. 17.

[4] Ibid., chap. 34.

by remaining as a hostage ; and he advised the King to have the bells rung for joy of those who had escaped, instead of their being tolled in sadness for the souls of the fallen.[1] In his virtues D. Fernando, the Holy Infant, as he is called, resembled Nuno Alvares Pereira ; he had the same cult of virginity, the same horror of impurity, which he considered the worst of sins, and the same love of the poor. He refused a Cardinal's hat, because he felt that the dignity would be too great a burden on his conscience, and during the six years' captivity which preceded his death in Morocco, he suffered many of the torments inflicted on our Lord in the Passion, and bore them with superhuman patience. Nothing was lacking to make this Grand Master of Aviz a perfect type of knighthood, for, like his brothers, he was expert in the games and sports of the day, as well as a lover of books, though not like Duarte and Pedro an author. If the sons of John I were complete men, much of the credit is due to their mother, Philippa, daughter of John of Gaunt, who gave them a wider education and severer discipline than was the custom in the Peninsula.

D. Pedro had a no less tragic end than D. Fernando ; driven by calumny and intrigue into rebellion against his nephew, King Alfonso V, he and his friend D. Alvaro Vaz de Almada, seeing no hope of life with honour, received Holy Communion and made a pact to die together. At the battle of Alfarrobeira (1449) D. Pedro fell, pierced by an arrow, while the Count of Avranches, after fighting till he could stand no longer, dropped, crying : "Body I feel you can do no more, and you my soul are lingering too long," and covered with wounds he sent his soul to accompany that of the Infant.[2] The Chronicler tells us that a friend cut off his head, and taking it to the King asked for a reward, and the honour of knighthood. History does not relate the reply, but we know that the Count's mutilated body lay long on the field, while that of D. Pedro was allowed to remain for three days in a cottage, without candles, covering, or public prayer. The ideals of chivalry suffered a total eclipse on that day,

[1] Ibid., cap. 36.
[2] Another victim was Ruy Mendes Cerveira, who in early years went to England to gain renown and took part in the battle of Agincourt, where he "acted like a noble knight". Zurara, *Chronica de D. Pedro de Menezes*, cap. 35.

but the chief blame must be laid on Pedro's enemies. Alfonso in later years won and deserved the title of the "Knightly King" by his expeditions against the Moors in Africa, which led to the capture of Alcacer Ceguer, Arzila, and Tangier, and he attracted to his Court distinguished foreigners bent on deeds of arms, like Jacques de Lalain, Companion of the Order of the Golden Fleece.[1] In 1447 he wished to lay down the sceptre and end his days at Jerusalem, and for some months before his death in 1481 he lived like a poor religious at the monastery of Varatojo. His only daughter, Joanna, was beatified. Alfonso joined modesty to courage; he would not allow Zurara to record his achievements, but ordered him to write those of D. Pedro and D. Duarte de Menezes, captains of Ceuta and Alcacer, and in these books we have two chroniclers of chivalry which by their truth are worth more than all the romances then in favour. These frontier fortresses constituted a school of arms, because warfare with the Moors never ceased for long. On the occasion of the siege of Alcacer in 1459, men of all ages hastened from Portugal to defend it; the young to gain honour fled there from home, while the old to keep what they had won could not stay away. At the capture of Arzila in 1471, Prince John, aged 16, accompanied his father and fought so hard that his sword was twisted by the blows he gave; the King knighted him beside the body of the youthful Count of Marialva, who had fallen in the assault, and after the ceremony said to him: "Son, may God make you as good a knight as this one who lies here."[2]

The race of medieval Kings and Knights ended with Alfonso V and the Count of Avranches; John II and his courtiers belonged to the new age of the Renaissance, but if chivalry as an institution was dead by the last quarter of the fifteenth century, much of its spirit survived, while its trappings were augmented.

At a much earlier date it had suffered a complete transformation outside the Peninsula; gallantry displaced religion

---

[1] His visit to the King at Evora and stay of a fortnight is described by the author of the *Chronique du bon Chevalier Messire Jacques de Lalain*, chaps. 38–42.

[2] In his *Chronica do Principe D. João*, cap. 27, Goes professes to give the discourse of the King on this occasion. Its importance lies in the fact that it shows the ideas prevailing in the middle of the sixteenth century as to the aims of chivalry and the obligations of knights.

KING ALFONSO V IN THE ATTACK ON ARZILA

From a tapestry at Pastraña.

CHIVALRY OF PORTUGAL

as its inspiration. Portugal did not escape the influence of this movement, but probably owing to her centuries of struggle with the Infidel, she preserved much of the crusading ideal, long after it had disappeared in the northern countries of Europe, and the licentiousness which went with the cult of women in France and elsewhere, though it existed during the first or Burgundian dynasty, was greatly diminished by the efforts of the English Queen Philippa. The early Kings had their mistresses, of whom the most famous was D. Ignez de Castro, and a crop of bastards, while those of the House of Aviz were far more faithful to the marriage vow. Gallantry had its origin in Provence, and was introduced into Portugal at the end of the twelfth century; the art of verse-making gradually became part of a knight's equipment, and the Courts of Alfonso III and Dinis (1248-1325) were centres of culture, whose literary output is found in three *Cancioneiros*, or song-books, containing erotic and satirical poetry. This movement apparently came to an end with the death of Dinis in 1325; Alfonso IV and Pedro I had no disposition to encourage such levity, but it is natural that individuals continued to celebrate their ladies in song, though none of their compositions have come down to us. A Lover's Wing fought at the battle of Aljubarrota in 1385, and some years later, a band of knights known as the Twelve of England repaired to London and successfully entered the lists in defence of the honour of as many English women.

The episode is related in *The Lusiads*, one of the great epics of chivalry, which was published as late as 1572, and it serves to while away an hour or two on the voyage of da Gama across the Indian Ocean. In these twenty-six stanzas [1] Camões contrives to make the past live again, and sound echo sense.

Here are two of them, as translated by Aubertin :—

> And now the very earth beneath appears
> To tremble with the chargers rattling sound;
> The anxious heart by turns leaps, hopes, and fears
> Within the breast of all beholders round;
> One from his charger flies, which onward bears:
> One, steed and all, is groaning on the ground,
> The shining arms of one are crimson made:
> On his steed's flanks another's plume is laid.

[1] Canto vi, stanzas 43-69.

>One falls to sleep for ever in the fight
>And makes of life a period short indeed ;
>Here runs some steed away without his knight
>And there is seen some knight without his steed :
>The English pride falls from its throne of might,
>For more than one beyond the bounds recede ;
>They who with sword are battle come to make
>Find more than armour, shield, and sword to break.

Gallantry had little scope at Court during the lifetime of Queen Philippa, nor in the short reign of her serious minded son Duarte (1433-38), but it revived in that of her grandson, Alfonso V (1438-81), and continued under his successor, John II (1481-95). In so far as it could be expressed in verse, we have a complete picture in the *Cancioneiro Geral* of Garcia de Resende.

The *serões do paço*, or palace evenings, had for their business *ouvir e glosar motes* ; a *mote*, or saying in one or more verses, usually of a satiric nature, was given to the poets, by a lady, to amplify or gloss. The *Cancioneiro* opens with a *tensão*, entitled *Cuidar e Suspirar*. Two poet-admirers of D. Leonor da Silva, meet, the one pensive, as he goes, the other uttering deep sighs. Each inquires the subject of the other's trouble, and the debate begins ; a crowd of versifiers joins in, taking one side and another, and their productions run to a hundred octavo pages of print, D. Leonor is asked to judge the contest, and orders each side to appoint pleaders, as in a lawsuit ; finally she decides in favour of sighing, but the god of love revokes the sentence after hearing Macias, Tarquin, and others, who give their experiences from the Limbo of love where they burn.

Most of the poems in the *Cancioneiro de Resende* deal with trivial subjects. We have verses on a lock of hair, a blue silk hat, an aged mule, a French cape, and a stout lady, but a few show inspiration and feeling and are a welcome relief to the effusions of *soi disant* lovesick courtiers ; the gem of the book is one on the death of D. Ignez de Castro by the collector. It would be unfair to judge Portuguese knights and ladies by the contents of this *Cancioneiro*, which for the most part are not poetry in the true sense, but the result of a mere game of wits. Many of the poets had won fame in the African wars, while as to the ladies, it would seem that they were less frivolous than their sisters in some countries, since Resende himself in his *Miscelanea*, written about 1531, says that

CHIVALRY OF PORTUGAL

they formerly considered it indecent to paint their faces, wear farthingales, or drink wine.

In the reign of King Manoel I and the early part of that of John III, representations of the plays of Gil Vicente entertained the Court, and every aspect of Portuguese life is faithfully and vividly portrayed in them. Two deal with heroes of chivalry, *Amadis de Gaula* and *D. Duardos*, whose actions were well-known by the prose romances, found admirers and inspired imitators. In a more serious piece, the *Boat of Hell*, one of a trilogy which recalls the medieval Dance of Death, we find an echo of the earlier religious chivalry; four *fidalgos*, Knights of the Order of Christ, who had died fighting the Infidel in Africa, are challenged by the Devil, who seeks to take them with him, but one boldly replies: "Look with whom you are speaking," and another: "We died in the parts beyond (the sea), and seek to know nothing else"; while an Angel welcomes them, for "those who fall in such a conflict, are saints and deserve eternal peace."

The prose romances are mostly of foreign origin, and cannot therefore instruct us about the details of chivalry in Portugal, but they were a source of inspiration and we have proofs of their influence, e.g. the names of their personages were bestowed on children at baptism, notwithstanding the rule that those of saints should alone be used.

Latter day chivalry found expression, not only in love, but also in the tournament and joust. As in the case of the Twelve of England, Portuguese knights repaired abroad to earn laurels in such encounters. The single combats, known as jousts, often became bloody duels, and they took place by preference in France, as being the country "where all noble and chivalrous men were the most honoured"; permanent lists, always open to combatants, existed in Paris and at Saint Inglevert, between Boulogne and Calais. The Knights of Spain and Portugal were highly renowned for their chivalry, says the *Journal of Paris under Charles VI*,[1] while in the *Chronique de Jean le Fèvre, seigneur de Saint-Rémy*[2] we have an account of various combats in 1414 and 1415 between Portuguese and Frenchmen. Alvaro Coutinho

---

[1] *Oeuvres complètes du Roi Réné*, Angers, 1844, vol. ii, p. xcv.
[2] Chap. 61, and cf. Monstrelet, *Chroniques*, bk. i, cap. 142.

fought Cluguet de Brabant with lance, axe, sword, and dagger at Bar le Duc, in the presence of the Duke of Bars and a squire Rumaindres (?) met Guillaume de Bars at Paris with the same weapons, each being allowed twelve blows. On another occasion the same two Portuguese, and a third, Pedro Gonçalves de Malafaya, were challenged by an equal number of Frenchmen to fight with axes, swords, and daggers, until one side or the other yielded, or were brought to the ground. The contest took place outside Paris, between St. Denis and Montmartre, the Duke of Guise acting as judge, and the Frenchmen won.

Jousts and tourneys were as much the fashion in Portugal as abroad, and to them she added *canas* and bull-fights; the former was a military game, played by bands of mounted men, who attacked each other with canes. The jousts held to celebrate the marriages of John I to Philippa of Lancaster, and of his granddaughter, Leonor, to the Emperor, are described by Fernam Lopes and Ruy de Pina in their chronicles, and deserve to be recorded, while those which took place at Evora on the occasion of the marriage of Prince Alfonso, son of John II, were magnificent; they lasted for many days, and were preceded by banquets and mimes, in which ships with their crews, castles, giants, animals, and birds came in. Resende describes at length these strange inventions, the rich dresses and jewels worn by the actors, the music, dances, and dishes, including two oxen roasted whole and yoked to a cart, which were made to walk as though alive, and afterwards given to the people; he says that if he were to tell all, it would seem a fable of Amadis or Esplandian. The King came as the *Knight of the Swan*, with eighty supporters, and won the two prizes offered for the most gallant knight and best jouster, a diamond ring and a gold collar.

From early times the exercise of the chase was considered the best means of developing physical robustness and agility in youths and accustoming them to the toils of war; John I compiled a classic treatise on hunting the wild boar, called *Livro da Montaria*, and his son produced a treatise on horsemanship in the *Livro da ensinança de bem cavalgar toda sella*.

We have said that the desire to spread the Faith inspired the navigations and the foundation of a colonial empire, which followed the voyage of Vasco da Gama,[1] though the Portuguese sovereigns were also incited to the great adventure by such mundane motives as thirst for dominion and trading profits. The history of the conquests in the East, while it contains episodes which disgrace the Christian name, has some worthy of the great days of chivalry, among them the exploits of Duarte Pacheco, the Lusitanian Achilles, the defence of Diu against the Turks, and the expedition of D. Christovam da Gama to Abyssinia, which, in the words of Gibbon, was saved by 450 Portuguese for Christianity. The Red Sea witnessed many combats between Portuguese and Mohammedans, and in 1541 D. Estevam da Gama disembarked at Tor and visited the monastery of St. Catherine of Mt. Sinai. He and his men were the first Europeans who with arms and a fleet had reached those parts, and in memory of that event (far more worthy of being exalted, remarks Couto, than the search of Jason for the Golden Fleece), the governor of India made knights of as many as desired the honour in the chapel. He celebrated the act with many joyful instruments and great salvoes of artillery, and above all with many thanks and praises, which all gave to God and the blessed St. Catherine, in whose house they were, for so great a favour.[2]

Portuguese rule in Asia was built up by a genius, Alfonso de Albuquerque, and maintained by some great captains, like D. Luis de Ataide, but in the list of Viceroys and Governors no one corresponds to the knightly ideal so well as D. John de Castro. Distinguished as a Christian, a scientist, and a soldier, he lives in the memory of thousands who know nothing of his achievements by two actions which struck the popular imagination. To obtain funds for the relief of Diu he wished to pawn the bones of his son, and actually raised money on some hairs of his beard from the municipality of Goa. Again, on his death-bed, in 1548, where he received the ministrations of so sure a pilot for the last journey as St. Francis Xavier, he was obliged to ask for money for food. He had spent his income on the royal service, and had not the wherewithal to buy a chicken to make him soup; what a contrast to the conduct of some of his predecessors and successors, who

[1] The discoverer of the sea road to India kept his vigil in the chapel of Our Lady of Bethlehem on the shore of the Tagus before commencing the voyage.
[2] *Asia*, dec. v, liv. 7, chap. 8.

used their position in India to fill their pockets by illicit means!

Chivalry in Portugal had a late flowering towards the end of the sixteenth century, in the person of King Sebastian. John III (1521-57) had devoted his energies to holding and developing his dominions rather than to extending them; he preferred missionary enterprises and the colonization of Brazil to war. He had even abandoned some of the African fortresses on the ground that they were not worth the expense and efforts their maintenance cost, but his peaceful policy did not win general approval, and the old crusading spirit reasserted itself at his death.

India, it was said, had proved a sieve of men and money; why, then, go so far, when the secular enemy was at the gate, and Morocco produced corn enough to make good the national shortage? Sebastian was educated in this current and exaggerated it; from childhood he nourished the ambition to be Christ's captain, and he felt that he had been called to be the champion of the Cross in Africa. Men of letters vied with one another in confirming his fixed idea, and promising him a new crown in those parts; among them was Camões, who, though old and broken in health, offered his sword to the youthful enthusiast. The King strove to be worthy of the vocation: he trained his body by every form of hard exercise, courted dangers by land and sea, and, like Galahad, preserved chastity as a means to the end. He has been compared to the Holy Constable, but there was a difference between them; the latter had the virtues of humility and prudence, while Sebastian was vain-glorious, reckless, and headstrong. The Pope, his relations, pious prelates, and priests, experienced soldiers and the representatives of the city of Lisbon, strove to persuade him that an expedition to Africa was inopportune; Morocco, even if conquered, could not be held and he had no right to risk his life until he had married and could leave a son to succeed him, if he died in the war. To these counsels he lent a deaf ear, holding his advisers as cowards, and one is tempted to apply to him the sentence: "Quem Deus vult perdere, prius dementat." But we, as Christians, may not hold God responsible for our errors, and the Portuguese felt that the disaster of Alcacer was permitted to happen on account of the sins of the nation;

KING SEBASTIAN

From a miniature belonging to His Majesty King Manoel II of Portugal.

[*face p.* 164

those committed in the East are dilated upon by St. Francis Xavier in his letters, and by contemporary writers, who do not spare their own countrymen. In the King's funeral oration Frei Miguel dos Santos truly said that the responsibility had to be shared by all, and it was not enough expiation that Portugal should lose her richest colonies; she could only make satisfaction by the loss of her independence.

In the battle Sebastian showed the bravery of a knight errant, dying like a hero of romance, but a total incapacity for command, and in two hours, on 4th August, 1578, his little army, surrounded by an immense host of Moors, was annihilated; not more than fifty men escaped death or captivity. The Portuguese gave proof of their unparalleled loyalty in following such a leader, for many of them felt no doubt of the result. Such was the end of what may be called the last Crusade.[1]

Thirty years previously, the historian João de Barros had said that God gave his countrymen the special gift, above all nations, of being defenders of the Faith and loyal in the service of their King.

[1] The accounts of its contemporary chroniclers are reprinted by Snr. Antonio Sergio in *O Desejado*, Lisbon, 1924.

SOME AUTHORITIES

Chivalry

Do Regimento da Guerra and *Dos Cavalleiros* (in the *Ordenações Afonsinas*, vol. i, pp. 285 and 360, Coimbra, 1786).
Historia da Ordem da Santa Cavallaria em Portugal. D. Thomas de Vilhena. Coimbra, 1920.

Military Orders

Definições e Estatutos dos Cavalleiros e Freires da Ordem de Nosso Senhor Jesus Christo com a historia da origem e principio d'ella. Lisbon, 1628.
Supplemento historico ou Memorias e noticias da celebre Ordem dos Templarios para a historia da Ordem de N.S. Jesu Christo. Dr. Alexandre Ferreira. 2 vols. Lisbon, 1735.
Historia da Militar Ordem de Nosso Senhor Jesus Christo. Frei Bernardo da Costa. Lisbon, 1771.
A Ordem de Christo. J. Vieira Guimarães. Lisbon, 1901.
Marrocos e tres Mestres da Ordem de Christo. J. Vieira Guimarães. Coimbra, 1916.
Regra da Cavallaria e Ordem Militar de S. Bento de Avis. Lisbon, 1631.
Nova historia da Militar Ordem de Malta. José Anastacio de Figueiredo. 3 vols. Lisbon, 1800.
Monarchia Lusitana, vols. iii–vii. See the indices under letter O.
Historia da Igreja em Portugal. Fortunato de Almeida. Coimbra, 1910 et seq. Vol. i, p. 313 et seq., vol. ii, p. 168 et seq., vol. iii, p. 551 et seq.
Historia da Administração publica em Portugal nos seculos XII a XV. Henrique da Gama Barros. Vol. i, p. 399 et seq. Lisbon, 1885.

CHAPTER VII

CHIVALRY IN MEDIEVAL ENGLISH POETRY

By Sir ISRAEL GOLLANCZ, LITT.D., F.B.A.,
Professor of English Language and Literature in the University of London.

I

OUR veracious historian, Professor Hearnshaw, acclaiming Clio as a Muse of Truth, has unsparingly probed beneath the gorgeous panoply of chivalry, and shown how under cover of high idealism men too often acted ignobly, and were false to their plighted vows. Evil was assuredly too often associated with an institution as exalted in its aims as in its origin, and the comment of the historian on the notorious instances of cruelty and want of honour which characterized the great religious military Orders is none too severe when this chivalry in action is tested by the standard of the ideal knight—

> " Who reverenced his conscience as his King ;
> Whose glory was redressing human wrong ;
> Who spake no slander, no, nor listen'd to it ;
> Who loved one only and who clave to her."

My theme is a brief survey of the ideals and portrayal of chivalry as found in medieval English poetry. The word itself, and much appertaining to the institution, belonged to Norman English. The old English " knight " eventually became identified with " chevalier ", and " knighthood " became the distinguishing mark of " chivalry ". In the older Teutonic heroic life there was a high ideal of conduct, and possibly some form of institutional ritual, from which the Order of Chivalry was perhaps ultimately evolved. Into these questions of origin and history it is not my task to enter. The Anglo-Saxon poem of " The Battle of Maldon ", at the end of the tenth century, breathes the spirit of exalted chivalrous idealism, with its picture of the great Chieftain accompanied by vassal Knights, unwilling to leave the field when their lord lay prostrate. The true Knight, as opposed to the craven coward false to his troth, is placed before us in epic dignity of word and deed. This late Anglo-Saxon poem, mirroring knightly heroism on the battlefield, harks back in sentiment to the greatest of Old English heroic poems, *Beowulf*, with its vivid protraiture of old English courtly life, interpenetrated by refined ideals as virile as any in later chivalry. The young warrior makes good his knighthood by fighting with monsters of the prime; and when, an aged monarch, he again goes forth to fight with a devastating monster, there stands undaunted beside him a young warrior, who will, where others fail, be steadfast to his vows of fealty. " Death were better for any warrior than a disgraced life "—such is the burden of this ancient English epic.

II

The literature of England is mainly French and Latin for some hundred and fifty years after the Norman Conquest, when at last the Muse of English poetry again awakens, endowed with new vigour and quickened by new sources of inspiration. Whatever germs of chivalry may be detected in Teutonic institutions, it is certain that by the date of the re-assertion of English speech as the medium of national literature, chivalry, with its three concomitants of war, religion, and gallantry, was the recognized ideal of all classes, both of Church and State.

Christianity had shaped and moulded the militarism from which chivalry had sprung, and in its religious aspects the institution owed much to its consecration by the Church. It soon linked itself to the allegory, and became an integral part of the literary devices of homilists and preachers. A most striking example is to be found in that fascinating thirteenth century book, *The Nun's Rule*—a masterpiece of various harmonics of prose, touched in part with the beauty of poetic thought, cadence, and diction. The love of Christ for the human soul is described in a tale, and as " a lesson under the cover of a similitude." "A lady was once besieged by her foes within an earthen castle, her land all destroyed, and she herself left poor. Yet the love of a powerful king was fixed upon her. He took upon him to fight for her and deliver her from those who sought her death ; and though he knew that he would receive a mortal wound, he would gladly receive it to win her heart. He showed by his knightly prowess that he was worthy of love, as knights were sometimes wont to do. He engaged in a tournament, and had, for his lady's love, his shield everywhere pierced in battle, like a valorous knight. This shield which covered his godhead was his dear body. . . . There are three things in a shield—the wood, the leather, and the painting. So was there in this shield . . . . After the death of a valiant knight, men hang up his shield high in the church, to his memory. So is this shield, that is the crucifix, set up . . . to remind us of Jesus Christ's knighthood." [1]

"The Bleeding Knight" inspired English religious song for long centuries, and is well exemplified in the old popular carol :—

> "Lully, lulley, lully, lulley.
> The falcon hath borne my make [2] away."
> He bare him up, he bare him down,
> He bare him into an orchard brown.
>
> In that orchard there was an hall,
> That was hanged with purple pall.
> And in that hall there was a bed,
> It was hanged with gold so red.
> And in that bed there lieth a Knight,
> His woundës bleeding, day and night.
> By that bedside kneeleth a may [3]
> And she weepeth both night and day.
> And by that bedside there standeth a stone,—
> *Corpus Christi* written thereon." [4]

In many ways were the formulæ and ideas of chivalry transferred to religious literature ; and allegory in close association with mysticism drew from chivalry some of its fairest embellishments.

[1] Cf. *The Nun's Rule*, Medieval Library (Chatto and Windus), pp. 204-8.
[2] Mate.   [3] Maid.
[4] Cf. *Ancient English Christmas Carols*, ed. Edith Rickert (Chatto and Windus), p. 103.

III

It was, however, "the matter of Britain," first potently revealed to the world by Geoffrey of Monmouth in his famed *Historia Regum Britanniæ*, completed by the year 1148, which provided for the age of Chivalry its most glorious literary materials. The Celtic inspiration derived from Arthurian legends was the great new force from which renewed strength came to the national literature at its re-awakening. Through Geoffrey's Latin history, directly and indirectly, chivalry transformed to its own ideals, through romance, these Arthurian traditions :—

> "British record long concealed
> In old Armorica, whose secret springs
> No Gothic conqueror ever drank." [1]

Geoffrey was himself working under the influences of the age when shaping his materials into literary form. Arthur's court, with all its splendours, gives him ample scope, though he confesses he cannot do justice to the pomp and ceremony that attended the monarch's coronation. All is orderly, according to highest precedent—"after the ancient custom of Troy"—but his description of the Knights who adorned that court portrays the consciousness of the ideals of chivalry. "For at that time," he writes, "Britain had arrived at such a pitch of grandeur that in abundance of riches, luxury of ornaments, and politeness of inhabitants, it far surpassed all other kingdoms. The Knights in it that were famous for feats of chivalry, wore their clothes and arms all of the same colour and fashion; and the women also, no less celebrated for their wit, wore all the same kind of apparel; and esteemed none worthy of their love, but such as had given a proof of their valour in three several battles. Thus was the valour of the men an encouragement for the women's chastity, and the love of the women a spur to the soldiers' bravery." [2] Prowess and gallantry and religion are all stressed in Geoffrey's History, and thereto also the glamour of Avallon, where was made his wondrous sword Caliburn, and where, when mortally wounded, Arthur departed to be cured. More noteworthy perhaps is the effort made by the historian to depict the great

---

[1] Wordsworth : *Artegal and Elidure*.
[2] Geoffrey of Monmouth's *British History*, translated by J. A. Giles, 1842.

King as the great Christian King *par excellence,* bearing on his shield " the picture of the blessed Mary, mother of God ... in order to put him frequently in mind of her." The Round Table and the Knights of the great Fellowship are not yet in Geoffrey's book. The Norman clerk, Wace, his contemporary, knew of " Breton " stories of the Round Table, and in his amplified rendering (made in 1155) of the *Historia* into French verse, *Geste des Bretons,* cursorily mentions that " the Bretons tell many a fable of the Table Round "; further, he gives a slight description of the Table, and tells that the fame of the Knights was known through all the world. To Layamon, priest of Arley Regis, Worcestershire, who flourished at the very beginning of the thirteenth century, belongs the meed of praise as the first who, in English speech, drawing from the French *Geste des Bretons,* embellished the story of Arthur, as derived from Geoffrey's world-famed Latin history. Celtic legends known to him concerning Arthur were evidently added by Layamon, perhaps the earliest of Englishmen in the south-west of England attracted by Anglo-Norman culture, and yet, at the same time, anxious to give, in his native English, " the matter of Britain " for the delight of his fellow-countrymen. Teutonic elements are in his *Brut* blended with the Celtic material, and his work, in movement and treatment, often recalls something of the dignity and stateliness of Old English epic poetry. The alliterative measure lives again, and with it, though rhyme obtrudes, we have much else that indicates the survival, through Layamon, of the spirit of pre-Norman England, while the British Arthur becomes " the best remembered among Englishmen before all other Christian Kings ". At his birth the elves " gave him power to be the best of Knights "; warrior Knights are at his side; the Round Table—" at which sixteen hundred men and more might sit "—though dealt with more fully than by Wace—has not yet found its destined elaboration. The poet knows more thereof than he cares to tell; and at his last battle, fought against Modred, leaving his kingdom to a trusty Knight, the wounded Arthur, " Christian King of England," the flower of chivalry—as Layamon, following Wace, portrays him—fares to the Island of Avallon. " To Avallon "— let us hear the music of the lines—

> " 'To the fairest of all maidens,
> To Argante the Queen, most beauteous elf.
> She will make my wounds all sound,
> And with a healing draught make me full well.
> Hereafter I will come to my realm again,
> And dwell among the Britons in great bliss.'
> Even with the words there came from the sea
> A little boat, floating with the waves;
> And two women therein, wondrously formed.
> And they took Arthur anon and brought him thereto,
> And laid him softly down, and forth departed."

The haunting beauty of Avallon, so intimately linked with the Arthurian romances of chivalry, is here for the first time pictured in English verse. But the early Arthurian romances take us far from the history of Arthur as found in Geoffrey, Wace, and Layamon. The Arthurian cycle, dealing with Gawain, Tristram, Lancelot, Perceval, and the Holy Grail—the ideal tales of chivalry—belong pre-eminently to French literature, even in cases where their place of composition may have been England, and their authors Anglo-Normans. English poets to the fourteenth century served a laborious apprenticeship in rendering some of the great French originals into English verse.[1] Other sources than those used by Geoffrey were known to these French "makers" of Arthurian romances. No romancer in England before the second half of the fourteenth century can claim to take his place by the side of the greatest of French medieval poets, Chrétien de Troyes, whose Arthurian romances on *Lancelot*, *Yvain*, and *Perceval* belong to the second half of the twelfth century.

IV

The poetry of chivalry attains in England its finest expression in " the spacious days " of Edward III. The glories of Creçy and Poictiers attest the national prowess of England, and on all sides we have manifestations of new-born national consciousness. In literature two distinct centres of poetical activity give evidence that while the diverse elements,

[1] Cf. Ten Brink: *English Literature*, vol. i, bk. iii, chap. 2; *Cambridge History of English Literature*, vol. i, chaps. xiii, xiv, xv; Gaston Paris: *Medieval French Literature*, chap. iv.

Teutonic and Romance, have become harmonized, yet, all the same, according to environment, the spirit of the one or the other may be detected as predominant. In the West of England the old English spirit re-asserts itself, whatever the materials used by the poets for their themes. In the East-Midland, with London as the seat of the Court and the ruling classes, the new forces, opposed to old-world provincial traditions, find voice through Chaucer, inspired by master-poets of France and Italy, until at last his genius fashions " The Canterbury Tales ".

Arthurian romance, as material for depicting chivalry or for other poetical purposes, had no attraction for Chaucer. The machinery was for him obsolete, and " th'olde dayes of King Arthour " made no serious appeal to his imagination. He saw the truest embodiments of chivalry among the Knights of his own day, and his picture of the Knight, whom he describes first among the pilgrims, was without doubt drawn from life :—

"He loved chivalryë,
Trouthe and honour, fredom, and curteisyë."

Chaucer's Knight had done actual service both in Christendom and "heatheness"; he was worthy and wise, and of his bearing as meek as any maid. Never had he spoken villainy to any man.

"He was a verray parfit gentil Knight."

Chaucer spends no time in telling of his array. There is nothing in his description of the pomp and glamour of Knighthood. His horse was good; his attire was not gaudy; his doublet of fustian was all soiled with the marks made by the habergeon which he had so lately worn over it. The poet obviously finds a special joy in his delineation of his perfect Knight, untouched by any of the glamour of romance, though the tale he tells is of chivalrous love and tourneying and death. When, however, mine host calls on the poet himself to tell a tale of mirth, Chaucer can but offer a rime which he had learnt long ago ; and his Tale of Sir Thopas, a parody of a large class of the metrical romances of chivalry, in " rime dogerel " (*rithmus caudatus*, with variations), is the best commentary on his attitude towards the popular treatment of courtly themes with their standardized machinery, in ballad-like metres, altogether far removed from the realms of poetry :—

> "Men spoke of romances of prys,
> Of Horn child and of Ypotis,
> Of Bevis and Sir Guy,
> Of Sir Libeux and Pleyn-damour :
> But Sir Thopas, he bereth the flour
> Of royal chivalry."

Sir Thopas was a doughty swain ; and we have a descriptive catalogue of the various items of face, lips, hair, beard, and robe. He could hunt and hawk, and was a good archer. He was a chaste lover. The rime tells how he rides forth set on adventure, with lance and long-sword. He fares through a forest wherein are wild beasts, and where there are blossoming herbs, great and small. The birds sing their songs. He falls in love-longing, and dreams that an elf-queen shall be his bride. His quest is the land of Faery where she dwells. He is there met by the terrible giant Olifaunt, who bids him begone from Faeryland. Sir Thopas threatens to meet him on the morrow, ere prime, when he will fight him to the death. Through God's grace, he escapes the stones hurled at him by Olifaunt. He then returns home, and prepares for the encounter with this three-headed giant, all for the sake of the lady fair. He bids his minstrels and tale-tellers entertain him while he dons his arms ; and thereto, wine, and gingerbread and spices are brought him. All details are given of his arms—his breeches, shirt, aketoun, habergeon, hauberk, cote-armour, his shield, all of gold with boar's head and carbuncle as armorial bearing, leg-armour, swords, helmet, saddle, bridle, spear, and steed. He thereupon sets out on his adventure. He will not rest in any house ; in his hood will he lie, and drink water of the well, as did the Knight Sir Perceval. Till on a day—. And the tale is at this point interrupted, and nothing more is told of the promised battle and " of chivalry and of ladies' love-drury ".

With inimitable skill Chaucer burlesquely touched all properties of so many of the romances of chivalry. But some of these popular poems of the period are not to be despised ; Sir Degrevant, for instance, is, to my mind, still attractive, both in respect of matter and manner. Anyhow, it was through the recital of these romances that the people got their delight in old-world chivalry.

There were finer achievements in the literature of chivalry than the best of these metrical romances. The finest of all was the poem of *Sir Gawain and the Green Knight*, written by an unknown contemporary of Chaucer, who may safely be credited with the authorship of *Pearl, Cleanness, Patience*, and possibly *St. Erkenwald*. *Sir Gawain* is the very gem of medieval English romance, and perhaps it may not be too much to claim for it as high a place in medieval romance generally. Whereas for Chaucer, the poet of London, Arthurian romance was a thing of the past, for the West-Midland poet of *Pearl* it was still a living source of inspiration. Of all the knights of the Round Table Gawain was the most popular along the Welsh marches and in districts near the Celtic border. The popularity was evidently traditional, though it is possible that some French original may have been utilized by the poet of this magical romance. Whatever the material he utilized, a master-poet has impressed on the workmanship his own genius and his own personality. In sheer poetic talent he is second only to Chaucer. His individuality differentiates him markedly from his more objective and more genial contemporary. It is as if the Teutonic seriousness, which in Anglo-Saxon times made poetry the handmaiden of religion, finds new opportunity in the attractive beauty and exalted idealism of Arthurian romance. The poet, undoubtedly an artist, has the obvious purpose so to use his gifts as to portray his ideal Knight as *chevalier sans peur et sans reproche*.

The story of Sir Gawain's adventure is too well known for me to summarize its vivid incidents, wherein are commingled many elements of chivalric life—adventure, gallantry, courtesy, Knight-errantry, the chase, and the picturesque life of medieval castle and hall. Attractive as any fairy tale, suffused with rarest glamour, the romance carries the hearer from episode to episode. Any didactic purpose on the part of the poet is lost sight of under the spell of the story, which is told in the revived alliterative verse, though the danger of monotony is avoided by the introduction of rhyming tags— the bob-wheel verse, as it is called, at irregular intervals. A brief quotation must suffice :—

> "O'er a mound on the morrow he merrily rides
> into a forest full deep and wondrously wild;
> high hills on each side and holt-woods beneath,
> with huge hoary oaks, a hundred together;
> hasel and hawthorn hung clustering there,
> with rough ragged moss o'ergrown all around:
> unblithe, on bare twigs, sang many a bird,
> piteously piping for pain of the cold.
> Under them Gawain on Gringolet glideth
> through marsh and through mire, a mortal full lonesome,
> cumbered with care, lest ne'er he should come
> to that Sire's service, who on that same night
> was born of a bride to vanquish our bale.
> Wherefore sighing he said: 'I beseech Thee, O Lord,
> and Mary, thou mildest mother so dear!
> some homestead, where holily I may hear mass
> and matins to-morrow full meekly I ask;
> thereto promptly I pray pater, ave, and creed.'
> He rode on in his prayer,
> And cried for each misdeed;
> He crossed him oft times there,
> And said: 'Christ's Cross me speed.'"

Even as Arthur, from Geoffrey of Monmouth onwards, stands forth as the Christian King, so, too, Gawain is depicted as the Christian Knight; originally he may have been even the Knight of the Holy Grail. In this poem one of the most striking passages describes the knight's shield, whereon was the pentangel, "the endless knot;" and, as Arthur in Geoffrey's *History*, so on the larger half of his shield Gawain bore the image of the Virgin, that when he looked thereon his strength might never be impaired. He is a gallant knight, a prince of nurture and courtesy, fearless and undaunted; yet in the end he fails. To save his life he accepts from the temptress the magic girdle, and falsely conceals the gift. He triumphs, however, in that he has resisted the lady's more serious wiles, and has successfully gone through temptations imperilling his ideals of chaste life. And here we have the poet's lesson. "Life is aye sweet," he wrote in another poem; though Gawain erred in thus loving life, yet he passed unscathed through the greater danger. The poet of *Cleanness* exemplified through Gawain that the knight's vows of chastity must be real, and that Gawain, pre-eminently gallant, shunned the easy morality which too often accompanied the external refinements of chivalry. The quaint lesson of *Cleanness* turns on the death penalty, for unchastity, which befell men at the Flood, and in Sodom and Gemorrah, and also the case of Belshazzar, who defiled the holy vessels of the Lord in his wanton debauchery. Even pride—the pride of Lucifer, and disobedience—the sin of Adam and Eve, did not receive a fatal doom. To the poet of the *Pearl*, the ideal Knight must be spotless and undefiled. The glorification of English chivalry—its highest idealism—is set forth in this greatest of all the romances of chivalry :—

> " As the pearl is of greater price than the white pea,
> So is Gawain, in good faith, than other gay Knights.
> But you lapsed a little, sir, and fidelity lacked ;
> But it was for nought wanton, nor for unlawful love,
> But for love of life—the less are you blamed."

Gawain and the Green Knight is not to be put in juxtaposition with Chaucer's burlesque *Sir Thopas*, but rather with the poet's greatest artistic achievement, *Troilus and Criseyde*, wherein we have his chief treatment of love. Without discussing whether or not " it is *at bottom* an earnest presentation of the circumstances and effects of idealistic passion," as Professor Schofield would maintain, the poem is primarily to be judged as a work of subtle art, and not as a moral tale. And this, indeed, the poet himself emphasized when, perhaps in a spirit of banter, he dedicated his finished work " to the moral Gower and the philosophical Strode ". I wish I could prove a theory I have hazarded that the philosophical Strode, whom I identify with the Common Serjeant of the City of London, and who lived over the gate at Aldersgate Street about the time when Chaucer lived over Aldgate, a poet as well as a great logician, was actually the gifted author of *Sir Gawain and the Green Knight*. This would, indeed, have been a fine tribute on Chaucer's part, though fraught with humour, to the greatest of that other school of poets, who dedicated their genius to the teaching of high morality as the essence of true chivalry. In the case of the poet of *Gawain and the Green Knight*, the love of the beautiful enhances the poet's love for what is goodly and righteous.

V

The origin of some great Order of Chivalry may have been associated with the theme of *Sir Gawain and the Green*

Knight. At the end of the unique manuscript of the poem we have the famous motto " Honi soit qui mal pense ", as though to suggest that the story bore on the Order of the Garter. In a later version of the romance we are distinctly told that hence arose the Order of the Bath. We are perhaps justified in holding that not only did the romance commemorate the foundation of some great Order, but that the figure of Gawain was drawn, however flatteringly, from some notable contemporary. In other Arthurian poems we can detect in the person of Arthur character sketches of Edward III, and an idealization of the Black Prince in the figure of Gawain. The pomp and lavish expenditure and display associated with the King's foundation of the Order of the Garter, in 1844–7 (in all probability to fulfil his vow that he would restore the Round Table of Arthur) evoked admiration on the one hand, but misgiving on the other. Social problems and economic conditions soon after the Black Death in 1349 made men weigh the cost of these external trappings of chivalry. Chivalric Honour went hand in hand with Waste, and the Waster had needs to be the Winner, or mere profiteer. An alliterative poet, in 1352, according to my dating, deals with this theme in a fascinating debate between two forces representing respectively *Winner* and *Waster*, who are both brought before the King ; he knows them well. It is a dream-poem, and the pavilion wherein the King is seen is covered with " besants ", bearing the only recorded English rendering of the motto of the Garter :—

" Hething have the hathel that any harme thinkes,"

i.e. "Scorn have the man who thinks any harm."

The most fascinating lines of the poem give us a life-like description of the Black Prince as but newly knighted. In a corrupt reading of the manuscript I have discovered the English equivalent of " Ich dien " (or, rather, " Ich dene," as the Prince himself wrote the words), viz. " I serve ". Notwithstanding his faults, the young prince was adored by his countrymen :—

" When that warrior I knew,
Lo, he was youngest of years and yarest of wit
That any wight in this world wist of his age." [1]

---

[1] Cf. *Winner and Waster*, edited I. Gollancz (Oxford, 1920).

In *Winner and Waster* we hear the first faint notes of the prophet-voice, which was destined in the *Vision of Piers Plowman* first to stir England some ten years later, and for many years after. In this denunciation of the corruption to be found in Church and State, there are many references to the duties of the knights, " who should faithfully defend and fight for truth " :— [1]

"The Knight," says Piers Plowman, "must keep Holy Church and myself
From wasters and from wicked men that this world destroy ;
And must hardily hunt the hares and foxes,
Boars and brocks that break down my hedges,
And train the falcons wild fowl to kill " ; [2]

He would not have that Knights should live austerely, nor would he wish them to waste their substance in foolish entertainment, and in giving their wealth to idlers and base buffoons. The poor are " God's minstrels ".[3] And turning from the knights to their ladies, he exhorts them to embroider vestments for the Church :—

"And ye, lovely ladies, with your long fingers,
With your silk and sendal sow, when time is,
Chasubles for chaplains, churches to honour." [4]

Piers Plowman is willing to swink and sweat and toil for those above him, if only they, on their part, will recognize their high responsibilities. The author is no leveller, but a serious prophet-poet, who calls the people to repentance and well-doing, and points to corruption beneath the tinsel and veneer of social life ; not least in dealing with those highly placed does he emphasize " Noblesse oblige ".

" Beguile not thy bondman, the better thou'lt speed ;
Though under thee here, it may happen in heaven,
His seat may be higher, in saintlier bliss,
Than thine, save thou labour to live as thou shouldst ;
Friend, go up higher ;
In the charnel at church, churls are hard to discern,
Or a knight from a knave there ; this know in thy heart." [5]

By their deeds they shall be known, not by any external pomp or dignity. This same voice declared that not the prayers of any bishop, no mere symbol of faith, won Trajan from purgatory. All righteous men had their chance of salvation.

[1] C. ii, 96, 99. [2] B. vi, 29. [3] C. viii, 100. [4] B. vi, 10.
[5] B. vi, 46. (The passages are modernized.)

VI

In the fifteenth century Chivalry had sunk to a low level. It has been truthfully said that "never had England had an aristocracy more proud and privileged, nor, it would seem, more corrupt, than in the fifteenth century." Yet the glory of English literature of that period is Malory's prose *Morte Arthur*. It is beyond the scope of this lecture to deal with this great book of Arthurian romance. When the need was greatest, the voice of Malory attempted to arrest the degradation :—

> "O ye Knights of England, where is the custom and usage of noble chivalry that was used in those days? What do ye now but go to the baynes and play at dice? And some not well advised, use not honest and good rule, against all order of Knighthood. Leave this, leave it! and read the noble volumes of Saint Graal, of Launcelot, of Galahad, of Tristram, of Perseforest, of Perceval, of Gawain, and many more. There shall ye see manhood, courtesy, and gentleness. And look in latter days of the noble acts since the Conquest, in King Richard's days Cœur de Lion, Edward the First and the Third and his noble sons, Sir Walter Manny; read Froissart, and also behold that victorious and noble King Harry the Fifth, the captains under him, his noble brethren, the Earls of Salisbury, Montagu, and many others whose names shine gloriously by their virtuous noblesse and acts that they did in the honour of the order of chivalry. Alas! What do ye but sleep and take ease, and are all disordered from chivalry?"

At the beginning of the next century the poetry of chivalry finds expression in the *Pastime of Pleasure*, by Stephen Hawes, wherein the education of the youth who is eventually to attain Knighthood is allegorically depicted with reference to the Trivium and Quadrivium which constituted the studies through which the youth had to pass before he could be qualified to enter the Tower of Chivalry. Grand Amour is incited to valorous deeds by the sight of La Bel Pucell, whom he wins in the end. Allegory has attained is last endeavour in the *Pastime*, which is not as unattractive as text-books are wont to assert. The aims of Knighthood as set forth by the poet are perhaps in inverse proportion to his poetic powers, but there is much of interest as regards the education preliminary to right manhood. The arms the Knight must carry are those of the good Christian as set forth by St. Paul.

It would be well to compare Grand Amour, before he becomes a knight, with the character of the Squire in Chaucer, and with that of Youth in the alliterative poem of the *Parlement of the Three Ages*, and generally to explore the Books of Nurture—the text-books of the fifteenth and sixteenth century—for the education of the young squire, hopeful of Knighthood in the process of years. Scott's lines, in *Marmion*, recur to one :—

> "Behind him rode two gallant squires,
> Of noble name and Knightly sires;
> They burned the gilded spurs to claim,
> For well could each a war-horse tame,
> And draw the bow, the sword could sway,
> And lightly bear the ring away ;
> Nor less the courteous precepts stored,
> Could dance in hall, and carve at board,
> And frame love ditties passing rare,
> And sing them to a lady-fair."

In Stephen Hawes we have tiresome descriptions of Grammar, Logic, Rhetoric, Arithmetic, Music, Astronomy, and the rest; and a giant with three heads is vanquished, and many other incidents illume the story of Grand Amour. But as we read the *Pastime* we instinctively see therein a far-off prophecy of the *Faerie Queene*, which in its turn owes so much to medieval romance, harmonized with the exalted philosophy of Neo-Platonism, both elements touched by the high poetical genius of one whom Milton characterized "as a greater teacher than Aquinas". Yet many, finding limitations in the greatest Elizabethan poet, are at a loss to understand the peculiar position of Spenser in the progress of English poetry. He it is who harmonizes the art of Chaucer with the didactic purposes of the West-Midland poets. If in the realm of poetic beauty he has affinity with Chaucer, in the subordination of this gift to the high morality he would teach his precursor is the author of *Sir Gawain and the Green Knight*. The Red Cross Knight is in very deed Sir Libius, the Fair Unknown, the son of Gawain, the peerless knight of medieval chivalry.

But here our theme must end !

CHAPTER VIII

Medieval Courtesy Books and the Prose Romances of Chivalry

By A. T. Byles, M.A.,
Lecturer in English at the Exeter Diocesan Training College.

CHIVALRY was the great ennobling force of the Middle Ages, consecrating the martial ardour of the period by enrolling it in the cause of religion and order. It showed to the feudal baron how the circumstances of his life could be raised from a base material level to a higher and more spiritual plane; how his skill in war could be used against the enemies of the Cross, his power devoted to the protection and government of the poor and helpless, and his lawless passion subjugated to the service of noble ladies. Chivalry was no less vital because it remained largely an ideal, which few completely realized and many scarcely approached. A great stride out of barbarism was taken when such an ideal was formulated and recognized as most worthy of attainment, while the men who furnished brilliant examples of any of the chivalric virtues, whatever their other faults may have been, merit high honour as pioneers in the march of civilization. In the eloquent words of John Addington Symonds:—

> "Whatever was most noble in the self-devotion of the Crusaders; most beneficial to the world in the foundation of the knightly orders; most brilliant in the lives of Richard, the Edwards, Tancred, Godfrey of Bouillon; most enthusiastic in the lives of Rudel, Dante, Petrarch; most humane in the courtesy of the Black Prince; in the gallantry of Gaston de Foix; in the constancy of Sir Walter Manny; in the loyalty of Blondel; in the piety of St. Louis—may be claimed by the evanescent and impalpable yet potent spirit which we call chivalry."

Though only the elect could fully exemplify chivalry in real life, fiction and legend could present the complete ideal. In this fact lies the peculiar importance of medieval literature. It did more than chronicle the deeds of chivalry; it inspired them, too. Familiar with the romances of chivalry from his childhood, the young knight yearned to emulate his favourite heroes and to enrol his name on the pages of the chronicles of his own day.

It is because of this intimate connection between chivalry and literature that the romances are accepted by all authorities as trustworthy evidence of chivalrous manners. Most of the English verse romances of the thirteenth and fourteenth centuries are translated or adapted from French originals. In the course of the next two centuries many of them were re-written in prose. Collections of romances such as Malory's *Morte Darthur* constitute one of the most important products of the first printing presses and were the chief delight of the reading public up to the time of Shakespeare. The earliest of the romances are the French " chansons de geste ", dealing mainly with the great family of conquerors, Charlemagne and his sire and grandsire, Pepin and Charles Martel. The most important and the oldest poem of this cycle is the famous *Chanson de Roland*, which the minstrel Taillefer sang as he rode before the Norman host at Hastings. Another cycle is concerned with a wise governor of Aquitaine and tutor to Charlemagne's son Louis, William of Toulouse, and his young nephew Vivien, who was slain at the great battle of Aliscans, in which William was defeated by the Arabs. The actual events are overlaid with legend and exaggeration. The only historical record of the redoubtable Roland is found in the chronicler Eginhard, who states that in 778, when a body of Gascon mountaineers surprised and defeated the rearguard of a French host, Roland, " the Count of the Marches of Brittany," was slain. Many romances, such as *Renaud de Montauban*, confuse the times of Charles Martel with those of Charlemagne. Nevertheless, the historical core is much larger than that of the Arthurian cycle, and as the original ballads, contemporary with the events described, were written down in their extant forms in the eleventh and twelfth centuries, they give a faithful reflection of the most flourishing period of French chivalry. It was from the " chansons de geste " that M. Gautier drew the materials for his great work, *La Chevalerie*. Some of these romances depict a state of society before the harshness of feudalism was relieved by the ideals of chivalry; in *Raoul de Cambrai*, founded upon actual events of the

COURTESY BOOKS, PROSE ROMANCES 185

year 942, one virtue only is emphasized, the fidelity of a vassal to his lord in spite of terrible injuries received at his hand. In the "chansons de geste" the elaborations of later times are wanting; the ceremonies of ordination are simple and the doctrine of courtly love had not yet been introduced into chivalry. Dr. Schofield records [1] that there are extant about 16,000 lines of Carlovingian romance in English translations of the age of Chaucer; "and this is but a small fraction of what formerly existed." At a later date, many of these romances appeared in prose redactions. *Charles the Great* and *Renaud de Montauban or the Four Sons of Aymon*, an account of Charlemagne's wars with his vassals, were translated and printed by Caxton, while *Huon de Bordeaux* was translated by Lord Berners and printed by Caxton's successor, Wynkyn de Worde, in 1534.

A number of poems resembling the old "chansons" were composed in honour of the heroes of the First Crusade, especially Godfrey de Bouillon. Early in the twelfth century the romances of King Arthur and the Round Table travelled from Wales through Brittany to France, where they became very popular and introduced a new note into the literature of chivalry. It was a note of love, enchantment, and faery. The old standards of conduct were maintained, but a fantastic code of courtly love was added. A sense of unreality pervades the whole mass of Arthurian romance, contrasting strongly with the impression of actuality given by the "chansons de geste", and in the popularity of this cycle M. Gautier sees one of the influences which contributed to the decay of chivalry. The great body of English Arthurian romances in the fourteenth century shows how this cycle superseded in favour the "gestes" of those somewhat crude and extravagant native heroes, King Horn, Beves of Hampton, and Guy of Warwick. By a most fortunate fate, at the very end of the Middle Ages, the best of Arthurian romance was preserved for ever in Sir Thomas Malory's classic prose redaction, *Morte Darthur*.

Two historians faithfully depict chivalry, not as it was idealized in the romances, but as it was actually practised. In Jean de Joinville's life of St. Louis we see the chivalry of the last Crusades, pure, high-souled, and earnest; in

[1] *English Literature from the Norman Conquest to Chaucer*, p. 155.

Froissart's chronicles we see the chivalry of the Hundred Years' War, elaborate, brilliant, and superficial. While Froissart had an eye only for the glittering display and splendid deeds of the age, his contemporary, Chaucer, looked on the world with keen, impartial, but tolerant gaze, discerning with equal clearness the nobility of the knight, squire, and parson, the coarseness of the churls, and the self-indulgence of the monk and friar.

In all the classes of literature which we have mentioned, the principles of knighthood are incidentally disclosed in narrative. During the long period of the decadence of chivalry, many treatises were written in which chivalry is analysed and its principles enunciated in didactic form. It is clear that the freshness and spontaneity of chivalry had passed when it could be formulated as a science, and when Ramon Lull could even complain that " grete wrong is done to the ordre of knyghthode, of this that it is not a scyence wreton and redde in scoles, lyke as the other scyences." [1]

One of the earliest of these " courtesy books " is the well-known little poem of the thirteenth century, *L'Ordène de Chevalerie*. It combines narrative and instruction in a most engaging way by describing how Saladin made his prisoner, Hugh of Tabarie, confer knighthood on him, afterwards releasing him with rich gifts and high honour. Hugh accompanies each ceremonial act by an account of its symbolic significance, and the poem shows clearly how elaborate the ritual and symbolism of chivalry had become by this time.

The Book of the Ordre of Chyualry, which Caxton translated and printed in 1484, has been recognized by all the chief writers on chivalry as the most compendious medieval treatise on the obligations of knighthood. It has always been incorrectly described as anonymous, although its authorship is now completely established.[2] It is the work of Ramon Lull, the apostle to the Saracens and indefatigable author, who was born at Palma in Majorca about 1285. He was the son of a wealthy and distinguished Majorcan soldier, and after marrying at an early age, he was made seneschal at the court of James II of Aragon. Here he lived the life of a gay worldling, but was probably no more profligate than the

---

[1] *Ordre of Chyualry*, E.E.T.S., p. 23.
[2] See *Ordre of Chyualry*, E.E.T.S., p. xiii.

average courtier of his day. The gift of poetry appeared in him in his youth, and the collection of Catalan poems, edited by M. Rosselló, is of more value to-day than the vast mass of his scholastic philosophy. His poetry was devoted to amorous and other secular themes until 1266, when the whole course of his life was changed by a vision of the crucified Christ, seen on five successive nights. He determined to devote himself to some great Christian service, and accordingly he essayed the task of converting the Saracens, chiefly in the north of Africa. He learnt Arabic from a Saracen slave, and commenced the long series of treatises in Arabic, or in vulgar Catalan, which only terminated with his death, and which are now extant mainly in Latin translations. The three objects of his life, besides his missionary journeys, were the establishment of colleges and professorships, by means of which men could learn Arabic and obtain missionary training; the organization of a Crusade which should have love and spiritual instruction rather than armed force as its basis; and the overthrow of the doctrines of the Moslem philosopher Averröes. In 1276 he founded the College of the Holy Trinity at Miramar in Majorca, where thirteen monks were enabled to learn Arabic. He lived there for ten years, during which he probably wrote *The Order of Chivalry* and many other books. Towards the end of his life, in 1311, he placed his favourite projects before the great Council of Vienne, and to his satisfaction it passed a decree establishing professorships in Oriental languages at several universities.

Lull's first journey to Africa took place in 1291, the year of the fall of Acre and the end of the Crusades. At the last moment his heart failed him, and he delayed his departure, but after his first venture, not banishment, nor privation, nor imprisonment, nor threats of death could keep him from the little colony of converts that he established in Tunis and Bugia. In his last years he was obsessed with a yearning for martyrdom, and in 1315, when he was eighty years old, he came into the open to preach at Bugia after living twelve months in secret with his disciples. The enraged Saracens stoned him to death on the sea-shore. His memory is deeply venerated to the present day by the Majorcans, who gave him the title of "Docteur illuminé et martyr".

The Order of Chivalry opens with a simple but pleasing little romance. The first chapter tells how a brave and distinguished knight, prevented by old age from further activity, retired from the world to live a hermit's life in a wood. One day a squire, riding to court to be knighted, fell asleep on his horse, and was carried to a meadow containing a fountain at which the horse began to drink. Awaking, the squire found himself in the presence of the hermit-knight, who was reading a little book.

The venerable and ascetic appearance of the knight awed the squire, who politely waited for him to speak. The knight received him kindly, and when they had sat down he asked him where he was going. When the squire told him, he fell into a deep meditation on the great honour and responsibility of knighthood. The squire asked him to instruct him on these subjects. After expressing surprise that the squire should be willing to accept knighthood without knowing his duties, the knight gave him the little book containing the required instruction, and told him to present copies to the king, who was also going to be made a knight, and to all the new knights. He also asked him to tell him on his return about his adventures at court. The squire gave copies to the king and his knights, but there is no record of his return visit to the hermit. The reader is left to understand that the following chapters comprise the contents of the little book.

The second chapter contains a very curious allegorical account of the origin of chivalry as a force to combat the anarchy of the era following the disruption of Charlemagne's empire.

> " At the begynnyng whan to the world was comen mesprysion, justice retorned by drede in to honour, in whiche she was wonte to be. And therefore alle the peple was deuyded by thousandes, and of eche thousand was chosen a man moost loyal, most stronge, and of most noble courage, and better enseygned and manerd than al the other." [1]

The remaining six chapters deal with the office of a knight, the strict examination of the morals and intentions of an aspirant for knighthood by a knight of blameless character, the ceremonies of ordination, and the spiritual significance of a knight's arms.

[1] *The Ordre of Chyualry*, p. 15.

THE HERMIT AND THE SQUIRE

Illustration to "L'Ordre de Cheualerie." British Museum: Royal MS. 14 E ii, p. 338. This MS. is one of the magnificent products of the Bruges craftsmen, and was compiled for King Edward IV of England. It contains many illustrations and decorated borders, all beautifully coloured.

Ramon Lull's life until the age of thirty well qualified him to compile a treatise on chivalry. He was familiar with every aspect of courtly life, which according to his own account he enjoyed to the full. The son of a soldier, he was doubtless skilled in horsemanship and martial pursuits, such as he prescribes for the education of a squire. His conversion from a life of pleasure to one of arduous missionary endeavour caused all his subsequent works to wear a devout and homiletic garb. The theme of this book could wear it with ease, because medieval Christianity in its militant form was the very essence of chivalry. "The Church Militant" had a more literal interpretation in the Middle Ages than it has to-day; it meant the Crusading hosts. Lull's religious enthusiasm is apparent in the central theme, which is constantly exemplified—" God and chyualry concorden togyder." His theological bias also appears when he takes advantage of the statement that a sermon is preached to the newly dubbed knight to give a complete list of the articles of the faith, the commandments and the sacraments. The list destroys the continuity of the account of the ordination, and is very wisely omitted by Sir Gilbert Hay. The seven virtues and the seven sins are also adapted to the subject, and provide material for the greater part of Chapter 7.

The offence with which Lull reproached himself most severely was the attentions, which he, a married man, had paid to the ladies of the court. It is not surprising, therefore, that he omits all reference to the doctrine of courtly love, which permitted relations that are now universally condemned and that must have appeared to Lull's austere mind in their true light as the most discreditable aspect of chivalry. He extols the virtue of chastity in more than one place, and his book concludes with an admonition to maintain the honour of knighthood by respecting the sanctity of marriage.

The central belief that inspired Lull's life, and the one great original idea that he gave to the world, was the conviction that the heathen could be conquered and converted, not by the sword, but by the Cross; not by force, but by love, teaching and persuasion. It is this belief, now shared by all who attempt to convert the heathen, that gives him his pre-eminent position as a pioneer among modern missionaries.

It is expressed in eloquent, though slightly ambiguous, language in the proposal which he laid before Pope Clement V and the Church Council at Vienne in 1811 :—

"Cum Sanctum Sepulchrum et sanctam terram ultramarinam, Domine, videatur debere acquirere per praedicationem melius quam per vim armorum, progrediantur sancti equites religiosi et muniant se signo Crucis, et impleant se gratia Sancti Spiritus, et eant praedicare infidelibus veritatem tuae Passionis, et effundant pro tuo amore totam aquam suorum oculorum, et totum sanguinem sui corporis, sicut Tu fecisti pro amore ipsorum." [1]

Lull cannot have intended that this spiritual Crusade, for which he agitated so earnestly in his last years, should be quite unarmed. In 1308 he had entreated Ferdinand IV of Castile to join Philip IV of France in a new Crusade, and Philip and Edward II of England actually pledged themselves to it, but finally decided to stay at home. These shrewd and worldly princes would not have paid the least attention to anything but a practical proposal. Lull was doubtless shocked at the wanton cruelty of the Crusaders and at the barbarous alternative—"Be baptised or die!"—which has been a blot on the history of Christianity from Clovis to the Inquisition, and which claimed its victims, as Sir Walter Scott points out, not only in the Old World, but among the American Indians of the New. He was distressed that the methods of Christ were never applied, and that the prophecy, "I bring not peace but a sword," was so relentlessly fulfilled; but in *The Order of Chivalry*—which was written, however, long before he formulated his project for a spiritual Crusade—there is no hint of disapproval of the attempt to wrest the Holy Places from the Saracens by force. On the contrary, he praises knights who, nurtured in the Catholic faith, go over the sea, " and there proue theyr strength and chyualry ageynst the enemyes of the Crosse, and ben martirs yf they deye. For they fyghte for tenhaunce the holy feythe catholyk." [2]

The Order of Chivalry was quickly translated into French

---

[1] Liber Contemplationis in Deum.
[2] *Ordre of Chyualry*, p. 91. Cf. St. Bernard—"Gaude fortis athleta, si vivis et vincis in Domino; sed magis exsulta et gloriare, si moreris et jungeris Domino."

COURTESY BOOKS, PROSE ROMANCES 191

and increased in size, while the number of extant MSS. testifies to its popularity. In 1456 it was translated into Scots, with many notable additions, by Sir Gilbert Hay, who also translated another popular and comprehensive work on medieval warfare and chivalry, the *Arbre des Batailles*, written about 1382 by Honoré Bonet, Prior of Salon in Provence. The translator, who worked under the patronage of William Sinclair, Earl of Caithness and Orkney, at the castle of Roslin, was the writer of the earliest literary Scottish prose now extant, while, as the author of the verse " Buik of Alexander the Conquerour ", he finds a place in Dunbar's *Lament of the Makars*. When Caxton issued his translation of the *Order*, the age of chivalry was passed, and in spite of the stirring epilogue, one of the best examples of the printer's original work, in which he challenges the decadent knights of England to emulate their great predecessors, no second edition was demanded, either in Caxton's lifetime or during the sixteenth century. In the two French prints of the early sixteenth century, it appeared in a misleading and surreptitious guise—in Vérart's and Michel's prints as an addendum to *Le Jeu des Eschecz Moralisé* (" The Game and Play of Chess "), in Portunaris' print as the work of Symphorien Champier.

Caxton's love of chivalry is testified by the number of books on the subject which he printed, besides *Morte Darthur*. One of the most important of these, *The Fayt of Armes and of Chyualry*, is the work of a woman, Christine de Pisan, who was one of the most original and versatile women of the Middle Ages. She was born in 1364, and, though an Italian by birth, she spent all her life in France. She was the first authoress to earn a livelihood by her pen, for the early loss of her father and of her husband, Etienne de Castel, made it necessary for her to live by her poetry and other writings, and she succeeded in building a great reputation for herself. She lived to hail Joan of Arc in inspiring lines as the liberator of France, and died in a convent at some time after 1429. *The Fayt of Armes* treats of the whole art of war in four parts. The former two are based on the " De arte militari " of Vegetius, whose work is the basis of more than one such treatise, in spite of the dissimilarity between Roman and medieval warfare. The two latter are largely derived from

Bonet's *Arbre des Batailles,* as Christine admits. She describes how a man appeared to her in a vision and invited her to pluck fruit from his tree of battles in order to complete her work, which was tiring her, saying that she is free to use his work, just as Jean de Meun used that of Guillaume de Lorris in *Le Roman de la Rose*—apparently an ingenious defence on Christine's part against the charge of plagiarism! In the third book Bonet answers Christine's questions on such matters as the payment of soldiers, the liability of English students in France to be imprisoned in wartime, and the immunity claimed for simple countrymen " that medle not of the werre ".

Two other notable books on knightly manners are the *Bréviaire des Nobles,* by Alain Chartier (1492–1529), " the father of French eloquence," and *The Book of Good Manners,* which Caxton translated from the French of Jacques le Grand.

From these " courtesy books ", of which Lull's *Order of Chivalry* may be taken as a typical example, much may be learnt of the ceremonies and obligations of knighthood, while the romances provide many concrete applications of their precepts. Lull's favourite theme is that

" the offyce of preesthode and of chyualry have grete concordaunce," [1]

and it is constantly emphasized throughout the book. As the order of knighthood is second only to that of the clergy, kings and barons ought to honour knights greatly, and choose their provosts and bailiffs from the ranks of knights alone; it is only the lack of special knowledge that prevents knights from being judges. Between no orders should there be more perfect accord than between knights and clergy, who both endeavour, the one by doctrine and the other by force of arms, to incline the people to a godly life. In the latter days of chivalry, the parallel was drawn so far that an elaborate symbolism was attached to the arms and garments of a knight, corresponding to the long-established symbolical interpretation of a priest's vestments, although it is probable that a spiritual significance was first given to armour through the influence of the passage beginning " Put on the whole armour of God ", in the epistle to the Ephesians (vi, 11–18). In *L'Ordène de Chevalerie* Sir Hugh explains to Saladin that

[1] *Ordre of Chyualry,* E.E.T.S., p. 76.

AN ORDINATION CEREMONY

Woodcut in Vincent Portunaris' print of "L'Ordre de Chevalerie," published with "Le recueil ou croniques des histoires des royaulmes daustrasie" (1510). A curious feature is the attitude of the candidates, with their backs to the King.

[face p. 192

each garment in which he is arrayed as a knight has its spiritual meaning—the white vest, purity; the red gown, the shedding of blood for God and his Church; the black breeches and hose, the remembrance of death; the white belt, chastity; the spurs, eagerness to serve God; the sword, a protection against sin; its two-edged blade, right and loyalty; and the white cap, the innocence of mind which all will desire at the Day of Judgment. Ramon Lull devotes his sixth chapter to explaining the symbolical meaning of the knight's arms and accoutrements, to the number of twenty. The sword, shaped like a cross, means that a knight should vanquish the enemies of God, as Christ on the Cross vanquished the devil. The spear signifies truth, its iron tip strength to overcome falsehood, and its pennon shows that truth is not afraid to be seen. The helmet stands for dread of shame, because it makes the knight look down; and as his helmet defends his head which is the most important part of his body, so does fear of shame preserve his honour. The tightly closed haubergeon is like a fortress against vice. As the iron chaces or leg-harness defend the knight's legs and feet, so he ought to defend the highways and punish malefactors. The spurs signify swiftness, and diligence in providing necessary equipment. The gorget teaches obedience, for as his neck is enclosed by the collar, so must the knight keep within his sovereign's commands.

Accounts in the "courtesy books" of the rite of ordination at different periods show clearly the growth of symbolism and elaborate ceremonial in chivalry. The one essential act was girding on the sword, and early acts of investiture consisted of no more than this, although the complete arming of the knight was soon added to the ceremony. A religious service was next combined with these secular acts, and priests as well as knights were authorized to ordain; in the reign of Edward the Confessor a nobleman named Hereward was knighted by the Abbot of Peterborough after mass and confession. This privilege of the Church was not regarded with favour in England and was short-lived, for in 1100 priests were forbidden to ordain knights. There was probably some dispute about the right of the Church for a long time after this, due to the absence of such a ruling on the Continent, and we hear an echo of it in Sir Gilbert Hay's repeated insistence that no man but the Pope may make a knight, unless he is himself a knight.

Symbolism is highly developed in the thirteenth century poem, *L'Ordène de Chevalerie,* but with the exception of the homily with which Sir Hugh concludes his investiture of Saladin, there is no trace of a religious ceremony. The preliminary bath, which at first had no symbolic meaning, is an emblem of regeneration, and even the bed on which Saladin reclines stands for the final rest of Paradise. Various interpretations are given to the garments in which he is clothed, but the only arms with which he is equipped are the sword and the spurs. Sir Hugh explains that it is customary to give the new knight a blow on the neck, but that it is not essential. He therefore withholds it, as it is improper for a prisoner to strike his captor. The significance which he attaches to the " colée " is very interesting :—

> " Sire, chou est li ramembranche
> De chelui qui la adoube
> A chevalier et ordene."

William Morris translates :—

> " Sir, 'tis the memory-stirring thing
> Of him who hath ordained the knight,
> And duly with his gear him dight."

It is a forcible reminder of the person who confers the order and therefore of all that the order implies. Sir Gilbert Hay's explanation is similar; it is intended to make the knight " think on the poyntis and defend his dewiteis ". It is certain that the blow was not " an emblem of the last affront which it was lawful for him to endure ", as Edward Gibbon supposed, since the squire was as jealous of his honour as the knight.

In his fifth chapter Ramon Lull describes the method of investiture which was most common in the twelfth and thirteenth centuries. It was a combination of religious and secular ceremonies. Vigil and confession are enjoined, but there is no mention of the bath. At a solemn mass on a great festival the squire swears an oath before the priest, devoting himself to the service of God and chivalry. He offers his armour at the altar and listens to a sermon. The actual investiture is performed not by the priest but by a knight, who girds him with a sword, kisses him, and hands him a palm.

COURTESY BOOKS, PROSE ROMANCES

The omission of all mention of the colée is noteworthy. Although it is frequently mentioned after about 1180, this blow with the hand or sword, from which is derived the single act of modern investiture, was not considered essential during the age of chivalry. Sir Gilbert Hay adds :—

" a strake with his hand, or with a drawin sword in the nek,"

to his version of Lull, and also remarks that the investing knight and the new knight, instead of kissing each other, may kiss the hilt of the sword, which is placed in the scabbard with suitable words of exhortation.

At the end of one of the two British Museum copies (1A 55071) of Caxton's *Ordre of Chyualry* there are three pages covered with MS. The writing is in a fine Tudor hand, and bears the heading " Making of Knyghte of the Bathe ". It comprises a fragment of an account of a knight's ordination, describing first the ceremony of the mass, at which the candidate offers at the altar a lighted taper with a penny " facked in "—" the taper to the worship of God and the penny in worship of him that shall make him knight "— and secondly the ceremonious robing of the squire after he has rested. The MS. then ends abruptly in the middle of a sentence.

After some investigations I found the complete MS in the British Museum MS., Cotton Nero C ix, a miscellaneous collection in which early MSS. are found together with statutes of Henry VIII.

The article on the making of knights is one of several which are written in the same hand and are concerned with the coronation of Henry VI on 6th November, 1429. In the article, " Coronatio regis Henrici VI ", it is stated that thirty-two knights of the Bath were created on this occasion, and that on the next day the Prince of Portugal was knighted in Westminster Hall. The article to which our fragment belongs is headed :—" Manner of making of a knight after the custom of England in time of peace, and at the coronation ; that is, Knights of the Bath."

It is therefore clear that this MS. is a contemporary account of the manner in which knights were made in 1429, and its historical value is increased by our ability to fix a definite date to it.

The tract is contained in Sir William Dugdale's *Antiquities of Warwickshire* [1] (1656), and also in the Harleian Miscellany,[2] the celebrated collection of papers from the library of Edward Harley, second Earl of Oxford. Dugdale's copy, which he says is derived from " an antient French tract ", is accompanied by twenty-three illustrations, copied from " a fair book " of Edward IV's time. The illustrations correspond to the twenty-three paragraphs into which the account is divided in Dugdale and the Harleian Miscellany. The copy in the latter is a reprint of a quarto of 10 pages, printed for Philip Stephens in 1661, " with a list of those honourable persons, who are to be created Knights of the Bath at his Majesty's Coronation, the twenty-third of April, 1661."

The article describes with much picturesque detail all the formalities by which a squire became a knight in the fifteenth century.

The knight designate is received at the royal court, and is provided with two squires of honour, or governors.

" And if the Esquire do come before dinner, he shall carry up one dish of the first course to the King's table."

In the evening a bath is prepared, and a number of knights and squires proceed with minstrelsy to the candidate's chamber. When he has entered the bath, the chief knight present sprinkles water on his shoulders and instructs him in the Order of Chivalry. When the squire is dried and clothed and his barber has taken the bath as his fee, he is conducted to the chapel, where the knights take leave of him. Only the two governors, the priest, the chandler, and the watch remain with him during his night-long vigil, which terminates with confession, matins and mass. The next day, after he has rested awhile and has been ceremoniously robed by attendant knights, he rides to court, preceded by a youth carrying his sword and spurs. The king himself awaits him ; he commands the two noblest knights to fasten the squire's spurs and girds on the sword with his own royal hands, saying " Be thou a good knight ". Even at this late date (1429) there is no " colée ". A solemn procession is then formed, and proceeds to the chapel, where the new knight pledges himself to maintain the rights of the Church and places his sword on the

---

[1] p. 531, et seq.
[2] Oldys-Park edition, 1808, vol. i, pp. 558-61.

THE COOK AND THE KNIGHT

"I, the King's master-cook, am come to receive your spurs as my fee; and if you do anything contrary to the Order of Knighthood (which God forbid!) I shall hack your spurs from your heels."

Illustration from a series depicting the "Making of a Knight of the Bath," in Sir W. Dugdale's "Antiquities of Warwickshire" (1656).

High Altar. "All which being accomplished, he is to take a draught of wine." As he leaves the chapel, the master-cook says: "I, the king's master-cook, am come to receive your spurs as my fee; and if you do anything contrary to the Order of Knighthood (which God forbid!) I shall hack your spurs from your heels." He then sits with the other knights at dinner, "but he must neither eat nor drink at the table, nor spit, nor look about him, more than a bride." Later, in his chamber, the knight is disrobed and his robes are given to the Kings of Arms. He is dressed in a blue robe, with "a lace of white silk" on his shoulder. He must wear this until he achieves some honour or renown in arms, when a prince "or most noble lady" will cut it off. The wearing of a token as a stimulus to the performance of valiant deeds is one of the oldest chivalrous observances and has been traced back to the customs of the German tribes, described by Tacitus. Malory tells [1] how the knight La Cote Male Taile explains why he wears the ill-fitting coat of his murdered father.

> "And this same coat had my father on the same time, and that maketh this coat to sit so evil on me, for the strokes be on it as I found it and never shall be amended for me. Thus to have my father's death in remembrance I wear this coat till I be avenged."

One of the most interesting and original passages in *The Order of Chivalry* is that in which Lull pleads with much earnestness that squires should receive formal instruction in their duties in schools devoted to the purpose.

> "So moche is hyhe and honoured the ordre of chyualrye that to a squyer hit suffyseth not only to kepe hors and lerne to serve a knyght, and that he go with him to tornoyes and batayles; but hit is nedeful that ther be holden to hym a scole of the ordre of knyghthode, and that the scyence were wreton in bookes, and that the arte were showed and redde in such maner as other scyences ben redde, and that the sones of knyghtes lerne fyrst the scyence that apperteyneth to the ordre of chyualry and after that they were squyers they shold ryde thurgh dyverse countrees with the knyghtes." [2]

This distrust of a training derived solely from practical experience is a remarkably modern idea. Lull's scheme was probably very little relished by the knights and squires of his day, and the education which they actually received in the astles of their fathers and neighbouring knights was

---

[1] *Morte Darthur*, bk. ix, ch. 1.
[2] *Ordre of Chyualry*, E.E.T.S., p. 22.

undoubtedly better adapted to their needs. Professor J. W. Adamson has even indicated that medieval education was in this respect more rational than our own. In his *Short History of Education* (p. 49) he writes :—

> " The men of the Middle Ages did not think that the only type of intelligence or capacity worth educating was that of the clerk . . . . (The) underlying principle (of medieval education) has not even yet been fully applied to public instruction, although modern conditions demand such an application. That principle is, in brief, that education should foster all sorts of capacity, not one only, however exceptional its occurrence among men and women."

The medieval priest confined himself to his books, but the squire, without altogether neglecting the arts, paid most attention to the active pursuits in which it was essential that he should excel. To-day all are compelled to be educated, but the contemplative and the practical alike have to partake of the same bookish fare.

The two men who translated the *Order* into the vernaculars of this island, the Scottish " makar " and the English printer, were both distinguished by decided literary talent. Both have left the mark of personality and opinions on their translations of *The Order*. Hay has amplified throughout, but Caxton has reserved his comments for the well-known epilogue. In one notable instance, however, the printer has altered the original, in order to bring it into agreement with his own views. This concerns the connexion between chivalry and aristocracy or noble birth. Theoretically knighthood was open to all, and was conferred purely for merit. It naturally happened that training and disposition alike practically confined the order to the well-born. The dubbing of " vilains ", however, was not uncommon, as in the case of Sir Robert Sale, the staunch governor of Norwich, who, at the time of Wat Tyler's revolt, was killed by the rebels for refusing to place himself at their head when they reminded him, as Froissart says, that " ye be no gentleman born, but son to a villain, such as we be ". Therefore, while Lull declares that chivalry and noble birth accord well, he does not fail to add that " elle puist auoir en cheuallerie aucun homme de nouuel lignage, honnourable et gentil." With this exception, Lull's view of knighthood is purely aristocratic. It is implicitly assumed that the lower orders are immeasurably inferior to the knights, and incapable of worthy motives or sentiments. While the common people till his fields, the knight occupies himself with sport and " thynges of whiche his men haue payne and trauayl ". The only motive which induces the labourers to work on the land is " fere lest they shold be destroyed " by the knights. A knight must have an adequate income, lest he should become " a robbour, a theef, traitre, lyar, or begylour ".[1]

Sir Gilbert Hay's humane and rational outlook is nowhere more evident than in the modifications which he introduced into such passages as these. He points out that while his serfs are working for him, the knight must not only seek recreation, but must also protect the labourers and enable students, clerics, and merchants to perform their several duties. A poor knight may be assisted by his lord, and the investing prince or lord should give the knight not merely ceremonial gifts, but substantial grants of land to support his new dignity. The order of knighthood is essentially democratic ; it is as noble and worthy of honour in the poorest knight as in the Emperor himself.

Caxton stresses the aristocratic conception even more than Lull. An ardent lover of chivalry, he insists that it is the preserve of a privileged class. In the Epilogue to *The Ordre of Chyualry* he writes : " [This] book is not requysyte to every comyn man to haue, but to noble gentylmen that by their vertu entende to come and entre in to the noble ordre of chyualry." Similarly he dedicates *Morte Darthur* to " all noble princes, lords, and ladies, gentlemen or gentlewomen ". It is very significant that almost the only original thought, outside the Epilogue, that Caxton introduces into his translation is concerned with the connexion between chivalry and noble birth. He omits Lull's single concession, that a man of lowly birth may be knighted if he is virtuous, and substitutes the following passage, which is found in no other version:—" Thordre of chyualry is most couenable and moche more syttynge [2] to a gentyl herte replenysshed wyth al vertues than in a man vyle and of euyl lyf." [3] The train of

[1] The harshness of this reflection is mitigated when it is remembered that many soldiers who were knighted on the field had insufficient means to sustain the dignity, and that while some enlisted in the service of richer knights, the more unscrupulous became a menace to the countryside by their lawlessness.
[2] = Most appropriate and much more suitable.
[3] *Ordre of Chyualry*, E.E.T.S., p. 59.

argument in this passage practically compels us to interpret "gentyl" and "vyle" as "well-born" and "lowly born" respectively.

Caxton considered that there was an innate connexion between nobility of birth and of character. In this belief he was in complete agreement with his contemporary, Sir Thomas Malory. In *Morte Darthur* knights like Sir Gareth and Sir Tor, who are at first supposed to be of humble origin, are found to derive their courtesy from their noble birth. The point is emphasized most heavily when King Arthur remarks that Sir Tor would be unmatched, if only he was as well born on his mother's side as on his father's. It is further enforced by Malory's severe comments on the two "vilains" who slew the noble knight Hermance,—"It is an old saw, Give a churl rule and thereby he will not be sufficed"; and by his statement that "Sir Launcelot is come but of the eighth degree from our Lord Jesu Christ; and Sir Galahad is from the ninth degree from our Lord Jesu Christ; therefore, I dare say that they be the greatest gentlemen of the world."

Contempt for the lower classes was one of the forces which contributed to the collapse of chivalry. The gulf between the orders of society was bridged much more successfully in England than in France, and this fact explains the survival of chivalry in England long after its practical extinction in the country of its origin. The disasters of Creçy, Poictiers, and Agincourt were all due to lack of co-ordination between the French knights and the despised soldiery, and to the harmonious relations between the English nobles and the redoubtable bowmen. The French attitude is accurately reflected in the pages of Froissart, who cared nothing about the troubles of the commons and dismissed the Black Death in three lines. By the end of the fifteenth century, chivalry was moribund in England, and the aristocratic attitude, fostered by the civil wars in which the commons were only pawns in the struggle between the rival Houses, had replaced the democratic patriotism of the days of Edward III and Henry V. Chivalry was sick beyond recovery, and Caxton and Malory, while honestly endeavouring to restore it to health, showed in themselves the causes of its decline.

The "courtesy books" and the prose romances together

provide us with a comprehensive account of the duties of a knight, the former by precepts, the latter mainly by examples.

> "For chyualry is not only in the hors ne in the armes, but hit is in the knyght, that wel enduceth and enseyneth[1] his hors, and acustommeth hymself and his sone to good enseygnements[2] and vertuouse werkes."[3]

The three principal objects of a knight's care are succinctly stated by Sir Gilbert Hay:—

> "that is one, the faith of Jhesus Crist; ane othir, his naturale lord; the third, the peple in thair richtis."

Faithfulness to an overlord was a paramount duty long before the days of chivalry,[4] and in the early feudal period the vassal was bound to his lord's service, even if he suffered cruelty and injustice. Thus Bernier in *Raoul de Cambrai* reproaches himself bitterly because he has slain his lord in self-defence, although Raoul has killed Bernier's mother and has heaped every insult on him. Lull gives no opinion on the duty of a vassal in such a situation, but Honoré Bonet, the wise Prior of Salon, advances enlightened views in his *Tree of Battles*. He maintains that a bondsman ought to defend his life against his lord's attack, and that he ought to defend his relations, even if by so doing he has to slay a priest. A bondsman ought not to commit murder at his lord's command. Bonet also remarks that it is cruel to make war on tillers of the soil, who serve all and harm none, and Lull states that one of the chief duties of a knight is the protection of poor, helpless, and oppressed people. A knight must always help the weaker side; when Sir Lancelot sees Kay beset by three knights, he cries:—

> "Yonder one knight shall I help, for it were shame for me to see three knights on one, and if he be slain I am partner of his death."[5]

Participation in tournaments, jousts, and manly sports is rightly regarded by Lull as incumbent upon a knight. Malory is more concerned with Tristram's renown as a hunter and harper than as a lover, and Caxton in his Epilogue deplores the lapse into disuse of knightly exercises and

---

[1] = Teaches and trains.   [2] = Instructions.
[3] *Ordre of Chyualry*, E.E.T.S., p. 114.
[4] Emphasis on this point is one of the most striking features of the oldest English poetry, *Beowulf*, *Widsith*, etc., and of the old Norse and German sagas.
[5] *Morte Darthur*, bk. vi, ch. xi, p. 121, in Globe ed.

exhorts King Richard III—a most unchivalrous king!—to revive tournaments and "Justes of pees" at least once a year.

Courage was the *sine qua non* of chivalry, but Lull wisely insists that it must be tempered with discretion. In *Morte Darthur*, book x,[1] Sir Tristram says:—

> "Be a man never so valiant nor so big yet he may be overmatched. And so have I seen knights done many times: and when they wend best to have won worship they lost it. For manhood is not worth but if it be meddled with wisdom."

So Bonet considers that to know the right time to assail, to stand firm, or to fly, is one of the cardinal virtues of a knight. Many famous knights, however, showed little of this quality, and the deeds of the bold Du Guesclin, or the death of the blind King of Bavaria at Creçy, kindle the imagination more than the records of more prudent warriors.

Lull's moderate and strictly rational attitude is again apparent, when he notes that the truly knightly virtue of generosity must not be carried beyond the donor's means. His favourite virtue is moderation:—

> "Attemperaunce is a vertu the whiche dwelleth in the myddle of two vyces, of whome that one is synne by ouer grete quantite, and that other is synne by ouer lytyl quantyte."[2]

In extolling restraint and self-control in all things, he is in agreement with the finest ideal of ancient Greece and with the practice of the noblest knights of medieval history and romance. Joinville records with admiration St. Louis' temperate habits. In a notable passage, Sir Gilbert Hay demonstrates that gluttony is the consummation of all the deadly sins. The restraint to which the noblest knights of the Round Table subject their passions, is most impressive. In the last sad quarrel between Lancelot and King Arthur, the taunts of Sir Gawain cannot shake Lancelot's attitude of magnanimous sorrow, nor make him injure his former friend and his liege lord. When Sir Tristram heard Sir Palamides singing of his love for Iseult

> "He was wroth out of measure, and thought for to slay him there as he lay. Then Sir Tristram remembered himself that Sir Palamides was unarmed, and of the noble name that Sir Palamides had, and the

---

[1] Ch. lix, p. 208, in Globe ed.
[2] *Ordre of Chyualry*, E.E.T.S., p. 108.

noble name that himself had, and then he made a restraint of his anger."

So he approached Sir Palamides, and made his quarrel known to him.[1]

Lull reprimands in contemptuous terms those knights who are proud of their "beaute of facion", their "body fayr, grete, and well aourned" and their fair hair, and who love "to holde the myrrour in the hand", and to affect "the other Jolytees".

He condemns pride, which he recognizes as a vice which is very apt to assail a knight, "armed and mounted upon thy grete hors." Vanity about personal adornment and an overweening pride and haughtiness to inferiors, were indeed vices which contributed largely to the decay of chivalry.

No vices were more abhorrent to chivalry than those of treachery and lying. The Charlemagne romance, *L'Entrée en Espagne*, contains an episode similar to *L'Ordène de Chevalerie*. Roland confers knighthood on a Pagan prince, Samson, and one of the maxims which he impresses on him is "Garde-toi de mentir."

Envy and sloth were regarded as almost identical in the Middle Ages, and Lull's description of an envious man is one of the best passages in his book.

"Slouthe is a vyce by the whiche a man is louer of wyckednesse and of euylle and to hate goodnesse. And by this vyce may be knowen and sene in men sygnes of dampnacion better than by ony other vyce. . . . A man that hath accydye or slouthe hath sorowe and angre the whyle that he knoweth that an other man doth wel; and whan a man dothe harme to hym self, he that hath accydye or slouthe is heuy and sorowful of that, that he hath not more and gretter. And therefore suche a man hath sorow both of good and of euylle of other men."[2]

It is significant that in King Mark, the character in *Morte Darthur* who represents all that a knight should not be, treachery, cowardice and envy are the vices most evident. He was treacherous to Sir Tristram; when Sir Lancelot attacked him, he would not fight, "but tumbled down out of his saddle to the earth as a sack"; he killed his brother

---

[1] *Morte Darthur*, bk. x, ch. lxxxvi, p. 323, in Globe ed.
[2] *Ordre of Chyualry*, E.E.T.S., p. 102.

through envy of his good name, and his hatred of Tristram is due more to spleen on account of his prowess than to resentment at his intrigues with La Beale Isond. With Lull's passage on envy may be compared the words of Queen Guinevere, when it was reported to her that Sir Palamides was " passing envious ".

"Then shall he never win worship, said Queen Guenever, for, and it happeth an envious man once to win worship, he shall be dishonoured twice therefore. For this cause all men of worship hate an envious man, and will show him no favour. And he that is courteous, kind, and gentle, hath favour in every place." [1]

The romances teem with examples of the courtesy, shown alike to friend and foe, which was one of the leading characteristics of chivalry. In the Charlemagne romances Roland exceeds all the paladins in the consideration that he shows to his opponents in single combat. He even allows the giant Ferragus to take a short nap, when he is wearied by fighting. In his combat with Sir Otuel, he refrains from taking advantage of his opponent, when his horse is slain under him and he is entangled in the trappings. A little later, when a like misadventure befalls Roland, his antagonist shows the same consideration. A good example of a typical chivalrous encounter is provided in the fight between Sir Gawain, "the mirror of courtesy," and Sir Galleroun, to settle their claims to the district of Galloway, which the latter had ruled until it was conquered by Arthur and given to Gawain. The stranger knight is royally received in a rich pavilion. In the combat he fights valiantly but admits defeat, generously declaring that Gawain is "matchless of might". Gawain, although victorious, willingly accedes to Arthur's request that the brave Galleroun should be left in possession of his territory, and his opponent, defeated but not dishonoured, is received into the fellowship of the Round Table. The story is told with much charm and vigour in one of the best English romances of the fourteenth century, *The Awntyrs of Arthur at the Tarn Wadling*. The courtesy of the Black Prince to the captive King of France is one of the best-known incidents in medieval history, and it was this courtesy, combined with reliance on a knight's honour and a sense of brotherhood even between knights on opposing sides, that made possible

[1] *Morte Darthur*, bk. x, ch. lxxxi, p. 318, in Globe ed.

the system, rarely if ever abused, by which a knight taken prisoner was allowed to depart on parole to obtain his ransom. In *L'Ordène de Chevalerie* Saladin is prepared to allow his prisoner to go home for his ransom. William Morris thus translates their conversation :—

> "'Hugh, unto me shalt thou make oath
> By that thy faith and by thy troth
> To come again unto this place
> Without fail in a two year's space,
> And then to pay thy ransom clear
> Or come back to thy prison here.
> Thuswise from hence forth art thou quit.'
> 'Sir,' quoth he, 'have thou thank for it,
> And all my faith I pledge thereto.'"

When such was the spirit of courtesy between knights whom the chances of war made enemies, it is scarcely surprising to learn that knights who were great friends would often enter into a bond of "brotherhood in arms" which was closer even than the ties of relationship. In the romance of *Amys and Amiloun* a knight is said even to have sacrificed his two children's lives to cure his friend of leprosy. Happily his devotion was rewarded by their miraculous resuscitation.

The universal comradeship of chivalry helps to explain why the "courtesy books" and the romances have very little to say about patriotism. Chivalry emphasized allegiance to the feudal lord and the international Church, rather than to king and country. Mr. Bernard Shaw recognizes in *Saint Joan* that the fierce opposition with which Joan was assailed on all sides was due to her championing the appeal of the motherland against the domination of these great forces of the Middle Ages. The comment of his Earl of Warwick exactly expresses the medieval point of view :—

> "If this cant of serving their country once takes hold of them, good-bye to the authority of their feudal lords."

"The age of chivalry is gone," cried Burke in despair during the darkest days of the French Revolution. The Order of Chivalry, with its ceremonies, its symbolism, its degrees, its aristocratic outlook and its militant Christianity, has indeed vanished with the age to which it belonged ; but chivalry as a moral force survives, because in every age there are men who love courtesy, faithfulness, courage, truth and moderation, just as in almost every age there has been a Spenser, a Shakespeare, a Milton, a Wordsworth, a Tennyson, to enshrine these ideals in imperishable verse. For the survival of the spirit of chivalry no small credit is due, not only to the medieval romances, but also to the " courtesy books ". These works circulated widely in manuscript in the later Middle Ages, and in printed texts in Tudor times. In his *Chivalry in English Literature* Dr. Schofield has adduced very plausible evidence to show that Shakespeare was probably acquainted with translations of both Bonet's *Tree of Battles* and Lull's *Order of Chivalry*. He quotes a large number of parallel passages from Bonet and Shakespeare, and he considers that some hints for Falstaff's character may have been derived from such phrases in the *Order* as—" A man lame or over grete or over fatte is . . . not suffisaunt to be a knyght ", and " A man that hath no rychesse for to make his dispences . . . shold peraventure happe for nede to be a robbour, a theef, traitre, lyar or begylour." [1] Whether a particular book came before the master's eye, however, is as much a matter of conjecture as what song the Syrens sang or what name Achilles bore when he hid himself among women, to quote Sir Thomas Browne's examples. The " courtesy-books ", like the burial urns of his " Hydriotaphia ", are fragments recovered from a remote age that is full of human interest, and many questions about their history and influence must perforce go unanswered. One thing at least is certain—it was due largely to them that, when medieval chivalry reached its end, the new age of the Renaissance received as a precious legacy the record of

" The goodly usage of those antique times
In which the sword was servant unto right."

[1] *Ordre of Chyualry*, E.E.T.S., p. 68. *Chivalry in English Literature*, pp. 290-292 and pp. 216-217. The following parallel, which I have taken from the *Ordre of Chyualry*, is perhaps close enough to be worth quoting :—
Lull : " A knyght beyng a theef doth gretter thefte to the hyhe honour of chyualrye in as moche as he taketh awey the name of a knyght without cause, than he doth that taketh awey or steleth money or other thynges. . . . For honour is more worth than gold or syluer withoute ony comparyson." (p. 50.)
Shakespeare :—
" Who steals my purse steals trash ; 'tis something, nothing ;
'Twas mine, 'tis his, and has been slave to thousands ;
But he that filches from me my good name
Robs me of that which not enriches him,
And makes me poor indeed." (*Othello*, iii, 3.)

CHAPTER IX

Chivalry and the Idea of a Gentleman

By A. W. Reed, M.A., D.Lit.,
Professor of English Language and Literature in the University of London.

I

"A GENTLEMAN is a man of ancestry . . . all other derivations seem to be whimsical. He is a man of birth, a man of extraction." Dr. Johnson follows up this uncompromising definition by a second equally emphatic: "*Nobility* is rank or dignity of several degrees conferred by sovereigns—as duke, marquis, earl, viscount, or baron." If he ever discussed this distinction with Boswell, it is pleasant to think that Boswell might well have illustrated it by the reply of James I to his old nurse: "I'll mak' your son a *baronet* gin ye like, Luckie, but the de'il himself coudna' mak' him a gentleman."

Nevertheless, Johnson was at fault, for the word gentleman, with its Latin equivalent *generosus*, had long before his day come to serve other ends than to indicate ancestry. Students of law, for example, were gentlemen of the Inns of Court. An utter barrister wrote himself Master, as we may see from a list of the printers and booksellers in London in 1526, when the King's Printer appears as plain Ricardus Pynson, but the lawyer-printer Rastell is described as *magister*.[1] Similarly certain offices carried with them the status and title of gentleman. The four chief personal officers of the Lord Mayor—the Sword Bearer, the Water Bailiff, the Common Crier, and the Common Hunt—ranked as *generosi* and enjoyed the title of Master, or even Esquire. The same distinctions were, of course, closely followed in the royal service; and it is of interest to observe that it was a distinction of material value, the *generosus* or gentleman being paid and pensioned at a different rate from the *valettus* or

---

[1] Mr. Rastell.

yeoman, whilst fines for offences were similarly graded. The penalties for " customable swearing "[1] in 1474 were 12d. for a " greate offycer ", 4d. for a gentleman, 2d. for a yeoman, 1d. for a groom, and ½d. (obolus) for a page. The same regulations enjoined " that every man knowe (i.e. recognize) other in his degree as yeoman, gentleman, etc." This distinction in " degree " between the gentleman (or *generosus*) and the yeoman (or *valettus*) is important, but it led to curious contradictions. Thus, while John Heywood, the Early Tudor dramatist, was by virtue of his office at Court, a gentleman, and his younger brother Richard, an eminent lawyer, was not only *generosus* but also *armiger*, their elder brother William described himself as yeoman, and actually was a tenant farmer.

In civic life we find the same distinction observed. John Shakespeare was plain John Shakespeare, Whittawer and Burgess, until he appears in 1567 among the Aldermen of Stratford, when he was nominated and elected Bailiff, and *ex officio* became a Justice of the Peace. Accordingly he is described in the Stratford Minutes of these proceedings as Master Shakespeare. One thinks of old Gobbo's denial of the right of his son to be called " Master Lancelot " ; " No Master, Sir ; but a poor man's son " ; and of the famous scene of the newly ennobled shepherd and clown at the end of the Winter's Tale.

If we observe this very distinct social differentiation, Thomas Fuller's lines take on a clearer meaning :—

> " Gentle blood fetcheth a circuit in the body of a nation running from yeomanry, through gentry, to nobility ; and so retrograde, returning through gentry to yeomanry again. My father hath told me, from the mouth of Sir Robert Cotton, that that worthy knight met in a morning a true and undoubted Plantagenet holding the plough in the country."

It must be observed, however, that the privileges enjoyed by the English gentleman were privileges of dignity and status rather than immunities of material value. In France, on the other hand, the immunity of the gentry and nobles from taxation created a class cleavage, and here we probably have one of the reasons why our French critics have sometimes flattered us. Taine explains the virtual absence of the word

[1] Regulations for the Household of Prince Edward (1474).

gentleman in France by the fact that they had not the thing; and

> "These three syllables, so used across the Channel, summarize the history of English Society ... The English have continued in communication with the people, they have opened their ranks to men of talent, they have taken recruits from the cream of the untitled, and these have continued as commanding or directing personages in the parish and state. They have been administrators, patrons, promoters of reforms, good managers of public affairs, diligent, instructed, capable men, the most enlightened, the most independent, the most useful citizens of the country. After this pattern has been formed the idea of a gentleman, quite different from that of the French *gentilhomme*."

I must not, however, pursue this interesting question of status too far, but refer my readers to a richly documented article by Sir George Sitwell, which appeared in the first number of the *Ancestor* in April, 1902, under the title *The English Gentleman*.

> "It is seldom," Sir George writes, "that we can trace the actual year in which a new word, or an old word in a new meaning,[1] was added to the language, but this may undoubtedly be done with our 'grand old name of gentleman'. As a description of rank or status or a class name, 'gentleman' is never found before 1413, and its sudden appearance must be attributed to the statute of 1 Henry V, cap. 5, which laid down that in all original writs of actions personal, appeals and indictments, in which process of outlawry lies, the 'estate or mystery' of the defendant must be stated."

In the following year, 1413–4, the Staffordshire indictments have yielded to Sir George his first record of a defendant describing his estate or degree as that of "gentleman". Robert Erdeswyke of Stafford, gentilman, "was charged with house-breaking, wounding with intent to kill, and procuring the murder of one Thomas Page, who was cut to pieces while on his knees begging for his life." If there is an earlier claimant than this ruffian, it will be found, predicts Sir George, within the same year and in connexion with some disreputable proceeding—assault, murder, robbery or house-breaking. Depression and the French wars of the fourteenth century had driven many a younger son of good family to become a soldier of fortune. On his return from France he became an idler or hanger-on. How could such a man declare his profession, dignity, or degree under the statute of 1413? It was false to class him as a yeoman or husbandman; he

[1] The word gentleman is common enough, of course, before 1413, but only as a term indicating ancestry, birth, or good breeding.

was not a knight or esquire like his elder brother, but he was of the same blood and he claimed accordingly to be a " gentleman of ancestry ". If Dr. Johnson had lived in 1400, the definition with which this paper opens would have been good ; what we have to bear in mind is that the term gentleman began to take on a new development in the reign of Henry V and that by Tudor times it represented a definite and recognized degree or status, inferior to nobility and superior to yeomanry or craftmanship, but not necessarily dependent on ancestry.

II

Alexander Barclay, the Early Tudor poet, in his Fifth Eclogue, tells an amusing tale. While Adam was pitching a sheepfold and Eve was sitting at her door surrounded by her thirty children, she saw Our Lord coming towards them across the fields ; and, ashamed that he should see how many children she had, she hid some under the hay, some in the chimney, and some in the drafftub ; but the best-looking, tallest, and most intelligent she kept within call. Our Lord explained his coming :—

> Woman let me thy chyldren see
> I come to promote eche after his degree.

He greeted them graciously and putting them courteously at their ease gave to the first " the sceptre of Rome imperyall ", to the second the kingly honour, to the third the leadership of an army and the title of duke ; and so on, promoting each to an office of dignity according to his age, as earls, lords, barons, squires, knights, and " hardy champions ". Further, he assigned to the emperor his sceptre, the king his crown, and to the others their appropriate arms, armour, standards, and shields.

> He taught them policy
> All things to govern concernynge chivalry.

The rest of Eve's more presentable children, though not of the chivalry, were, nevertheless, granted offices of honour as judges, mayors, governors, and merchants ; and pleased

PUBLIUS CORNELIUS AND GAYUS FLAMINIUS ASK OF FULGENS
THE HAND OF HIS DAUGHTER

Royal Library, Brussels, MS. 10977. (See p. 212.)

with her good fortune Eve brought out the children she had hidden, saying that these also were her very children and praying that to them, too, might be granted offices of honour.

Our Lord looked troubled, and said :—

> Ye smell all smoky, of stubble and of chaff,
> Ye smell of grounde, of weeds and of draff,
> And after your scent and tedious savour
> Shall be your rooms and all your behaviour
> * * * * *
> I will not make, howbeit that I can
> Of a vile villain a noble gentleman.

These, therefore, were made ploughmen, swineherds, shepherds, threshers, butchers, tinkers, costermongers, and hostlers, and to them were assigned the goad, whip, mattock and wheelbarrow, with the warning that they must never " grutch at labour ".

The fable of Eve's "unlike children" belongs to the fifteenth century, and is first found, as far as I know, in the Eclogues of Mantuan, from whom Barclay took it. It became popular, particularly among the reformers. Melancthon used it, and the Protestant schoolmaster of Augsburg, Sixt Birck, made a Latin school play out of it in the third decade of the sixteenth century. It appears also in Hans Sachs' delightful version *Die ungleichen kinder Eva's*. As Barclay's translation belongs to the time of More's *Utopia*, we may assume that among the social problems that were interesting that age was the simple question, " What is a gentleman ? " but one wonders how those who used Mantuan's fable reconciled it with the old tag attributed to John Ball :—

> When Adam delved and Eve span,
> Who was then the gentleman ?

The best answer to the tag would be to recite the fable. They certainly do not tell the same story. The one looks back to the time of Adam and Eve for the origin of social divisions, the other for their absence as in a Golden Age.

Mantuan was born in 1448 and died in 1516 ; but early in the fifteenth century a treatise had been written by the Italian humanist Bonaccorso of Pistoja that had a great vogue. It was a debate, written in Ciceronian Latin, on the theme *De vera nobilitate* : on what constitutes a gentleman. It was dedicated to Carlo Malatesta of Rimini, the austere uncle of the famous Sigismondo, whose illegitimacy may have prompted Bonaccorso's *controversia*. The story tells of a Roman senator, Fulgens, his daughter Lucrece, and two lovers, one of noble birth, Publius Cornelius Scipio, the other of obscure origin, Gaius Flaminius. The well-born youth is an idler, the other studious and active in public affairs. The daughter declares that she will marry the suitor who is found to be the more noble. This question Fulgens declines to decide; and the lovers debate their claims to true nobility before the Senate; Cornelius urging the claims of his inherited nobility, the fame of the Scipios, Flaminius pleading his achievements. What the decision of the Senate was we are not told. The subsequent history of Bonaccorso's debate is interesting. It was translated into French by Jean Mielot, one of the secretaries of Philip the Good, Duke of Burgundy, and three beautifully illustrated MSS. of Mielot's translation may be seen in the Royal Library at Brussels.[1] Caxton's friend Collard Mansion printed this French version, and the English nobleman, John Tiptoft, Earl of Worcester, translated it into English. Caxton printed Tiptoft's English version at Westminster in 1481, and not long afterwards Cardinal Morton's chaplain, Henry Medwall, dramatized it as an Interlude. Medwall's modifications of the original Italian story are particularly interesting. He cut out the Senate and introduced two boys and a maid. His cast, therefore, consisted of seven players. Instead of appearing before the "fathers conscript", the lovers plead their causes before Lucrece, and she boldly declares for the man of obscure origin and personal merit. The two boys in an underplot make love to the maid, while their masters make love to the mistress. It will be seen that whilst the Italian story left the matter open, Cardinal Morton's chaplain gave a dramatic decision in favour of the man of humble merit. And this may be taken, I think, to represent the atmosphere of the Cardinal's household, where, it will be remembered, Thomas More spent some part of his boyhood, and where he must have known Medwall, the dramatist.

And just as Sixt Birck made a school play out of the fable of Eve's children, so, again, he made a play from Bonaccorso's *De Vera Nobilitate*; and like Medwall, he rejects the "gentleman born", and gives a dramatic decision in favour

[1] See illustrations facing this page and pp. 214, 218, 224.

of the "churl's son". On the other hand, while Medwall leaves the decision to Lucrece, Birck, having a school full of boys to draw on, stages the Senate, and each senator gives his reasons for voting for the man of merit.

III

The question whether ancestry and inheritance are essential to gentility is very old, and, broadly speaking, the philosophers have held that there can be no true gentility without virtue. Plato and Plutarch, discussing the same problem as Bonaccorso, urged that it is dishonourable to rest one's claims to regard merely on the honour due to ancestors. Aristotle, however, in his shrewder way, facing facts, claimed that it is everywhere counted honourable to be well descended and of wealthy parentage; whereas Horace praised Mæcenas as one who discriminated between true and false gentility :—

Non pâtre præclaro sed vita pectore puro.

"If aught else be good in philosophy it is this," says Seneca, "that it regards not nobility or descent." "Who is a gentleman? One naturally disposed towards virtue. It is not a hall filled with time-darkened portraits that enobles one, but character, in the strength of which one rises above one's fortune from any condition of life."

Between the classical and the medieval worlds of letters Boethius built a bridge; and the views of Boethius on the question of gentility Chaucer came to be familiar with as the translator of the *De Consolatione Philosophiæ*. "Why bosten ye your elders?" asks Boethius; and he replies in effect in the passage: "If there be any good in gentilesse, I trow it be only this, that it seemeth that a kind of necessity is imposed on gentle men that they should not degenerate from the virtue of their noble kindred?"

What contribution had Christianity to offer to this much debated question, and what had it to add to the conception of the gentleman? One would have expected the claims of birth to fail before the teaching of the Gospel story. Yet, strangely enough, it was used by the heraldic writers as their great support. "Of the offspring of the gentleman Japheth come Abraham, Moses, Aaron, and the prophets, and of the right line of Mary that gentleman Jesus was born." So wrote Dame Juliana Berners, who tells us in another place that "Christ was a gentleman of his mother's behalf and bore cote-armure of aunseturis. The apostles were Jewys and of gentlemen come by the right line of that worthy conqueror Judas Machabeus, but that by succession of tyme the kynrade fell to poverty and then they fell to labours and were called no gentlemen." (1486.)

In Tudor treatises on heraldry this conception of the gentility of Christ kept its place, and it is possible that it survives, unsuspected, either by its writer or by the children who sing it, in the hymn "Gentle Jesus, meek and mild".

But at this point Chaucer's *Ballad of Gentilesse* should be read as our comment on the naïvety of Dame Juliana.

> The first stok, fader of gentilesse [1]
> What man that claymeth gentil for to be,
> Must folowe his trace, and all his wittes dresse
> Vertu to serve and vices for to fle.
> For unto vertu longeth dignitee,
> And noght the revers, saufly daur I deme,
> Al were [2] he mytre, croune, or diademe.
>
> This firste stok was ful of rightwisnesse
> Trewe of his word, sobre, pitous, and free.
> Cleene of his goste, and loved besinesse.
> Ageinst the vyce of slouthe, in honestie;
> And but his heir love vertu, as did he,
> He is noght gentil, though he riche seme,
> Al were he mytre, croune or diademe.
>
> Vyce may wel be heir to old richesse;
> But ther may no man, as man may wel se,
> Bequethe his heir his vertuous noblesse;
> That is appropred unto no degree,
> But to the firste fader in magistee,
> That maketh him his heir, that wol him queme,
> Al were he mytre, croune, or diademe.

Chaucer's argument in this little poem should be followed closely. He who claims to be of gentle birth must shew himself to be a follower of Christ, from whom, as the first stock, all gentilesse derives. He must eschew evil and pursue virtue; for to virtue alone appertains dignity. And the virtues of Christ are righteousness, truth, soberness, pity, freedom, purity of heart, and ceaseless labour. Old wealth cannot

[1] Christ.   [2] Wear.

LUCRES DECLARES TO HER FATHER HER DECISION TO WED
THAT SUITOR WHO IS THE MORE NOBLE

Royal Library, Brussels, MS. 9278-80. (See p. 212.)

CHIVALRY: IDEA OF A GENTLEMAN

ensure gentility, for it may fall into the hands of a vicious heir; and no father, however virtuous, save Christ, can bequeath to his son his good qualities.

His best essay on true gentility is found in the *Wife of Bath's Tale*, whose prosperous opening, though familiar, is always worth recalling:—

> In th' olde dayes of the Kynge Arthour
> Of which that Britons speken great honour
> Al was this land fulfild of fairye;
> The elf queene with her joly compaynye
> Daunced ful ofte in many a grene mede.
> This was the old opinion as I rede.

It is the tale—told also, in his naïve way, by Gower—of a knight whose life depended on his finding within a twelvemonth the answer to the question what it is that women most desire. An old hag revealed the answer to him on condition that he wedded her; and Chaucer's essay on gentilesse is delivered by the old woman to the unhappy knight in bed on the night of the marriage, as a prelude to her miraculous transformation. The situation shows Chaucer at his best.

> Thou art so loothly, and so oold also
> And ther-to comen of so low a kynde
> That litel wonder is thogh I walwe and wynde.[1]

It is to these words of the knight that the wife answers:—

> Swich arrogance is nat worth a hen
> Looke, who that is moost vertuous alway,
> Pryvee and apert, and moost entendeth ay
> To do the gentil dedes that he kan,
> Taak hym for the grettest gentil man.
> Crist wole we clayme of hym oure gentilesse
> Nat of oure eldres for hir old richesse.
>   *   *   *   *   *   *
> Redith Senek,[2] and redeth eek Bocce[3]
> Then shul ye seen expresse, that no drede is,
> That he is gentil that dooeth gentil dedis.

It would be pleasant to discuss this interesting tale at greater length. The knight owed courtesy to the old woman and learns from her in circumstances that Chaucer knew how to make the most of, the doctrine of the making of a gentleman. The subject was one that clearly had more than ordinary interest for him. He gathers his supports from a wide

---

[1] "Walwe and wynde" = turn and toss.
[2] Read Seneca.
[3] Boethius.

field of authorities, including Dante, whom he translates; and he seizes so many occasions to introduce his views, that one can only conclude that he held them firmly. In the *Parson's Tale* he defines the marks of gentleness with preciseness: "eschewing of vice and ribaudrie and servage of sin in word and in work and contenance; and using virtue, as courtesie and cleanesse, and to be liberal, that is to say large by measure, to remember him of bounty that he of other folk hath received; and to be benigne to his subjects."

The reference here to liberality is interesting. In other places Chaucer uses the word *freedom*. The Knight of the Prologue—

" loved chivalry
Truth and honour freedom and courtesy."

Freedom implied liberality, or generosity, as well as franchise, frankness and the state of freedom by birth. It is a word of wide implication, but liberality was an important element in the virtue of freedom.

Perhaps, however, the quality that Chaucer most often emphasizes in the perfect gentleman is *pity*. Four times in his works there occurs the line:—

For pity renneth sone in gentil herte.

It occurs in the *Knight's Tale*, and might well stand as its motto; it occurs in the *Squire's Tale*, and in the *Legend of Good Women*.

If it be asked what place in his chivalric qualities Chaucer assigns to "high kindred", it is not enough to say that he does not place it as high as virtue. He includes it in the catalogue of endowments that go to make the ideal servant of chivalric love, as distinct from that higher service that looks to Christ as the "Father of gentilesse". He therefore includes it among the qualities of Palamon given in the dying speech of Arcite:—

To speken of a servant [1] properly
With all circumstances trewely,
That is to seyn, trouthe, honour, and knighthede
Wysdome, humblesse, estaat and *hye kynrede*,
Fredom and all that longeth to that art
So Jupiter have of my soule part
As in this world right now no know I non
So worthy to be loved as Palamon.

[1] Lover.

CHIVALRY : IDEA OF A GENTLEMAN

Nevertheless, it is in the *Wife of Bath's Tale* that Chaucer arrives at his most comprehensive definition of a gentleman.

<blockquote>He is gentle that doeth gentle deeds</blockquote>

One feels that something more than the chivalric virtues is necessary to explain the essential gentility of his Poor Parson, his Clerk of Oxenford, and his Ploughman ; and his comprehensive definition provides for this. This becomes clearer if we turn to a famous passage in Malory :—

> " Ah, Sir Lancelot," said he, " thou wert head of all Christian knights : and now I dare say, there [1] thou liest thou wert never matched of none earthly knights hands : and thou wert the curtliest knight that ever bare shield ; and thou wert the truest friend to thy lover that ever bestrood horse, and thou wert the truest lover of a sinful man that ever loved woman ; and thou wert the kindest man that ever strook with sword : and thou wert the goodliest person that ever came in the press of knights : and thou wert the meekest man and the gentlest that ever sate in hall among ladies : and thou wert the sternest knight to thy mortal foe that ever put speare in the rest."

This, surely, is as great a passage as any in our chivalric literature ; yet we feel that if Lancelot is the gentleman of chivalry, there yet has to be found a place for those other gentlemen, the Poor Parson, the Clerk and Ploughman. For it was not to them, or their like, that Malory was writing when he closed his *Morte Darthur* with the words :—

> " I pray you all gentlemen and gentlewomen that read the book of Arthur and his knights from the beginning to the ending, pray for me while I am on live that God send me good deliverance, and when I am dead, I pray you all pray for my soul : for this book was ended the ninth year of the reign of King Edward the Fourth by Sir Thomas Malorye knight as Jesu help him for his great might as he is the servant of Jesu both day and night.

IV

About the year 1528 John Rastell, the brother-in-law of Sir Thomas More, wrote an Interlude of *Gentleness and Nobility*, which he describes as a *Dialogue between the Merchant, the Knight, and the Ploughman, disputing who is a very Gentleman, and who is a Nobleman, and how man should*

[1] There = where.

come to authority. The knight, whose ancestors for five hundred years have inherited the same lands and borne the same name and arms, considers that it is presumptuous of the merchant to claim precedence because of his great riches. The ploughman enters and undertakes to show that though the knight is one of the chivalry, ever ready at the command of his prince, and the merchant has laboured successfully for his own profit, he himself nevertheless is more noble than either. The noblest thing of all is that which stands in least need of any other thing. God is the noblest thing that is. He who needs for his living that which another provides, is less noble than he who provides for his needs. In so far as man owes his food or clothing to the lower animals, he would be less noble than they, were it not that he is superior to them in having what they have not, "a soul intellective." The ploughman finds that the merchant stands in greater need of him than he of the merchant. He cannot see that there is anything the knight does for the common weal that any other man, being in authority and "having the wit", might not do as well. And since both the knight and the merchant stand in more need of him than he of them, the ploughman claims to be nobler than either of them. They debate the origin of property in goods and lands, and of the strife that has arisen consequently. The knight claims that his ancestors, being men of wisdom, studied to make laws that the people might live in peace; they defended from their enemies the tillers of the ground, and were rewarded by gifts of lands and possessions. The ploughman retorts that the first possessors of land were those who preferred violence and robbery to labour, and that possession began by extortion. The extortioners then established the laws of inheritance, and in his opinion it is against all good reason that there should be any inheritance in the world. He admits that the charitable deeds of wealthy merchants are laudable; to build churches, to mend the highways, to build almshouses, are good deeds; but commonly the wealthy merchant lacks learning, and when he is promoted to authority his judgments are prejudiced. The ploughman is insistent that inheritance and the entailing of lands are indefensible. They then return to the question "What is a gentleman?" and the ploughman concludes that as music maketh the musician, grammar the

PUBLIUS CORNELIUS ADDRESSES THE SENATE

(See p. 212.)

[*face p.* 218

grammarian, geometry the geometrician, and churlish conditions the churl, so gentle conditions make a gentleman, and these are meekness, patience, charity, liberality, abstinence, honest business and chastity, and he claims that in respect of these he is superior to the other two. Rastell's Ploughman is a man of modern notions.

Born about the same time as Rastell, there was, however, an Italian, Baldassare Castiglione, who was destined to influence the Tudor evaluation of the gentleman much more deeply than More's brother-in-law. In his delightful edition of Hoby's translation of Castiglione's *Il Cortegiano*, Raleigh has the passage :—

> "It was a shrewd remark of Dr. Johnson's that manners are best learnt at a small Court: 'You are admitted with great facility to the prince's company, and yet must treat him with much respect.' The best book that ever was written upon good-breeding, *Il Cortegiano*, by Castaglione, grew up at the little Court of Urbino, and you should read it."

Here in this little city of Urbino, the ladies and gentlemen of the Court used to join the Duchess after supper in lively talk and discussion. In order to make their debates edifying as well as entertaining, they considered what topics were likely to be most agreeable and finally agreed to "shape in words a good courtyer, specifying all suche condicions and particular qualities, as of necessitie must be in him that deserveth this name." It is not possible in the space at our disposal to give any adequate account of the delightful intimacy and naturalness of the talks that followed, nor of the wit and point of the illustrations and anecdotes that enlivened the discussions, but there is time for one of Castiglione's prettiest anecdotes.

Count Lewis is arguing that though arms be the profession of the courtier, yet he must not wed his armour. There was, he says, such a man whom a gentlewoman invited to dance with her. He refused not only that, but to hear music, or any other entertainment, "always affirming such trifles not to be his profession." At last the gentlewoman asked him: "What, then, is your profession?" With a frown he answered: "To fight." Then said the gentlewoman: "Seeing you are not now at the war nor in place to fight, I would think it best for you to be well besmeared [1] and set

---
[1] Greased.

up in an armory till time were that you should be occupied, lest you wax more rustier than you are."

Raleigh remarks that whilst few great Englishmen of the nineteenth century were intimately connected with the court, there were few great Elizabethans who were not. The names of Darwin, Browning, and Gordon on the one hand, of Bacon, Spenser, and Sydney on the other sufficiently point the contrast. Tudor literature was as much a literature of the Court, as the literature of Anne was a literature of the town. Yet, when Tudor Englishmen like Sir Thomas Eliot discussed the question of the education and training of a gentleman, they had in mind, not so much the perfect courtier as the efficient counsellor. Whilst Castiglione was concerned with describing only his man of grace and culture, Eliot was bent upon inquiring into the system of education best calculated to produce the good servant of the commonweal. And this, too, with a particularly patriotic orientation was the intention of Ascham's *Scholemaster*. Yet both Ascham and Eliot were aiming at producing the perfectly rounded character that Castiglione had in mind. That Eliot should write an admirable essay on dancing and Ascham a treatise on archery is therefore not surprising. The *Faerie Queen* derives both from Castiglione and from English humanism, yet Spenser's own schoolmaster, Mulcaster, belongs only to the English tradition. One observes, nevertheless, that the minor English reformers tended, unlike Spenser, to lose sight of " the ideal of the gentleman, perfect in character, general accomplishments and bearing ", and to become moralists and pedagogues. Even Milton lost here as elsewhere something of his sense of proportion, by demanding too much of those that were too young. The fact is that Puritanism was blind to the virtue of many of the normal activities of healthy youth. Thus John Cleland in the *Institution of a Young Nobleman* allows recreation only in so far as it does not take the place of some worthier pursuit. " As for the common Play-houses, which may be called the very sink of the City, he would have his disciples never resort thither." He was afraid of poetry, and of the fashions of his day ; the influence of Castiglione is seen, nevertheless, even in Cleland, for he tells us that a young man can learn more at court in a month than he would in a year should he run over all France and Italy; and this writer was speaking of the court of James I.

His contemporary, Henry Peacham, however, in his *Compleat Gentleman*, provided the cavaliers of the next generation and the Tories of the eighteenth century (including Dr. Johnson) with a book to their liking; a book, which still keeps its freshness. Valorous and virtuous men are never ashamed, he tells us, of their mean parentage. " I remember when I lived with Sir John Ogle at Utrecht "—where resorted scholars and soldiers from all the northern nations, English, Scotch, French, and Dutch—" the reply of that valiant gentleman, Colonel Edmonds, to a countryman newly come out of Scotland, who desiring entertainment of him told him that My Lord his father and the Knights and Gentlemen his cousins and kinsmen, were in good health. Quoth Colonel Edmonds, Gentlemen, believe not one word he says; my father is but a poor baker of Edinburgh, and works hard for his living, whom this knave would make a lord to curry favour with me and make you believe I am a great man born."

This we may take to be Peacham's answer to his own first question: Is nobility a matter of ancestry? To his second question—whether one of noble birth may lose his nobility by vice, he has no answer but to say that " to be drunk, swear, wench, follow the fashion, and to do just nothing are the marks nowadays of a great part of our gentry." His third question—whether poverty stains nobility is answered by his reflection that there often lies more worth under a threadbare cloak than the richest robes. Advocates and physicians he allows to be gentlefolk by profession, but not surgeons, mountebanks, empirics, and women doctors. The danger of these is worse than the disease itself. As for merchants, he admits that the Spartans had a law that no one was honourable in their commonwealth who had not, ten years before, given over trading. He himself, however, is of opinion that God has so distributed His blessings over the whole earth that no one country provides us with all that we require. We owe it to the honest merchant that he exposes his life and goods to the hazard of the sea to bring us those things of which we have need; and as one who was interested in painting, he includes amongst his necessities colours of all sorts for painting and dyeing. His last question is interesting because it is still vexed. What are we to think of those who make it their profession as painters, stage players, musicians, swordsmen, dancers and the like, to follow these arts? These, our modern professionals, he would in no wise admit to gentility. We have, I think, admitted painters, actors, and musicians, but the line of division in our more popular games is still giving us some trouble. It is interesting to find that he is of opinion that if masters took an active part in school games, they would soon cease to be the deadly enemy of the boy. His admiration for Sir Thomas More, and More's friend Lyly, the author of the Latin Grammar, is hardly greater than his respect for the learning of More's daughters; to whom, along with the learned daughters of Sir Anthony Cooke, and some other ladies of his acquaintance then living, he pays the pretty compliment of praying that before their fair faces time will never draw the curtain. That he was not a Puritan we may learn from his anecdote of "Politian, a canon of Florence," who, when asked if he had ever read the Bible through, replied: "Yes, once I read it quite through, but never bestowed my time worse in my life."

Since speech is the interpreter of a man's mind, and writing the image of speech, Peacham would have us remember that whenever we speak or write, we submit ourselves to the judgment of others. He praises Sir Nicholas Bacon and Lord Burleigh, not merely for their good matter, but their graceful, clear, and distinct pronunciation. He would have gentlemen scrupulous in their care for the preservation of all records and documents, and he charges Polydore Virgil, the early Tudor historian, with burning and embezzling the best and most ancient records and muniments of our abbeys and cathedral churches. A gentleman does not sell his books secondhand, nor suffer them through neglect to mould and be moth-eaten, or lose their strings and covers. The purpose of his admirable chapter on cosmography is to show how delightful a subject it might become if teachers were not dull dogs. He manages to intrude the following merry tale of two poor scholars and an innkeeper.

Two scholars in Germany, having lain so long in an inn that they had run into a debt of two hundred dollars, told their host of Plato's great year, and how that in 86,000 years the world should be again as it was and they should be in the same inn and chamber again, and desired him to trust them till then. Mine host replied: "I believe it to be true, and I remember six and thirty thousand years ago you were here, and left just such a reckoning behind to pay: I pray you, gentlemen, discharge that first, and I will trust you for the next."

In his rather perfunctory essay on poetry he omits all reference to Ben Johnson and Shakespeare on the ground, I suppose, that he was concerned strictly with gentleman-poets. He includes, of course, "our Phœnix, the noble Sir Philip Sydney." He deals heavily with the sectaries, who deny that the service of God is advanced by singing and instruments. He is a great believer in the cultivation of the taste through the intelligent study of antiquities, and being himself a skilful draughtsman and painter, he not only writes an admirable chapter on the value of proficiency in these arts, but adds to it the first account we have in English of the great Italian painters. The quaint enthusiasm of his chapter on the exercise of the body makes very good reading. "Leaping is an exercise very commendable and healthful for the body, especially if you use it in the morning. Upon a full stomach, or to bed-ward, it is very dangerous and in no wise to be exercised." "Old Lord Gray" he tells us, "when he was deputy of Ireland, would cause his sons to be roused from bed at midnight in frost, snow, or rain to go out hunting till the next morning; then come wet and cold home to breakfast off a brown loaf and a mouldy cheese, or, which is ten times worse, a dish of Irish butter. This, he adds, was to "inure his sons for the war". Hawking and hunting were forbidden, he tells us, by canon law to the clergy, though he sees no reason why they should not have their recreation as well as others. He regrets that the bishoprics have lost their parks: Norwich used to have thirteen; if they had left one, "it had not been indifferent, but to rob the Church of all is more than too much."

Finally Peacham anticipates in his last chapter the good Isaak Walton. "I have taken so much delight in the art of angling, that I may well term it the honest and patient man's recreation." Unfortunately, it is a short chapter, but the instructions he gives for making flies still hold good.

V

Peacham died a poor man on the eve of the outbreak of the Civil War, and civil war is surely the severest strain that can be put upon the essential virtues of a gentleman. Here were none of the chivalric formalities of war and combat; there could be none. The King, the fount of honour, was himself the object of attack; and his execution, a deliberate and considered act, aroused passions that must, one would think, break down all the defences of gentility. It was inevitable that men of refinement should seek consolation in philosophical detachment or the quieter recreations. Sir Thomas Browne's *Religio Medici* and *Urn Burial*, Walton's *Compleat Angler* and his *Lives*, the poems of Crashaw, Vaughan, and Marvell may be taken to represent this search for peace of mind in a world that appeared to have lost its sense of spiritual values.

It was into this world of strife that Dorothy Osborne and William Temple were born. Dorothy's father, Sir Peter, held Guernsey for the King, and it was on his way to France that Temple first met Dorothy in the Isle of Wight, when he was twenty and she twenty-one. His father was a Parliamentarian, and it is not surprising that the courtship ran a chequered course of seven years. Its story we may read in Dorothy's letters, from which I extract the following account of a day in the country in the month of May.

"I rise in the morning reasonably early, and before I am ready, I go round the house till I am weary of that, and then into the garden till it grows too hot for me. About ten o'clock I think of making me ready, and when that's done I go into my father's chamber, from thence to dinner where my cousin Molle and I sit in great state in a room and at a table that would hold a great many more. After dinner we sit and talk till Mr. B. comes in question, and then I am gone. The heat of the day is spent in reading or working, and about six or seven o'clock I walk out into a common that lies hard by the house, where a great many young wenches keep sheep and cows and sit in the shade singing of ballads. I go to them and compare their voices and beauties to some ancient shepherdesses that I have read of, and find a vast difference there: but trust me, I think these are as innocent as those

GAYUS FLAMINIUS REPLIES

(See p. 212.)

could be. I talk to them and find they want nothing to make them the happiest people in the world, but the knowledge that they are so. Most commonly, when we are in the midst of our discourse, one looks about her and spies her cows going into the corn and then away they all run, as if they had wings at their heels. . . . and when I see them driving home their cattle, I think 'tis time for me to retire, too. When I have supped I go into the garden, and so to the side of a small river, where I sit down and wish you were with me. (You had best say, this is not kind neither.) 'Tis a pleasant place, and would be much more so to me if I had your company. I sit there sometimes till I am lost with thinking, and were it not for some cruel thoughts of the crossness of our fortunes that will not let me sleep there, I should forget that there were such a thing to be done as going to bed."

My only comment on this charming letter is that it might have been written in the time of Jane Austen. Later in the same year she tells him of the many ingredients that she looked for in a husband. " First, he must have that kind of breeding that I have had, and used that kind of company. That is, he must not be so much a country gentleman as to understand nothing but hawks and dogs, and be fonder of either than of his wife, nor of the next sort of them whose aim reaches no further than to be Justice of Peace, and once in his life High Sherriff; who reads no books but statutes, and studies nothing but how to make a speech interlarded with Latin that may amaze his disagreeing poor neighbours. He must not be a thing that began the world in a free school, was sent from thence to the University and is at his furthest when he reaches the Inns of Court, has no acquaintance but those of his form in these places, speaks the French he has picked out of old laws, and admires nothing but the stories he has heard of the revels that were kept there before his time. He must not be a town gallant neither, that lives in a tavern and an ordinary . . . that makes court to all the women he sees, thinks they believe him, and laughs and is laughed at equally. Nor a travelled Monsieur whose head is all feather inside and outside, that can talk of nothing but dances and duels. He must not be a fool of no sort, nor peevish, nor ill-natured, nor proud, nor covetous; and to all this must be added that he must love me and I him as much as we are capable of loving. Without all this, his fortune, though never so great, would not satisfy me ; and with it a very moderate one would keep me from ever repenting my disposal."

In another place she writes : " You cannot imagine how often I have been told that I had too much franchise in my humour, and that it was a point of good breeding to disguise handsomely ; but 'twas not to be expected I should be exactly bred that had never seen a court."

"Do you remember Arme and the little house there ? Shall we go thither ? That's next to being out of the world. There we might live like Baucis and Philemon, grow old together in our little cottage, and for our charity to some ship-wrecked strangers obtain the blessing of dying both at the same time. How idly I talk : 'tis because the story pleases me. I remember I cried when I read it." Arme is the island of Herm, as it is now called, two or three miles from Castle Cornet which Dorothy's father, the gallant cavalier Sir Peter, had valiantly defended.

There is much good talk in these letters of the long French romances of Calprenède and Scudéri, which she used to send to Temple, a few volumes together as she had finished them. Later, in her courtship she turned to Jeremy Taylor's *Holy Living*, a book she loved and knew well.

The last of the letters of courtship is dated October, 1654. The wedding was prepared, but Dorothy at the last moment caught smallpox. They were married in December at St. Giles in the Fields. Thirty years later one of their children an only daughter, died of smallpox and was buried in Westminster Abbey. There is extant a letter from the little Dorothy thanking her father for a present " of fine things ". "If Papa was here," she says, "I should think myself a perfect Pope, though I hope I should not be burnt, as there was one at Nell Gwynn's door, the 5th of November, who sat in a great chair with a red nose half a yard long, with some hundreds of boys throwing squibs at it."

Sir William Temple holds a secure position in English history as one of the greatest ambassadors we have had. Macaulay in an essay that shows an inadequate sense of his high character, nevertheless describes him as the greatest negotiator of his age. He won the confidence of that blunt and great Dutch patriot, the Grant Pensionary, de Witt, and together they defeated the Franco-phile intrigues of Charles and his Cabal by the creation of the Triple Alliance. Assisted by Dorothy, he negotiated the marriage of William of Orange and Mary, and thus made possible the constitutional control of the events of the revolutionary year 1688. Dorothy was a lady of sixty when Mary became Queen at the age of twenty-six, and they remained close friends. The Queen died six years later, and Dorothy her confidential adviser, outlived her only by a month.

There surely can be no doubt that the qualities for which we admire Sir William Temple and his wife are closely akin to those that Chaucer found in his knight; wisdom and discretion, truth and honour, freedom and courtesy; in a word, *gentilesse*.

As an English gentleman Temple loved his garden at Sheen and Moor Park, and as an amateur of letters the high praise is his that he is the subject of Lamb's charming essay, *On the Genteel Style in Writing*. Nor is it his own writings only and the reputation he enjoyed in his old age as an arbiter of literary taste that give him a place in English letters. Two years before Dorothy died, young Jonathan Swift came to Moor Park, to act as his amanuensis, and so became Temple's literary executor. Like Doctor Johnson, Swift was punctilious in all points of gentle behaviour, but unlike Johnson, he was scrupulously clean and neat in dress.

> But then a parson so genteel,
> So nicely clad from head to heel :
> So fine a gown, a band so clean,
> As well become St. Patrick's Dean.

We have now reached a point in our paper at which we find ourselves in a world that is curiously modern. Old-fashioned it may be, but it is much nearer to us than the Tudor age was to it. There was, however, a problem emerging in Temple's day that now is vital : the problem of national education. The first Charity Schools were being opened. The question that John Rastell debated in his *Gentleness and Nobilitie* in 1529 is, after all, the psychological problems of the labour movement of to-day. Rastell's ploughman argued that he was more noble than the knight or the merchant because he had less need of them than they had of him. To-day the miner believes that he is more necessary to the merchant and the knight than they are to him. *Gentilesse* was never more needed in England than now; but looking back at the feeble beginnings of elementary education in the Charity Schools in the last years of Temple's life, one cannot resist the feeling that our present problems are educational, and that we have progressed. The London County Council recently opened a new Secondary School at Tooting—the Bec School. The manor of Bec was once a fee of the Abbey in Normandy, which sent us Lanfranc and Anselm. Henry VI assigned it to Eton. The Lower Master of Eton told this to the parents assembled for the opening of the school and explained that that was why the lilies of Eton find a place in the arms of Bec School. He suggested that the two schools should make games fixtures. Another speaker, alluding to a foolish remark that " all one learnt at places like Eton was to hand a cup of tea to a lady and to tie a bow tie ", added that rightly understood this surely was no mean achievement; it implied respect for others and respect for oneself. I do not know that I can find a more appropriate conclusion for my paper *Chivalry and the Idea of a Gentleman*.

INDEX

Albuquerque, Alfonso de, 163
Alcántara, Order of, 128
Alfonso Henriques, King of Portugal, 147 ff.
Alfonso V of Portugal, 157
Alfonso X (the learned), 122, 142
Anglo-Saxon Chronicle, 4, 5
Antioch, Bohemund of, 10, 46
Antioche, Chanson d', 41, 42
Arbre des Batailles, 191, 192
Arthur, King, 170
Aue, Hartmann von, 89, 92
Aviz, Order of, 151

Barbarossa, 85, 183
Barclay, Alexander, 210
Bath, Knights of the, 195
Bayard, 79
Bibliographies, 34, 107, 131, 132, 166
Birth and knighthood, 198
Black Prince, the, 72, 73, 178
Blois, Peter of, 19, 20 n.
Böethius, 71, 213
Bonaccorso, 211
Bouillon, Godfrey of, 10, 12, 21
Brantome, 79
Bremen, Adam of, 20
Broadstone of Honour, 29
Byron, 110, 112

Calatrava, Order of, 126, 127
Cambrai, Raoul de, 5, 43
Cancioneiro de Resende, 160
Carrion, lords of, 116 ff.
Castiglione, Baldassare, 219
Castro, D. John de, 163
Caxton, William, 28, 186 ff.
Cervantes, 110, 111
Charlemagne, 59, 82
Charles VI, 74 ff.
Chartres, Fulbert, of, 42
Chaucer, 173, 214
Chivalry, books about, 29, 184; Church's attitude, 7, 40 ff.; deeds of, 153; decline of, 25, 78, 101, 200; defects of, 30; definitions, 1; golden age of, 18, 25, 45 85; in England, 53; in English poetry, 167; in France, 57 ff. ; in Germany, 81 ff. ; in literature, 89, 167 ff.—

183 ff. ; in Portugal, 142 ff. ; in Spain, 109 ff. ; influence of, 21, 27 ; interest during Romantic Movement, 29, ,104 ; and love, 49, 66, 97, 159 ; origin of, 8, 37 ; medieval, 37 ff. ; religion and, 59 ff. ; rules for, 41 ; virtues of, 29, 32, 183, 202 ; women and, 51, 66 (*See also* knighthood.)
Christ, Order of, 151, 155
Church, attitude towards war, 7, 40 ff., 123 ; to the Crusades, 10 ; to the knights, 47 ; duties of the knights to, 41
Cid, the, 113 ff. 132 ff.
Clement V, 15
Clermont, Council of, 8, 10
Compleat Gentleman, The, 221
Cortegiano, Il, 219
Cortes, 110
Courtesy, 71, 204
Courtesy Books, 186
Crusades, in the East, 8, 9, 41, 62 ff. ; in Portugal and Spain, 146
Crusading Orders, 11, 15, 62

De vera nobilitate, 211
Defoe, 110
Digby, Kenelm, 29
Dupuy, Raymond, Master of the Hospitallers, 12

East, influence on Spanish civilization, 119
Edward III, 26
England and the Spaniards, 137
English literature and chivalry, 167
Erec, 93
Eschenbach, Wolfram von, 94
Eve's children, fable of, 210

Fastolf, Sir John, 54
Feudalism, 6, 81, 82, 122 n.
Fougères, Etienne de, 61
France, chivalry in, 57
Frederick I, 85
Froissart, 19, 26, 69, 71, 73, 75, 180

Gallantry, 15 ff., 67, 160
Gamez, Diaz de, 134, 136
Gawain, Sir, 175

229

INDEX

Gentility, 213 ff.
Gentleman, definition of, 207 ff.; qualities of, 213 ff.
Gentleness and nobility, 217
German scholars, the two, 222
Germany, chivalry of, 81; lyrics, 97; romances, 91
Goethe, 104
Golden Age of Chivalry, the, 18, 25, 45, 85
Gonçalves, Nuno, 153
Gregory VII, Pope, 9, 41

Hadloub, Johannes, 97
Hamton, Bevis of, 1, 6
Hay, Sir Gilbert, 191 ff.
Henry VI (of Germany), 86
Henry of Portugal, 155
Hohenzollern, Albert of, Grand Master of the Teutonic Knights, 18, 88
Horse, the, in chivalry, 117
Hospitallers, Order of the, 11
Hundred Years' War, 26, 68, 70

Infanzones de Fuero, 117
Isabella of England, 69
Iwein, 93, 94

John I of Portugal, 154; sons of, 155 ff.
Joinville, 19, 62 ff., 75, 186

Knighthood, Church and, 41, 47, 192; consequences of, 45; duties of, 15, 28, 201 ff.; feudal, 4; how it was lost, 145; orders of, 15, 28, 72, 124 ff.; ordination, 23, 43 ff., 74, 142 ff., 193, 195 ff.; origin of, 82; preparation for, 22, 38 ff.; patterns of, 153; rules of, 41 ff.; training for, 22, 38, 197; virtues of, 32, 202

Lackland, John, 42
Lancelot, Sir, 217
Lateran, Council, 123
Layamon, 171
Lay of the Shadow, 67
Lichtenstein, Ulrich von, 100
Literature, earliest, 184; English, 167; German, 88 ff.; influence on Spanish chivalry, 182; Portuguese, 159
Love, cult of, 49, 66, 97
Lucrece and her suitors, 212
Lull, Ramon, 186 ff.
Lusiads, The, 159

Mandeville, Geoffrey de, 5
Mantuan, 211
Marriage, 51
Mauni, Olivier, 68
Maximilian I, 103
Meistersingers, 103
Minnesingers, 97
Moniz, Egas, 147
Monmouth, Geoffrey of, 170
Moors, expulsion from Spain, 138, 146
Morte d'Arthur, 180, 184, 185

Niño, Don Pedro, 134
Nobility, *see* Gentleman
Nun's Rule, The, 168

Ogier, the Dane, 5
Ordene de Chevalerie, 41, 43, 186, 188 ff.
Orders of knighthood, 15, 28, 124 ff., 151
Ordre of Chyualry, *see Ordene de Chevalerie*
Osborne, Dorothy, 224

Parzival, 94
Pastime of Pleasure, 180
Peacham, Henry, 221
Pereira, D. Nuno Alvares, 153
Petit Jehan de Saintré, 22, 77
Philip VI, 26
Piers Plowman, 179
Pisan, Christine de, 54, 79, 101
Poema de Mio Cid, 118 ff.
Portugal, chivalry in, 142; conquests in the East, 163; exemplary knights, 153 ff.; literature of chivalry, 159; rise of the kingdom, 146, 148
Prisoners, treatment of, 73
Prussia, consolidation of by the Teutonic Knights, 87

Rastell, John, 217
Roland, 47, 58 ff., 118 ff.

Sachs, Hans, 103
Saladin, 61
St. Augustine, 8
St. Benedict of Aniane, 39
St. Bernard, 14, 47
St. Inglevert, 76, 101
St. James of Compostela, Order of, 128 ff.
St. John of Jerusalem, Order of, 127
St. Louis, 19, 62 ff.
Salisbury, John of, 20, 48
Scott, Sir Walter, 29
Sebastian, King of Portugal, 164
Seljuk Turks, 9, 11
Sicily, Tancred of, 10, 21
Spain, chivalry 109 ff.; influence

of French and Celtic romances, 132; literature, 113; orders of knighthood, 15
Straszburg, Gottfried von, 96
Templars, Order of the, 11, 13, 124 ff.
Temple d'Honneur, 70
Temple, Sir William, 224
Teutonic Knights, Order of the, 11, 13, 87
Thopas, Sir, 173
Toledo Cathedral, 138
Tournament, description of, 75; in Portugal, 161
Tours, Gregory of, 38
Troubadours, 17

Troyes, Chrétien de, 93, 94
Troyes, Council of, 14

Urban II, Pope, 9

Valour, 72
Veldeke, Heinrich von, 85, 91
Vicente, Gil, 161
Villon, 52
Vogelweide, Walther von der, 90, 99

Wace, 171
Women, change in position, 16; chivalry and, 50 ff., 66 ff.; under feudalism, 16, 51

For Product Safety Concerns and Information please contact our EU
representative GPSR@taylorandfrancis.com
Taylor & Francis Verlag GmbH, Kaufingerstraße 24, 80331 München, Germany

www.ingramcontent.com/pod-product-compliance
Lightning Source LLC
Chambersburg PA
CBHW051630230426
43669CB00013B/2248